THE MATERIALITY OF LITERATURE

This book retraces the emergence of conceptions of authorship in late-eighteenth-century Germany by studying the material form of Immanuel Kant's 1785 essay, 'On the Wrongfulness of Reprinting'. Drawing upon book history, media theory and literary studies, this book analyses the essay's paratexts as indices of literary production in the German Enlightenment. Far from being an idealist proponent of intellectual property, Kant is shown to be a media theorist and practitioner, whose critical negotiation with the evolving print machinery in his time helps to illuminate our present struggle with digital technology and the mounting pressures borne by copyright as a proprietary institution. Through its novel perspective on established debates surrounding authorship, this book critiques the proprietary conception of authorship in copyright law and proposes an ethical alternative that responds to the production, circulation and reading of literature. This title is also available as open access on Cambridge Core.

Benjamin Goh is Assistant Professor in the Faculty of Law, National University of Singapore. He was awarded the 2024 Zipporah B. Wiseman Prize for Scholarship on Law, Literature, and Justice.

CAMBRIDGE INTELLECTUAL PROPERTY AND INFORMATION LAW

As its economic potential has rapidly expanded, intellectual property has become a subject of front-rank legal importance. Cambridge Intellectual Property and Information Law is a series of monograph studies of major current issues in intellectual property. Each volume contains a mix of international, European, comparative and national law, making this a highly significant series for practitioners, judges and academic researchers in many countries.

A list of books in the series can be found at the end of this volume.

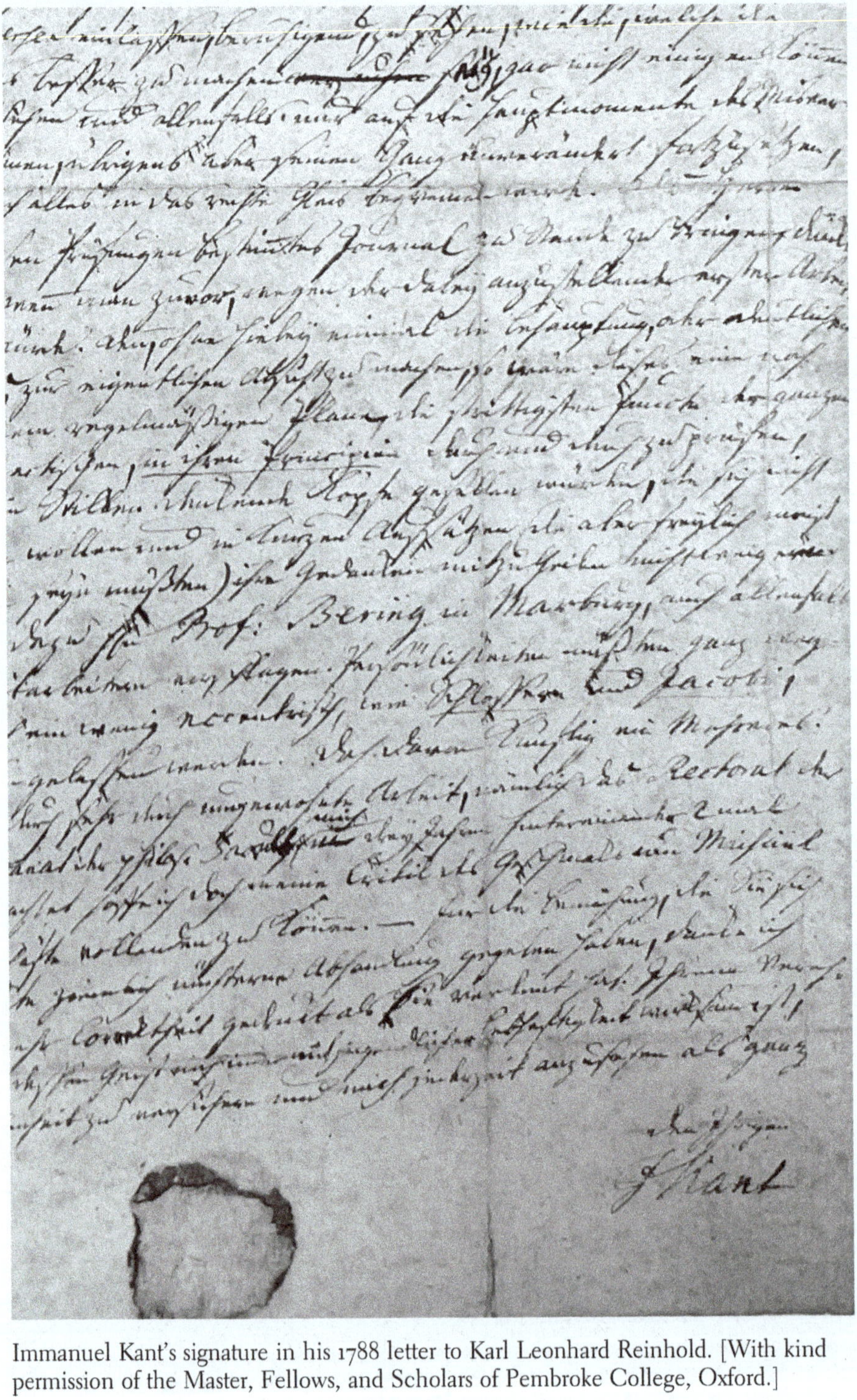

Immanuel Kant's signature in his 1788 letter to Karl Leonhard Reinhold. [With kind permission of the Master, Fellows, and Scholars of Pembroke College, Oxford.]

The Materiality of Literature

REREADING AUTHORSHIP AND COPYRIGHT WITH KANT

BENJAMIN GOH
National University of Singapore

CAMBRIDGE
UNIVERSITY PRESS

CAMBRIDGE
UNIVERSITY PRESS

Shaftesbury Road, Cambridge CB2 8EA, United Kingdom

One Liberty Plaza, 20th Floor, New York, NY 10006, USA

477 Williamstown Road, Port Melbourne, VIC 3207, Australia

314–321, 3rd Floor, Plot 3, Splendor Forum, Jasola District Centre, New Delhi – 110025, India

103 Penang Road, #05-06/07, Visioncrest Commercial, Singapore 238467

Cambridge University Press is part of Cambridge University Press & Assessment, a department of the University of Cambridge.

We share the University's mission to contribute to society through the pursuit of education, learning and research at the highest international levels of excellence.

www.cambridge.org

Information on this title: www.cambridge.org/9781009654319

DOI: 10.1017/9781009654296

When citing this work, please include a reference to the DOI 10.1017/9781009654296

First published 2025

Cover image: Immanuel Kant's signature in his 1788 letter to Karl Leonhard Reinhold: With kind permission of the Master, Fellows, and Scholars of Pembroke College, Oxford.

A catalogue record for this publication is available from the British Library

A Cataloging-in-Publication data record for this book is available from the Library of Congress

ISBN 978-1-009-65431-9 Hardback

Contents

List of Figures — *page* ix
Acknowledgements — xi

Introduction: Literary Materiality and the Question of Authorship — 1

1 **Two Ways of Looking at a Printed Book** — 21

2 **From Paratexts to Print Machinery** — 52

3 **Materialities of Type** — 77

4 **A Biography of I. Kant** — 116

Conclusion: The Ethics of Digital Authorship — 167

Index — 187

Figures

1.1	Footnote on the opticality of books in Kant's 1785 essay	*page* 43
1.2	Title page of Kant's 1784 essay on enlightenment	49
2.1	First page of Kant's 1785 essay and the verso facing it	68
2.2	Frontispiece and title page of the fifth volume of the *Berlinische Monatsschrift*	71
3.1	First page of Fichte's 1793 essay	89
3.2	Last page of Fichte's 1793 essay	113
4.1	List of contributors in Schiller's foreword to the first issue of *Die Horen*	136
4.2	Last page of Kant's 1785 essay	140
4.3	Title page of the May 1785 issue of the *Berlinische Monatsschrift*	143
4.4	Last page of the editors' preface to the first issue of the *Berlinische Monatsschrift*	144
4.5	Title page of Kant's *Zerstreute Aufsätze*	150
4.6	Contents of Kant's *Zerstreute Aufsätze*	151
4.7	Original contents of the May 1785 issue of the *Berlinische Monatsschrift*	152
4.8	Master contents of the May 1785 issue of the *Berlinische Monatsschrift*	153
4.9	Kant's 1790 public notice in the *Allgemeine Literatur-Zeitung*	155
4.10	Kant's 1799 public notice in the *Allgemeine Literatur-Zeitung*	164
C.1	Main page of Wikipedia	169
C.2	Author page of Wikipedia	172
C.3	Revision history of the author page of Wikipedia	174
C.4	Contents of Wikipedia	178

Acknowledgements

This book is indebted to many hands. I am grateful to Alain Pottage, Fiona Macmillan, Brad Sherman, Jose Bellido, and other wondrous ISHTIP colleagues for their support, critique, and reception of the work. For this open-access publication funded by NUS, I thank my encouraging colleagues in the faculty and university. I must also thank Cambridge University Press and everyone whose anonymous labours made it possible.

This book is dedicated to my beloved wife, family, and friends.

Introduction: Literary Materiality and the Question of Authorship

RE-MATERIALISING AUTHORSHIP

This book attends to the materiality of literature as a vital dimension of literary production from which conceptions of authorship, including the proprietary author of modern copyright law, have emerged. The material form of books and other textual publications not only index the densely historical conditions in which they have been received and recently brought under the copyright categories of 'work' and 'author' but also prompt their rethinking beyond the proprietary paradigm. Recognising the current legal orthodoxy of 'literary property' to be a contingent effect of medial-material configurations, largely even if not solely surrounding the eighteenth-century printed book, may yet accede to more ethically robust understandings of books, authors and their importance in public cultures.

To advance this claim, I perform an extended analysis of Immanuel Kant's *Von der Unrechtmäßigkeit des Büchernachdrucks* ('On the Wrongfulness of Reprinting'), an essay originally published in the May 1785 issue of the *Berlinische Monatsschrift*.[1] Though now a celebrated classic in copyright history, Kant's text has mostly been read on the level of its semantic content – that is, for its proposal of a non-proprietary regime of author's rights as a solution to the problem of reprinting in eighteenth-century Germany.[2] The periodical essay's printed form and medium, which exceeds

[1] For a digitised version of the fifth volume of the *Berlinische Monatsschrift* with Kant's essay stored in the Bavarian State Library, see www.digitale-sammlungen.de/en/view/bsb10926844?q = %28berlinische+monatsschrift+1785%29&page = ,1 (accessed 9 September 2024). This book also refers to the following English translation: Immanuel Kant, 'On the Wrongfulness of Unauthorized Publication of Books (1785)', in *Practical Philosophy*, ed. Paul Guyer and Allen W. Wood, trans. Mary J. Gregor, The Cambridge Edition of the Works of Immanuel Kant (Cambridge: Cambridge University Press, 1996), 27–35. See also 'Kant: On the Unlawfulness of Reprinting, Berlin (1785)', Primary Sources on Copyright (1450-1900), eds L. Bently & M. Kretschmer, www.copyrighthistory.org/cam/tools/request/showRepresentation.php?id = representation_d_1785 (accessed 9 September 2024).

[2] On Kantian copyright scholarship, see Chapter 1.

its putative message, is otherwise ignored. Drawing upon the insights of book history, media theory and literary studies, I apprehend some of the essay's paratexts, including its catchwords, signature marks, front matter, typesetting and printed authorial name, as indices of literary production in the German Enlightenment. For its presentation before the eighteenth-century German reading public, Kant's text depended on such peripheral matters, which extended from a print machinery that he sought to steer even as it preceded, and threatened to engulf, his authorial interventions.[3] Both the historical period in which Kant was writing and the gesture in his writing are especially pertinent to our critique of copyright qua proprietary authorship. As copyright historians are familiar, the eighteenth century with its burgeoning book trades across Western Europe is often affirmed to be the vital period that precipitated modern understandings of the author as Romantic genius and proprietary author.[4] Whether or not the proprietary author predated the eighteenth century,[5] and regardless of discernible tensions between genius and copyright,[6] this historical period offers us a privileged look at the role of print in propagating, and potentially contesting, the proprietary understanding of authorship. Further and relatedly, as critical intellectual property scholars have begun to observe, Kant's publications registered their author's acute awareness of the medial-material conditions in which he was writing, so much so that he may be viewed as a media theorist *avant la lettre*.[7] For Kant, print was the very medium that put into relation authors and public readers, the mediated interaction between whom he situated at the heart of enlightenment practice. As we shall learn in regard to the form and placement of Kant's authorial name, Kant exhibited a critical, and markedly ethical, understanding of authorship that well surpasses the utilitarian-proprietary account in copyright law.[8] It is this ethical instance of the author-function, I argue, that our return to Kant and eighteenth-century Germany offers as a richer substitute for the proprietary conception that legal scholars have tended to

3 On the print machinery of late eighteenth-century Germany, see Chapters 2–4.

4 See, for instance, Martha Woodmansee, 'The Genius and the Copyright: Economic and Legal Conditions of the Emergence of the "Author"', *Eighteenth-Century Studies* 17, no. 4 (1984): 425–48; Martha Woodmansee, *The Author, Art, and the Market: Rereading the History of Aesthetics* (New York: Columbia University Press, 1994); Mark Rose, 'The Author as Proprietor: Donaldson v Becket and the Genealogy of Modern Authorship', *Representations* 23 (1988): 51–85; Mark Rose, *Authors and Owners: The Invention of Copyright* (Cambridge, MA: Harvard University Press, 1993).

5 For a persuasive argument that it did, see Roger Chartier, 'Foucault's Chiasmus: Authorship between Science and Literature in the Seventeenth and Eighteenth Centuries', in *Scientific Authorship: Credit and Intellectual Property in Science*, ed. Mario Biagioli and Peter Galison (London: Routledge, 2003), 13–31.

6 For an illuminating account of the Romantic genius as copyright's *pharmakon*, see Mario Biagioli, 'Genius against Copyright: Revisiting Fichte's Proof of the Illegality of Reprinting', *Notre Dame Law Review* 86, no. 5 (2011): 1847–68.

7 See Alain Pottage and Mario Biagioli, 'What Is a Book? Kant and the Law of the Letter', *Critical Inquiry* 49, no. 4 (2023): 605–25.

8 See Chapter 4.

stress in Michel Foucault's landmark theoretical intervention,[9] and which presently prevails across copyright regimes. Far from being an idealist proponent of intellectual property,[10] Kant is better understood to be a media theorist and practitioner, whose critical negotiation with the evolving print machinery in his time helps to illuminate our present struggle with digital technology and the mounting pressures borne by copyright as a proprietary institution.

The material form of Kant's eighteenth-century essay and its present implications on copyright qua proprietary authorship may seem to be of limited interest to doctrinal lawyers and others who accede to the hegemonic law of intellectual property. Copyright law is a predominantly proprietary institution that grants authors (and other statutorily prescribed owners) economic rights, including the right to exclude others from reproducing their works, so as to reward and incentivise their production of literature and other cultural goods while facilitating the public's access to these goods.[11] On the utilitarian-proprietary perspective, a printed book largely matters only as the material embodiment of literary property, whose ownership by its author serves the societal goal of promoting the production and consumption of the literary good.[12] However, it is my argument that Kant's essay, when read across the levels of medium and content, discloses that the ascendancy of the proprietary paradigm was neither inevitable nor necessarily desirable. It remains imaginable for literary and other forms of cultural reproduction to be articulated and regulated through non-proprietary idioms that illuminate instead the social and ethical significance of books, culture, and authors. Kant also recognised that inherited practices that have become institutional dogma are to be radically questioned rather than exempt from critique. Kant's rousing preface to the original edition of the *Kritik der reinen Vernunft* ('Critique of Pure Reason') remains instructive:

9 Michel Foucault, 'What Is an Author?', in *Language, Counter-Memory, Practice: Selected Essays and Interviews: Selected Essays and Interviews by Michel Foucault*, ed. Donald F. Bouchard (Ithaca, NY: Cornell University Press, 1977), 113–38. I argue alongside Chartier that Foucault more importantly offers a material understanding of the author-function, which commentators have tended to elide.

10 For various (mis)readings of Kant as an intellectual property proponent, see Robert P. Merges, *Justifying Intellectual Property* (Cambridge, MA: Harvard University Press, 2011); Leslie Kim Treiger-Bar-Am, 'Kant on Copyright: Rights of Transformative Authorship', *Cardozo Arts & Entertainment Law Journal* 25, no. 3 (2008): 1059–103; William Fisher, 'Theories of Intellectual Property', in *New Essays in the Legal and Political Theory of Property*, ed. Stephen R. Munzer (Cambridge: Cambridge University Press, 2001). For critiques of these accounts, see Anne Barron, 'Kant, Copyright and Communicative Freedom', *Law and Philosophy* 31, no. 1 (2012): 1–48; Maria Chiara Pievatolo, 'Freedom, Ownership and Copyright: Why Does Kant Reject the Concept of Intellectual Property?', *Società Italiana Di Filosofia Politica*, 2010, 1–10.

11 We should note that there are also moral rights that protect the reputation of authors (which, as we will see in Chapter 4, might interest Kant), though these are fairly limited and rarely the objects of dispute. On moral rights in the United Kingdom, see Lionel Bently et al., 'Moral Rights', in *Intellectual Property Law* (Oxford: Oxford University Press, 2022), 303.

12 On utilitarian copyright, see Chapter 1.

> Our age is the genuine age of criticism, to which everything must submit. Religion through its holiness and legislation through its majesty commonly seek to exempt themselves from it. But in this way they excite a just suspicion against themselves, and cannot lay claim to that unfeigned respect that reason grants only to that which has been able to withstand its free and public examination.[13]

Having acquired the authority of law, proprietary authorship now needs to be publicly reviewed rather than unquestioningly affirmed as the cornerstone of modern and contemporary copyright law. My suggestion is that the medium of print, in particular Kant's 1785 essay, affords a critical rereading of authorship and copyright that suspends, even refutes, the proprietary paradigm.

FOUR FACES OF KANT IN AUTHORSHIP AND COPYRIGHT

This book returns to Kant and his essay on author's rights about four decades after Martha Woodmansee's landmark genealogy of the modern author as an effect of the eighteenth-century print markets in which European writers like Kant were working.[14] Between then and now, the proper name 'Kant' has come to stand for varying positions within authorship and copyright studies, four of which may be adumbrated here. My present intention is as much to clarify the distinctiveness of this book's contribution as to acknowledge its indebtedness to a tradition of critical and cross-disciplinary legal scholarship.

First, in Woodmansee's germinal contributions to the history of authorship, Kant appears as the principal theorist of aesthetics whose concepts shaped the interventions of late eighteenth- and early nineteenth-century writers, including Johann Adam Bergk's *Die Kunst, Bücher zu lesen* (1799) ('The Art of Reading Books') and Samuel Taylor Coleridge's 'On the Principles of Genial Criticism concerning the Fine Arts' (1814).[15] This account of Kant as an aesthetician with insights into the social significance of authorship may be less familiar to copyright scholars, who have mostly focused on Woodmansee's 1984 study of the economic and legal conditions of the emergence of modern authorship.[16] In Woodmansee's classic response to

[13] See Immanuel Kant, *Critique of Pure Reason*, ed. and trans. Paul Guyer and Allen W. Wood (Cambridge: Cambridge University Press, 1998), 101–2.

[14] Woodmansee, 'The Genius and the Copyright'; Woodmansee, *The Author, Art, and the Market*.

[15] See, especially, chapters 4 and 6 of Woodmansee, *The Author, Art, and the Market*. For a digitised version of Bergk's work, see www.digitale-sammlungen.de/de/view/bsb10400331?page = ,1.

[16] As Kathy Bowrey has sharply observed, this tendency amongst legal scholars to focus on the authorship essay without regard for the surrounding book chapters on the fine arts, poetry, reading habits and gender has inadvertently suppressed Woodmansee's insights into the importance of considering copyright law alongside and within debates surrounding the social and cultural significance of literature and art: see Kathy Bowrey, 'Law, Aesthetics and Copyright Historiography: A Critical Reading of the Genealogies of Martha Woodmansee

Foucault's prior appeal to historicise the modern individualisation of authors and works,[17] Kant's name was only ambiguously cited alongside his student Johann Gottlieb Fichte's as one of the German discussants to have elaborated on Edward Young's proto-Romantic theory of original authorship while contributing to the late eighteenth-century debate over the nature of books and problem of reprinting.[18] Whereas Fichte's distinction between the privately owned 'form' of ideas and the commonly owned 'ideas' was carefully reprised and further claimed to be the conceptual basis of subsequently enacted copyright laws, no mention was made of Kant's 1785 essay on the wrongfulness of reprinting. Only in the revised chapter of Woodmansee's 1994 monograph do we find an accompanying endnote referencing Kant's essay in the *Berlinische Monatsschrift* alongside more than ten other titles contributing to the late eighteenth-century German debate on books.[19]

Notwithstanding the strange elision, and perhaps inadvertent suppression, of Kant's legal-theoretical contribution, Woodmansee crucially positions Kantian aesthetics as an influential tradition of intellectual thought that has evolved alongside the burgeoning book trades of late eighteenth-century Europe and further sought to shape the reading habits of German and English reading publics. Consider the context of late eighteenth-century Germany: alarmed by the indiscriminate, diversionary reading practices that accompanied the proliferation of books,[20] Bergk joined other European contemporaries (a forerunner being the English writer Joseph Addison)[21] in advancing corrective modes of reading that stressed instead the cultivation of aesthetic judgement or taste: that is, the 'ability to judge nature and art so as to become acquainted with these in terms of the feelings they inspire in us'[22] through serious literary forms such as poems, plays and novels. Bergk's account of taste was conceptually indebted to Kant's analytics of the beautiful and the sublime in *Kritik der Urteilskraft* (1790) ('Critique of Judgment').[23] What Kant had understood to be the universal feelings of beauty and sublimity invoked in persons by cultural artefacts and natural phenomena were similarly stressed in Bergk's

and Mark Rose', in *Research Handbook on the History of Copyright Law*, ed. Isabella Alexander and H. Tomás Gómez-Arostegui (Cheltenham: Edward Elgar Publishing, 2016), 29.

17 See Foucault, 'What Is an Author?'. For more on Foucault's work, see Chapter 4.

18 Woodmansee, 'The Genius and the Copyright', 440. See 'Fichte: Proof of the Unlawfulness of Reprinting, Berlin (1793)', Primary Sources on Copyright (1450-1900), eds L. Bently & M. Kretschmer, accessed 9 September 2024, www.copyrighthistory.org/cam/tools/request/showRecord.php?id = record_d_1793.

19 Woodmansee, *The Author, Art, and the Market*, 161.

20 On the problem of print surfeit in eighteenth-century Germany, see Chapter 2.

21 See Joseph Addison, 'The Pleasures of the Imagination', in *The Spectator*, ed. Donald F. Bond, vol. 3 (Oxford: Clarendon Press, 1965).

22 Woodmansee, *The Author, Art, and the Market*, 95, citing Bergk, 176.

23 Immanuel Kant, *Critique of the Power of Judgment*, ed. Paul Guyer, trans. Paul Guyer and Eric Matthews (Cambridge: Cambridge University Press, 2000). See also Kant's preceding 1764 essay: Immanuel Kant, *Observations on the Feeling of the Beautiful and Sublime and Other Writings*, ed. Patrick Frierson and Paul Guyer (Cambridge: Cambridge University Press, 2011).

exposition on taste as the faculty of discriminating between pleasing and displeasing objects that elicited those very affective responses in viewers.[24] Further drawing upon Kant's account of taste as consisting of wholly 'disinterested and free'[25] judgements – that is, the contemplation of works without concern for their utility or advantage to the perceiver – Bergk differentiated the popular literary forms in his time (including sensationalist, sentimental and moralist fictions) from the more esteemed masterpieces (for instance, 'Johann Wolfgang Goethe's *Die Leiden des jungen Werthers* (1744) ('The Sorrows of Young Werther') and Christoph Martin Wieland's *Geschichte des Agathon* (1766) ('The History of Agathon')) that evidenced and fostered the free play of the imagination and understanding.[26] Against the passive and extensive consumption of popular printed matter, Bergk relied upon Kant's theory of aesthetics to articulate, demonstrate, and promulgate a more active and intensive mode of reading that, ultimately, empowered readers to derive pleasure from the formally accomplished classics. In other words, Kant was the leading intellectual authority to whom Bergk (and, later, Coleridge in respect of early nineteenth-century England)[27] sought recourse to instruct the reading public on both the value and means of (re-)immersing in the literary classics that offered the highest forms of aesthetic experience.

Woodmansee's appreciation of Kant's influence over the early modern European literary imagination is vital to this book because it anticipates the present resituation of proprietary authorship alongside other conceptions of authorship that had coexisted in the late eighteenth-century. Though the putative continuity between the Romantic genius and copyright's proprietary author was one of the central claims in 'Genius and the Copyright', Woodmansee's more insightful, and arguably more robust, contribution was to disclose the multiple, and often competing, senses of authorship that circulated during that historical period. Bergk and other Kantian aestheticians saw the book neither as consisting in something ideal that was perpetually owned by its author (Fichte's position) nor as an intangible work whose reproduction and use was to be so regulated as to simultaneously reward and incentivise its creation while ensuring public access to it (the logic of utilitarian copyright). Rather, late eighteen-century writers recognised that books and other printed matter had larger pedagogical, social and potentially ethical roles to play in respect of personal and collective human development. Kantian aesthetics went

[24] Bergk, 176, cited in Woodmansee, *The Author, Art, and the Market*, 95.

[25] Kant, *Critique of the Power of Judgment*, 95.

[26] Woodmansee, *The Author, Art, and the Market*, 98. See also Kant, *Critique of the Power of Judgment*, 103.

[27] Samuel Taylor Coleridge, 'On the Principles of Genial Criticism Concerning the Fine Arts, More Especially Those of Statuary and Painting, Deduced from the Laws and Impulses Which Guide the True Artist in the Production of HIs Works', in *Biographia Literaria*, ed. John Shawcross, vol. 2 (Oxford: Oxford University Press, 1907). See also Woodmansee's discussion of Coleridge's transposition of Kant to England in Woodmansee, *The Author, Art, and the Market*, 111–47.

beyond the liberalist, proprietary and self-interested authorial subject. Bergk himself stressed that the literary cultivation of taste was part of one's psychical maturation so as to 'fulfil [one's] responsibilities as a human being and a citizen'.[28] As sharply observed by Kathy Bowrey, reading Woodmansee's 'Genius and the Copyright' alongside her other book chapters allows us to see 'a much larger social and cultural project in train'[29] during the late eighteenth century than the self-centred and industry-oriented paradigm of literary property. In step with Woodmansee, I argue that proprietary authorship was neither the only understanding of authorship nor the most desirable one in Kant's time. Indeed, Kant's 1785 essay directs us to the very technological and medial-material conditions from which conceptions of authorship emerged, and which Woodmansee, insofar as the printed book opened and undergirded her analysis,[30] recognised as accompanying, even preceding, the legal and economic conditions that generated the modern author.

The second way in which Kant has been interpreted in authorship and copyright history is as an intellectual property forerunner or proponent. For Robert P. Merges and other advocates of intellectual property, it is Kant's property theory rather than his philosophical aesthetics that affords a Kantian rethinking of authorship (and, relatedly, inventorship).[31] Dissatisfied with the utilitarian grounds on which the proprietary edifices of copyright, patent and trademark have tended to be justified, Merges has sought to extend Kant's concept of property (advanced in *Rechtslehre* ('Doctrine of Right') (1797)), from the domain of physical objects to that of so-called intangibles such as literary or artistic works.[32] On Merges's reading, Kant was at heart a liberal philosopher who prioritised property rights and obligations as the means with which to secure the individual's exercise of will. 'As a legal right, the essence of property for Kant is this: other people have a duty to respect claims over objects that

[28] Bergk, 107; cited in Woodmansee, *The Author, Art, and the Market*, 93.

[29] Bowrey, 'Law, Aesthetics and Copyright Historiography', 34. Bowrey also observed that Woodmansee was more interested in writing a genealogy of aesthetics than in a genealogy of authorship or law. Whilst this might be true, it remains open to us to unpack the implications of her rich study of Kantian aesthetics on authorship and the limits of proprietary authorship through this return to Kant's elided 1785 essay.

[30] See Woodmansee's reference to an encyclopedia entry on the eighteenth-century printed book as 'the motto' (p. 48) of her chapter: Woodmansee, *The Author, Art, and the Market*, 35.

[31] Merges, *Justifying Intellectual Property*, 68–101. Other than Merges's work, see Riccardo Pozzo, 'Immanuel Kant on Intellectual Property', *Trans/Form/Ação, São Paulo* 29, no. 2 (2006): 11–18; Fisher, 'Theories of Intellectual Property'. For two critiques of these accounts, see Barron, 'Kant, Copyright and Communicative Freedom'; Pievatolo, 'Freedom, Ownership and Copyright'.

[32] Merges, *Justifying Intellectual Property*, 72. Merges refers to the translation in Immanuel Kant, 'The Metaphysics of Morals (1797)', in *Practical Philosophy*, ed. Paul Guyer and Allen W. Wood, trans. Mary J. Gregor (Cambridge: Cambridge University Press, 1996), 353–603. Other than to Kant's philosophical works, Merges refers to those of John Locke, John Rawls, Robert Nozick and Jeremy Waldron in the initial half of the book dedicated to 'a search for foundations' of intellectual property law: Merges, *Justifying Intellectual Property*, 2.

are bound up with the exercise of an individual's will.'[33] Property rights in objects are necessary to affirm the autonomy of individuals, who rely on their use of such objects to carry out their projects in the world. Whilst recognising Kant's focus on physical property in the doctrine of right, Merges opts to extend Kant's insights to such 'intellectual creations' and 'intangible media' as literature and other cultural works: 'We are … free to apply Kant's idea to the building blocks of intellectual creations, just as we do for other assets such as blocks of marble or land. Many people in the modern world may choose to express themselves in intangible media.'[34] For Merges, Kant's idea of property and its relationship with autonomy could be readily reconciled with, and more robustly justify, the prevailing regimes of intellectual property.

For now, suspending judgement on the (im)propriety of Merges's citation of Kant,[35] let us note that Merges neglects the 1785 essay in which Kant had proposed a distinctly *non-proprietary* solution to the problem of reprinting in late eighteenth-century Germany. In 'On the Wrongfulness of Reprinting', Kant had eschewed the language of literary property, opting instead to see the printed book as a communicative medium to be regulated according to a system of publishers' and authors' rights that was grounded in the author's 'innate right in his own person'.[36] For Kant, a print publication did not consist in an intangible object of property owned by its author, but rather served to relay to the public a speech made 'simply and solely in the author's name'.[37] The legitimate publisher was an agent empowered by the author to communicate with the public. It was from the perspective of public communication, not literary property, that Kant argued against the unauthorised publication of books and other texts in his time. Contrary to Fichte's claim, Kant and he were not fellow travellers 'on the same road'[38] leading up to a commonly endorsed legal system of proprietary authorship. Rather, Kant's argument against unauthorised reprinting was based on an account of the book as a speech act, extending from the author's personhood, whose addressee was the reading public.

Kant's conception of the book as public address has facilitated critical reimaginings of the copyright sphere, from an instituted space governed by the logic of incentives and rewards to one where social ends, including those of egalitarian authorship, truth seeking and collective emancipation, could be realised.[39] This third face of Kant is as a non-proprietary proponent of author's rights who recognised the potential emancipatory significance of publications as speech acts. For instance, Anne Barron reads the essay's system of publishers' and authors' rights as the

33 Merges, *Justifying Intellectual Property*, 72.
34 Ibid., 73–74.
35 On Barron's critique of Merges, see Chapter 4.
36 Kant, 'On the Wrongfulness of Unauthorized Publication of Books (1785)', 35.
37 Ibid., 30.
38 'Fichte: Proof of the Unlawfulness of Reprinting, Berlin (1793)'.
39 On Kantian copyright scholarship, see Chapter 1.

juridical arrangement for securing the public use of reason which Kant had theorised as the practice of enlightenment in another essay published in the *Berlinische Monatsschrift* just a year prior.[40] A non-proprietary system of rights in literary (re) production was one of the legal-empirical conditions of possibility for ensuring the 'communicative freedom'[41] of authors and a culture of 'free public criticism'.[42] For Barron, though Kant's idea of author's rights was proposed as a solution to a specific problem in eighteenth-century Germany, it nonetheless paves the way for our re-evaluation of contemporary copyright regimes, which remain bound to utilitarian and proprietary modes of organisation.

Helpful as Barron and other Kantian copyright scholars have been in constructing more socially involved imaginings of copyright based on Kant's non-proprietary understanding of the book, they have tended to focus on the rhetorical content of the 1785 essay (and other related works), and even then only on those parts concerning the book's operation as public speech act (*opera*). If we revisit the essay for what it 'says', we shall find that it oscillates between two senses of the printed book, the other of which has tended to be suppressed in contemporary interpretations of the text.[43] Not only was the book understood to be a communicative act (*opera*) in which the personhood of the authorial speaker was involved; it was also recognised to be a manufactured object (*opus*) whose printed letters afforded its reading. In a key footnote, Kant described the book as a 'mute instrument',[44] distinguishing it from acoustic media such as the 'megaphone'[45] or 'mouth'[46] that 'delivers speech by sound'[47] and underscoring its status as an optical medium that operated 'by letters'.[48] Since it is by means of the visible letters of Kant's essay that it is read for what it 'says', this material dimension of the text could be understood as that which affords the production of its meaning. Even at the level of its 'content', Kant's essay registered the visual-corporeal basis on which printed texts like itself operated during the late eighteenth century (and beyond). And yet, the medial-materiality of the 1785 essay was not discussed by its contemporary legal readers, as if it had nothing to do with our understanding of the text and its place in the history of authorship and copyright. Ceding priority to (parts of) its ostensible 'message', the medium of the text, along with its conscious turn to its own mediality, remains

40 Immanuel Kant, 'An Answer to the Question: What Is Enlightenment? (1784)', in *Practical Philosophy*, ed. and trans. Mary J. Gregor (Cambridge: Cambridge University Press, 1996), 15–22.

41 Barron, 'Kant, Copyright and Communicative Freedom', 39.

42 Ibid., 38.

43 On these two senses of the printed book, see Chapter 2.

44 Kant, 'On the Wrongfulness of Unauthorized Publication of Books (1785)', 30.

45 Ibid.

46 Ibid.

47 Ibid.

48 Ibid.

below what Cornelia Vismann had separately referred to as 'the perception threshold of the law'.[49]

What if Kant was a media theorist and, indeed, a media practitioner? In their recent return to Kant's 1785 essay and related works, Alain Pottage and Mario Biagioli come closest to presenting the fourth face of Kant as a thinker of media.[50] Inverting the traditional prioritisation of persons over things in the discourses of intellectual property and law more generally, Pottage and Biagioli underscore Kant's attendance to the print medium as the material basis on which various eighteenth-century literary roles, be they authors or public readers, were generated. It is the print typeface and typeset pages, rather than the personal visage, that their rethinking of Kant foregrounds. Whereas Barron and other Kantian copyright scholars have stressed the non-proprietary legal arrangement of author's rights proposed by Kant as a socially richer yet no less viable alternative to contemporary regimes of intellectual property, Pottage and Biagioli more crucially recognise such legal solutions to be possibilities technically prescribed by the printed book qua optical medium. If Kant had advanced a law of agency with which to apprehend the legitimate publisher's role in remediating and transmitting the author's speech as print, then this law was also one premised upon 'the medial agency of print itself',[51] that is, on the capacity of print both to bring into existence and register on its pages (for instance the title page)[52] print actors such as authors, publishers, and public readers. The authors put it well: 'As Kant appreciated ... [the] medium of print is alive; through its own agency, it configures the roles of author and reader and represents each to the other.'[53]

This book renews Pottage and Biagioli's medial rethinking of Kant by taking seriously the print medium in which Kant's intervention was advanced. My argument is that the most productive and satisfactory way in which to assess the place of Kant in authorship and copyright history is through the printed pages that bear his authorial name, 'I. Kant'.[54] Kant's essay on author's rights, his earlier and more famous contribution on enlightenment practice, and other eighteenth-century publications have yet to be studied collectively for what they disclose about the medial-material conditions in which conceptions of authorship arose. However insightful, the commentaries surrounding Kant's philosophical aesthetics, property

[49] Cornelia Vismann, *Files: Law and Media Technology*, trans. Geoffrey Winthrop-Young (Stanford, CA: Stanford University Press, 2008), 11.

[50] Pottage and Biagioli, 'What Is a Book?'. See also Alain Pottage, 'Literary Materiality', in *Routledge Handbook of Law and Theory*, ed. Andreas Philippopoulos-Mihalopoulos (London: Routledge, 2019), 409–29; Alain Pottage, 'The Materiality of What?', *Journal of Law and Society* 39, no. 1 (2012): 167–83; Alain Pottage and Brad Sherman, *Figures of Invention: A History of Modern Patent Law* (Oxford: Oxford University Press, 2010).

[51] Pottage and Biagioli, 'What Is a Book?', 606.

[52] On the 'jurisprudence of the title page', see Pottage and Biagioli, 'What Is a Book?', 614–17.

[53] Pottage and Biagioli, 'What Is a Book?', 610–11.

[54] On Kant's authorial name, see Chapter 4.

theory and author's rights theory are unfinished inasmuch as they have yet to reckon fully with the author's conscious dealings with the print machinery in his time. As a result of this medial disinterest, authorship and copyright history studies have not been able to unpack the potential implications of Kant's 1785 intervention on the digital public sphere. It is my present task to re-materialise Kant's text(s) and the multiple conceptions of authorship at play in late eighteenth-century Germany to pave the way for further investigations into the digital afterlife of Kant's works.

EXCURSIONS INTO BOOK HISTORY, MEDIA THEORY AND LITERARY STUDIES

My rereading of authorship and copyright alongside Kant draws upon the intersecting traditions of book history, media theory and literary studies. Consolidating some of the key works and authors here, otherwise cited across the book, may clarify the theoretico-historical bases of this interest in the materiality of literature.[55]

When read alongside Roger Chartier's book history, Foucault's founding study of the author-function suggests itself to be as much interested in the materialities of authorship as it was in the author's function of limiting the proliferation of meaning in discourse.[56] As a critical archaeologist keen on excavating the rules according to which knowledge was produced, disseminated and received,[57] Foucault took an interest in the role of the author in the existence, circulation and operation of discourses. Roland Barthes's projected supersession of the 'Author-God'[58] with the anonymous reader, one 'without history, biography, psychology ... simply that *someone* who holds together in single field all the traces by which the written text is constituted',[59] was less interesting than his opening observation about the production of the author as a 'modern figure',[60] one emergent from history, asserting its tyrannical monopoly over textual interpretation despite the challenges issued by French literary modernism during the late nineteenth and early twentieth centuries. Rather than calling for a desertion of the author-figure (as if that were possible),

55 For two examples of other media-oriented studies in the law of copyright and patents, see Monika Dommann, *Authors and Apparatus: A Media History of Copyright*, trans. Sarah Pybus (Ithaca, NY: Cornell University Press, 2019); Alain Pottage and Brad Sherman, *Figures of Invention: A History of Modern Patent Law* (Oxford: Oxford University Press, 2010).

56 Roger Chartier, 'Figures of the Author', in *The Order of Books: Readers, Authors, and Libraries in Europe between the Fourteenth and Eighteenth Centuries*, trans. Lydia G. Cochrane (Stanford, CA: Stanford University Press, 1994), 25–59; Chartier, 'Foucault's Chiasmus'; Roger Chartier, *The Author's Hand and the Printer's Mind*, trans. Lydia G. Cochrane (Cambridge: Polity Press, 2014); Michel Foucault, 'What Is an Author?'.

57 See Michel Foucault, *The Archaeology of Knowledge* (London: Routledge, 2002).

58 Roland Barthes, 'The Death of the Author', in *Image Music Text*, trans. Stephen Heath (London: Fontana, 1977), 146.

59 Ibid., 148.

60 Ibid., 142.

Foucault recognised the importance of attending to its mutable historical conditions of possibility and variable discursive functions.

> Perhaps the time has come to study not only the expressive value and formal transformations of discourse, but its mode of existence: the modifications and variations, within any culture, of modes of circulation, valorization, attribution, and appropriation. Partially at the expense of themes and concepts that an author places in his work, the 'author-function' could also reveal the manner in which discourse is articulated on the basis of social relationships.[61]

It was to enable 'an historical analysis of discourse',[62] one attentive to such controlling practices as the bibliographic and hermeneutic classification of works under the names of individual authors, that Foucault made a preliminary sketch of four key features of the author-function.[63]

Though studies in authorship and copyright have tended to centre upon Foucault's first comments on the *proprietary* and *penal* understanding of authorship,[64] Foucault's theorisation of the author-function was by no means limited to its operation in legal discourse. Read alongside the remaining pages, Foucault's discussion of the mutual imbrication of cultural understandings of authorship with those enforced in private and public law simply anticipated, by way of illustration, his subsequent remarks on what appear to be more fundamental facets of the author-function. Provisionally localised within legal discourse and presented as bifurcated into its penal and proprietary instantiations in two successive periods of history, authorship was shown to be a discursively specific and historically contingent formation.[65] Further, depicted as bound up in the machinery of law, itself enmeshed with religion, politics and the economy, the author-function revealed its indebtedness to a material complex of procedures, practices and protocols, without which there is no authorship.[66] Lastly, by excavating multiple social understandings of the author, prior or current, legal or non-legal, Foucault staged the dispersal and multiplication of the author-function, suggesting its meaning to be gleaned from the continuities and tensions between varying discursive sites.[67] The law of authorship, however exemplary and indubitably pertinent to the history of authors and works, is but one of the many sites where the author-function derives, and discloses, its significance.

New materialist readings of Foucault often surround the late concept of *dispositif*: an historical assemblage composed of both discursive and non-discursive elements, 'a thoroughly heterogenous ensemble consisting of ... the said as much as the

[61] Foucault, 'What Is an Author?', 137.
[62] Ibid.
[63] On these four features of the author-function, see Ibid., 124–31.
[64] See, for instance, Woodmansee, 'The Genius and the Copyright'; Rose, *Authors and Owners*.
[65] Foucault, 'What Is an Author?', 125–27.
[66] Ibid., 127–29.
[67] Ibid., 129–30.

unsaid',[68] the critical mapping of which is the key to understanding power as it has been exercised in any given locality. But already in Foucault's discussion of the author-function and its dependence on such material features as the names of authors we glean his acute awareness of the interplay between verbal and non-verbal elements of the scene of reading. Far from being a merely passive object of action, the book was recognised to be vitally constitutive of the presently dominant legal-cultural understanding of authors as personal creators and owners of intangible works. '[T]hese aspects of an individual, which we designate as an author (or which comprise an individual as an author), are *projections, in terms of always more or less psychological, of our way of handling texts*.'[69] It is in the encounter with books that readers have come to see themselves and others as authors, actual or potential, standing over against them. Authorial names affixed to books, as if they were authoritative identifiers of their makers, belong to 'a series of precise and complex procedures'[70] by which texts were attributed to individual creators.

Despite having conceptualised authorship as a discursive function, then, Foucault already understood authorship to be 'also a function of the materiality of the text'.[71] Through a series of book-historical investigations into the history of authorship,[72] Chartier succeeded in demonstrating not only the material indebtedness of the author-function but also its uneasy coexistence with other historical forces indexed in the printed pages of books. Whilst rightly wary of the book's potential complicity in the silencing of marginal voices ('the silences of those who never wrote; the silences of those whose words, thoughts, and acts the masters of writing thought unimportant'[73]), Chartier understood its material form to be a privileged index of the historical processes from which it emerged, including those pertaining to the socio-technological system of print, the regimes of print regulation and financing, and their interactions with subsisting ideas of authorship.

For instance, by returning to various front matter and paratexts of Migel de Cervantes's *Don Quixote*, Chartier showed how the typographical form and placement of the proper names of author, patron, printer and publisher on the original 1605 title page of Part I of the book pointed to the techno-institutional network in

[68] Michel Foucault, 'The Confession of the Flesh', in *Power/Knowledge: Selected Interviews & Other Writings 1972-1977*, ed. Colin Gordon (New York: Pantheon Books, 1980), 194. For instance, see Gilles Deleuze, 'What Is a Dispositif?', in *Michel Foucault, Philosopher: Essays Translated from the French and German*, trans. Timothy J. Armstrong (New York: Routledge, 1992); Giorgio Agamben, *What Is an Apparatus? And Other Essays*, trans. David Kishik and Stefan Pedatella (Stanford, CA: Stanford University Press, 2009).

[69] Foucault, 'What Is an Author?', 127; emphasis added.

[70] Ibid., 130.

[71] Chartier, 'Foucault's Chiasmus', 28.

[72] Chartier, 'Figures of the Author'; Chartier, 'Foucault's Chiasmus'; Chartier, *The Author's Hand and the Printer's Mind*.

[73] Chartier, *The Author's Hand and the Printer's Mind*, xi.

which multiple print actors of early seventeenth-century Spain had contributed to its production.

> [The] visual space of the title page shows the three things that commanded all literary practice in the Golden Age: a claim to a paternity of the text that the prologue, and then the fiction of Cide Hamete Benengeli, ironically deny; the patronage relationship linking the writer to the duke of Béjar, whose various titles occupy four lines of type; the economic realities of the edition that implied the royal authorization [*Con privilegio*], the work of the printshop (represented on the title page by Juan de la Cuesta's imposing device) and the enterprise of the bookseller/publisher who had financed the edition and sold the copies ('*Vendese en casa de Francisco de Robles, librero del Rey nuestro Señor*').[74]

Well before the first copyright laws of Europe, texts such as *Don Quixote* attributed texts to authors as their creators whilst also evidencing the assemblage of actors and technologies involved in their making. Far from being irrelevant or secondary in importance to the history of authorship and copyright, the material form of books matters as indices of the concrete practices that shaped and reproduced such bibliographic, cultural, economic and legal phenomena.

The second field driving this book's turn to the materiality of literature is that of German media theory, particularly the works of Vismann and Friedrich Kittler. In contrast to mainstream legal scholarship, German media theory takes the medial-technical conditions of meaning and culture seriously, stressing the importance of studying the interplay between the medium and the message. Marshall McLuhan's famous injunction, 'the medium is the message',[75] obtains its afterlife in myriad investigations into the medial or technical a priori of culture and society, past and present, European and non-European.[76] In Vismann's provocative reformulation of the theory of media and cultural techniques in grammatical terms, we find a methodological reversal in the positions occupied by the human and non-human: 'If media theory were, or had, a grammar, that agency [of media and things] would find its expression in objects claiming the grammatical subject position and cultural techniques standing in for verbs. Grammatical persons (and human beings alike) would then assume the place assigned for objects in a given sentence.'[77] In media theory, the non-human thing frees itself from the merely passive role assigned to it in

[74] Chartier, *The Author's Hand and the Printer's Mind*, 139.

[75] Marshall McLuhan, *Understanding Media: The Extensions of Man* (Cambridge, MA: The MIT Press, 1994), 7.

[76] Other than Vismann's and Kittler's works discussed below, see also Bernhard Siegert, *Cultural Techniques: Grids, Filters, Doors, and Other Articulations of the Real*, trans. Geoffrey Winthrop-Young (New York: Fordham University Press, 2015); Wolfgang Ernst, *Digital Memory and the Archive*, ed. Jussi Parikka (Minneapolis: University of Minnesota Press, 2013); Jussi Parikka, *What Is Media Archaeology?* (Hoboken, NJ: John Wiley & Sons, 2012).

[77] Cornelia Vismann, 'Cultural Techniques and Sovereignty', *Theory, Culture & Society* 30, no. 6 (2013): 83.

and by the juridical fiction of the sovereign human actor, and instead assumes its fundamental position as that which actively defines the permissible course of action in a given situation. The term 'cultural techniques' describes those procedures or operations executed by and in reference to medial objects. Examples of such mediated procedures that define modern and contemporary culture include the traditional print-based 'cultural techniques of education, alphabetization, reading, writing'[78] but also extend to 'those [digitally enabled] techniques dictated by computers and the internet'.[79]

When brought to bear on the question of authorship and copyright, the vocabulary of media and cultural techniques enables, even invites a study of the medial-historical conditions under which authors come to be recognised as creators and owners of intangible works. Woodmansee had traced the emergence of the proprietary genius to the professionalisation of German writers within an expanding book trade that lacked adequate legal protection for authorised publishers and writers. In Friedrich Kittler's diagram or 'blueprint'[80] of eighteenth-century German literary culture, on the other hand, the media theorist disclosed the centrality of the predominant communicated medium of that time, namely the printed book, to the prevalent understanding of authorship.

Whereas Fichte and other contemporary proponents of Romantic authorship had overlooked the material surface of the book in preference to the 'mind'[81] that generated it, Kittler recognised that books themselves were involved in the turning of persons into Romantic authors. For instance, Kittler noted that it was through the mass printing, distribution and use of state-sanctioned ABC books or primers around the turn of the nineteenth century that German mothers were enlisted as primary instructors in their children's education.[82] Other than ensuring a general alphabetisation of future authors and readers, these primers from which German mothers read aloud specifically contributed to the making of authors who, like Fichte, were drawn to 'a voice between the lines'.[83] Romantic authorship, a legacy that Woodmansee (and, later, Mark Rose) suggested to be the ideology underpinning today's law of copyright qua intellectual property, was shown to be a phenomenon mediated by print publications and print actors. Vismann's remark on 'the cultural techniques of education, alphabetization, reading, writing'[84] might well have been an allusion to Kittler's medial-historical study of eighteenth-century Germany.

78 Ibid., 89.

79 Ibid.

80 Friedrich Kittler, 'Unpublished Preface to Discourse Networks', trans. Geoffrey Winthrop-Young, *Grey Room* 63 (2016): 93.

81 'Fichte: Proof of the Unlawfulness of Reprinting, Berlin (1793)'. On Fichte's proprietary account of the book, see Chapter 3.

82 See Friedrich Kittler, *Discourse Networks 1800/1900*, trans. Michael Metteer and Chris Cullens (Stanford, CA: Stanford University Press, 1990), 27–53.

83 Ibid., 34.

84 Vismann, 'Cultural Techniques and Sovereignty', 89.

Anticipating Chartier's book-historical investigations into the material evolution of the author-function, Kittler excavated the medial basis of Romantic authorship, where printed matter executed their cultivating and subjectivising operations.

Kant did not feature strongly in Kittler's study. Amongst the prominent German philosophers of the period, it was instead Fichte and Hegel whose works and biographies were cited as examples of a philosophical idealism that collaborated and cohered with the Romantic-genius approach to books and authors advanced by Johann Wolfgang von Goethe and other poets.[85] But as Chad Wellmon has shown, Kant critically contributed to the cultural milieu's negotiation of the problem of print proliferation and its impact on human society, which mirrors our present anxieties about information overload pursuant to the emergence of new digital channels of communication such as social media, blogs, and *Wikipedia*.[86] The contemporary epistemic crisis, in which the research university plays the continuing role of generating and legitimating knowledge, could be productively compared to preceding concerns with print saturation in late eighteenth-century Germany represented in and instantiated by the texts of German intellectuals such as Kant, Fichte and Friedrich Wilhelm Joseph Schelling.[87]

In the opening page of Kant's essay on enlightenment we find Kant's characterisation of the book-object, alongside other personal subjects of authority, as a threat to enlightenment culture: 'It is so comfortable to be a minor! If I have a book that understands for me, a spiritual advisor who has a conscience for me, a doctor who decides upon a regimen for me, and so forth, I need not trouble myself at all.'[88] Having thus identified the agency of print in obstructing the emancipatory process of the human being's exit from immaturity, the essay proceeds to clarify what its proposed solution of the public use of reason entailed, which paradoxically relied on the same print medium that imperilled the freedom of its user. The book was seen to be a critical technology that addressed its own contribution to the problem of readers being unable to distinguish between 'truths' and 'falsehoods', 'good' and 'bad' knowledge practices. Coinciding with Kant's appeal for persons to use their own understanding instead of reproducing dogma, the research university was reimagined by his contemporaries, including Schelling, as an institution directed at cultivating subjects of knowledge competent to navigate the surfeit of print.[89] Rather than being alien to present-day concerns with digital saturation and its

85 Kittler, *Discourse Networks 1800/1900*, 124–73.

86 See Chad Wellmon, *Organizing Enlightenment: Information Overload and the Invention of the Modern Research University* (Baltimore, MD: Johns Hopkins University Press, 2015), 1–19, 123–50.

87 Ibid., 15–16.

88 Kant, 'An Answer to the Question: What Is Enlightenment? (1784)', 17. See Wellmon, *Organizing Enlightenment*, 357; Brad Pasanek and Chad Wellmon, 'Enlightenment, Some Assembly Required', in *The Eighteenth Centuries: Global Networks of Enlightenment*, ed. David T. Gies and Cynthia Wall (Charlottesville: University of Virginia Press, 2018).

89 See Wellmon, *Organizing Enlightenment*, 169–75.

impact on the university, Kant's work and the wider discourse surrounding print proliferation in late eighteenth-century Germany has much to add to our understanding of the relationship between technological change, institutional structures and knowledge practices.

The third field facilitating my investigation into the material form of Kant's essay is literary studies, particularly Gérard Genette's poetics and concept of the paratext.[90] Whereas the doctrinal triad of 'work', 'originality' and 'author' focus on the *literary property* embodied in the book, and whereas Kantian copyright scholarship centres upon the *speech act* of the book, Genette's paratext directs us to the *peripheral matters* or 'thresholds'[91] of the text that present it as an interpretable unit of meaning. The internal sequence of statements forming the signifying contents of a given text on which we tend to focus our interpretive efforts is noted to be dependent upon an open set of auxiliary features – 'the paratext is what enables a text to become a book and to be offered as such to its readers, and, more generally, to the public'.[92] In other words, 'paratext' refers to certain material conditions – front cover, title page, typesetting, page numbers and so forth – on the basis of which a text is presented as a book to be read. To become the book *Paratext* (or the original *Seuils*), Genette's text has had to acquire the printed title and authorial name that afford our identification and interpretation of it. Paratext is a heuristic figure that calls attention to the peripheral matters of the book that tend to escape the conscious reflection of readers – intellectual property lawyers as well as critical copyright scholars – despite their fundamental role in facilitating and shaping its reception.

Of the five characteristics of the paratext outlined by Genette, two are of especial importance to my extended analysis of the material form of Kant's essay. The first feature is defined in reference to the spatial dimension of the publication at hand. Where a paratext is found 'within' or as being physically appended to the book, it is called a 'peritext'.[93] Besides the front cover, examples of the peritext include other front matter such as the title page and various prefaces, the material form of the book such as its typesetting and paper, and other sectional or marginal elements such as intertitles and notes. Conversely, if the paratext appears 'outside' the book, it is referred to as the 'epitext'.[94] In this subcategory of more remote elements, Genette locates 'public epitexts'[95] – that is, epitexts that are addressed by the author and/or the author's associates to the public or a segment of it, such as author interviews, book advertisements and other promotional activities undertaken by the publisher –

[90] Gérard Genette, *Paratexts: Thresholds of Interpretation*, trans. Jane E. Lewin (Cambridge: Cambridge University Press, 1997).
[91] Ibid., 2.
[92] Ibid., 3.
[93] Ibid., 5.
[94] Ibid.
[95] Ibid., 9.

and 'private epitexts',[96] namely those with more specific, individual addressees, such as the personal letters, even diary entries, of the author. The other aspect of the paratext of interest to this book concerns its substantiality or 'mode of existence',[97] an understanding of which similarly points us to a range of paratextual elements that could be studied alongside a text such as Kant's. Most of the paratexts reviewed in Genette's encyclopaedic study are 'of a textual, or at least verbal, kind',[98] meaning they are composed of legible letters not unlike the main text. However, Genette also notes that paratexts could be 'iconic'[99] (for instance, a cover image or frontispiece), 'material'[100] (for example, the typeface or typesetting), or even 'purely factual'[101] (that is, some known fact that influences a given reader's interpretation of the text). Genette gives the example of Proust's commonly known half-Jewish and homosexual identities, the biographical facts of which necessarily inform our reading of the relevant passages in *A la recherche du Temps perdu* ('In Search of Lost Time').[102] Though these facts concern the author, they are not communicated by him or his publishers, but instead form part of the larger historical background or context in which the book is (re)produced and disseminated. They belong to the 'implicit contexts that surround a work and, to a greater or lesser degree, clarify or modify its significance'.[103] Known facts about authorial life and generic conventions alter the way books are read. The historical background, 'the context formed [citing the example of Balzac's *Le Père Goriot* (1835)] by the period known as "the nineteenth century"',[104] is no less involved in the question of the text's significance. It may well be that any posited communicative situation pertaining to the text and its constitutive paratexts only owes its significance to the historical period(s) and context(s) in which they participate, notwithstanding the structural possibility of every mark being cited out of the context (or what Derrida calls its 'iterability'[105]).

Informed by Genette's notes on these spatial and substantial aspects of paratexts, my paratextual reading of Kant's 1785 essay covers not only a selection of peritexts in the essay and other issues of the *Berlinische Monatsschrift* but also some factual epitexts surrounding the period of late eighteenth-century Germany and the genre of the periodical. Considered collectively, these paratexts enable us to grasp some of the historical and medial-material conditions of literary production and to displace the epistemic limits of copyright discourse.

96 Ibid.
97 Ibid., 4.
98 Ibid., 5.
99 Ibid.
100 Ibid.
101 Ibid.
102 Ibid., 8.
103 Ibid., 7.
104 Ibid.
105 Jacques Derrida, 'Signature Event Context', in *Limited Inc* (Evanston, IL: Northwestern University Press, 1988), 12.

OVERVIEW OF THE BOOK

Chapter 1 reconstructs the contexts of mass digitisation and the Kantian copyright debate in which Kant's 1785 essay is to be reread. First, I consider the Google Books project as an emblematic case for our urgent need to rethink authorship, copyright and their profound co-evolution with media technologies. Then, I review the recent debate surrounding the utilitarian-proprietary approach to copyright and its limits as suggested by three readers of Kant's 1785 essay. After that, I propose an alternative media-theoretical way of looking at a printed book, one that focuses on the paratexts of Kant's 1785 essay to illuminate the medial dimension of literary production and the limits of proprietary authorship. My contention is that although the three Kantian copyright scholars have demonstrated the power of Kant's essay and its concept of the book as communicative act to reshape our understanding of authorship and copyright, they have also underestimated the material dimension of the text that affords the production of its meaning. A more adequate understanding of Kant's text and how it could illuminate the present digital transformation of authorship and copyright would require that we attend closely to its medial-materialities.

Chapters 2–4 respond to this call for a renewed attention to the printed pages of Kant's essay. Chapter 2 juxtaposes the myth of proprietary authorship embodied in the legal idiom of 'work', 'author' and 'originality' with the realities of print production in late eighteenth-century Germany. I problematise the conventional view of the literary work as an intellectual creation of a personal author through a paratextual reading of Kant's 1785 essay that reconstructs its underpinning historical processes and conditions. This analysis includes not only the epitextual background of the German Enlightenment and the role therein played by periodicals such as the *Berlinische Monatsschrift* but also the peritextual features of catchwords, signature marks and front matter that appeared within and alongside Kant's text. I argue that these paratexts lead us back to the print machinery of the German Enlightenment: a socio-technological assemblage of human actors interacting with technologies, which Kant and others sought to steer to address the problem of print saturation. The existence of such a machinery, one that preceded the authorial figure, perturbs copyright law's attachment to original authorship. Insufficient to deal with the complexities of the book's emergence, the terms and doctrines of copyright law tend to suppress the deep historicity of literary production.

Chapter 3 both deepens and problematises the legal understanding of literature by attending to the making and perception of typefaces, particularly the Breitkopf Fraktur typeface in which Kant's 1785 essay was set. Close reading a 2001 House of Lords decision, *Newspaper Licensing Agency Ltd v Marks & Spencer Plc*, allows us to see that literary copyright and published edition copyright, though pertaining to the respective labours of authors and publishers, nonetheless share an originalist aesthetics of the book that affirms the myth of proprietary authorship. To dislodge copyright's originalist aesthetics, I revisit and compare Fichte's and Kant's accounts of the printed book in late eighteenth-century Germany, which, in their own ways, anticipate and undermine the contemporary legal perspective. Unlike Fichte, Kant recognised the visual materiality of the book, including the perceptibility of its typeface and typesetting, which pointed to an historical domain of embodied interactions. Guided by Kant, I attend to two aspects of the material history of the Breikopf Fraktur typeface: the history of its production and the history of its perception. This material history of the typeface, which reveals the deep interactions between human actors and print technologies, acts as a counter-image to copyright's originalist aesthetics.

Chapter 4 charts a biography of Kant's printed authorial name, 'I. Kant', to disclose its ethical function in late eighteenth-century Germany. Drawing on Foucault's and Chartier's studies of the materialities of authorship, I consider uses of the authorial name at the rhetorical level of Kant's 1785 essay alongside its textual and typographical displacements, both within and outside the May 1785 issue of the *Berlinische Monatsschrift*, and during and beyond the author's lifetime. Other texts to be analysed include Kant's 1784 essay on enlightenment, his 1795 and 1798 letters addressed to Friedrich Schiller and Friedrich Nicolai, a 1790 pirated edition of Kant's writings, two 1790 and 1799 public notices in the *Allgemeine Literatur-Zeitung*, and the 1996 Cambridge edition of Kant's 1785 essay. In so tracing the anthumous and posthumous movements of 'I. Kant', I clarify the authorial name's role in implementing an ethical author-function that Kant understood to be responsive to the demands of enlightenment practice. I contend that Kant not only recognised the importance of printed authorial names to the enactment of authorial responsibility but also so deployed his own authorial name as to hold himself and others accountable for the print publications that contributed to the public discourse in his time. I argue that this ethically and socially concerned author-function in the German Enlightenment discloses the limits of copyright's proprietary understanding of authorship and its material constitution.

This book concludes by analysing a contemporary digital text, Wikipedia's article on authorship, based on the prior insights into literary production gleaned from Kant's 1785 essay. I clarify the fundamental challenge issued by Wikipedia's multitudinous authorship to copyright's proprietary model by turning to some of its digital paratexts. The dispute tags, hyperlinks, footnotes and revision history of Wikipedia's article on authorship are read as indices of the digital machinery that constituted it and keeps it open to revision. I further discuss the ethical dimension of Wikipedia's production by situating the digital encyclopaedia alongside, and against, some of its print predecessors in Roman antiquity and the European Enlightenment. Pliny the Elder's *Historia Naturalis*, Denis Diderot's and Jean d'Alembert's *Encyclopédie* and other eighteenth-century encyclopaedic projects are read as presenting prior models of the encyclopaedia that could clarify Wikipedia's function as an information technology and its mass-participatory ethos. This analysis of Wikipedia closes with an invitation for the writing of a media history of the encyclopaedia, one that could account for its ethics and communicative function in the digital present.

1

Two Ways of Looking at a Printed Book

RETHINKING COPYRIGHT IN MASS DIGITISATION

On 18 April 2016, the US Supreme Court declined to hear the appeal against the Second Circuit Court of Appeals' decision in favour of Google's mass digitisation of books and other printed matter,[1] thereby conclusively affirming Google Books and the Library Project as involving the 'fair use'[2] of copyrighted works.[3] As authors, the plaintiff-appellants owned copyrights in works that had been digitally scanned and made publicly available for search and snippet view without their permission pursuant to bilateral agreements between Google and its partner libraries. According to the decision, however, Google's copying of the literary works for those 'transformative purposes'[4] fulfilled the copyright system's broad objective of advancing public knowledge by making available to the public significant information about those works without offering any effectively competing substitute for each of them. In other words, it was a fair use of works that did not require any authorisation from the copyright owners – a defence against alleged copyright infringement recognised in section 107 of Title 17 of the United States Code.[5] The 'exclusive control over copying of their works'[6] granted to authors under the copyright system as an incentive to produce those works for public consumption did not restrict the

[1] The decision is *Authors Guild v Google, Inc* No. 13-4829 (2d Cir. 2015).

[2] The doctrine of fair use is codified in Title 17 of the United States Code, section 107. For the Supreme Court's recent discussion of fair use as applied to Google's partial copying of a computer program, see *Google LLC v Oracle America, Inc* 593 U.S. 1 (2021).

[3] Adam Liptak and Alexandra Alter, 'Challenge to Google Books Is Declined by Supreme Court', *The New York Times*, 18 April 2016.

[4] *Authors Guild v Google, Inc*, 16. The meaning of 'transformative purpose' is based on the Supreme Court's discussion of the four statutory factors of fair use in *Campbell v Acuff-Rose Music, Inc* 510 U.S. 569 (1994).

[5] Title 17 of the United States Code, section 107.

[6] *Authors Guild v Google, Inc*, 12.

technology company's creation and exploitation of a universal database of digitised books.

For readers drawn to a renewed Library of Alexandria, this authoritative recognition of Google's mass digitisation project as fair use might come as a relief from the strictures of modern copyright. In October 2009, when Google was still in the midst of negotiating a final settlement with the Authors Guild and the Association of American Publishers, its co-founder Sergey Brin had justified the project as fulfilling the double goals of preserving and improving accessibility to the world's cultural heritage in books.[7] The thrice burning of the ancient Library was cited as one of the prime historical instances of the fragility of material books, which was a condition to be overcome by Google's and its partners' assembly of 'a [digital] library to last forever'.[8] Once mostly confined within elite academic libraries, the vast majority of literary works not yet in the public domain could now be scanned, indexed and made publicly searchable without any risk of infringing copyrights held by their authors or assignees. One of the most prominent legal scholars to have long argued for both the lawfulness and desirability of the Google Books search function is Lawrence Lessig.[9] When the project still bore the early name of 'Google Print', Lessig already extolled its potential to radically democratise our access to knowledge and culture: 'Google Print could be the most important contribution to the spread of knowledge since Jefferson dreamed of national libraries. It is an astonishing opportunity to revive our cultural past, and make it accessible.'[10] With all the world's books increasingly copied to a single database, Google promises to facilitate access to these books by any user in possession of a digital device, including those underserved by analogue copies for geographical, socio-economic or other reasons. As understood by the techno-futurist Kevin Kelly, however, the mass digitisation of books is but preparatory for the expedited user-led processing of books, which has to some extent already been enabled by the digital innovations of link and tag: 'The real magic will come in the second act, as each word in each book is cross-linked, clustered, cited, extracted, indexed, analyzed, annotated, remixed, reassembled and woven deeper into the culture than ever before.'[11] In Kelly's view, the ultimate significance of Google Books extends from its potential to collapse the instituted boundaries between literary works: 'the universal library becomes one very, very, very large

7 Sergey Brin, 'A Library to Last Forever', *The New York Times*, 8 October 2009.

8 Ibid.

9 Lawrence Lessig, *Is Google Book Search 'Fair Use'?* (YouTube, 16 January 2006).

10 Lawrence Lessig, 'Google Sued', *Lessig Blog Archives* (blog), 22 September 2005. Whilst initially endorsing the terms of the Google Book Search settlement for securing greater access to books than if the lawsuit were won by Google, Lessig withdrew his support for the revised proposal a year and a half later, mostly on the grounds that it excessively regulated and juridified our access to culture: compare Lawrence Lessig, 'On the Google Book Search Agreement', *Lessig Blog Archives* (blog), 29 October 2008; and Lawrence Lessig, 'For the Love of Culture', *The New Republic*, 26 January 2010.

11 Kevin Kelly, 'Scan This Book!', *The New York Times Magazine*, 14 May 2006.

single text: the world's only book'.[12] Alexandria 2.0, 'a single liquid fabric of interconnected words and ideas',[13] could seem less distant a future with the present balance struck between the putatively competing interests of proprietary authors and the public at large, which ostensibly favours the latter.

Nonetheless, Google's mass digitisation project has also been criticised for its fundamental challenges to the tradition of authorship, the copyright system and the global economy of books, information and culture, which persist despite the latest judicial decision. Just a month after Kelly's essay was published in the supplementary magazine to *The New York Times*, John Updike's reply would appear in the newspaper.[14] In the novelist's view, Kelly's prophesised dissolution of the borders between books implied 'the end of authorship'[15] – a tradition of communication between authors and readers prescribed by the written word and print technology. Against the prospect of 'a huge, virtually infinite word stream accessed by search engines populated by teeming, promiscuous word snippets stripped of credited authorship',[16] Updike affirmed the printed book's 'old-fashioned function of … communication from one person to another'.[17] The print medium affords an intimate relation between author and reader that threatens to be permanently disrupted by the next suggested phase of the digital revolution. 'The printed, bound and paid-for book … is the site of an encounter, in silence, of two minds, one following in the other's steps but invited to imagine, to argue, to concur on a level of reflection beyond that of personal encounter.'[18] Google Books is a medial event that spurs the obsolescence of our print-based understanding of authors and readers, no less than that of booksellers and other intermediaries on whom we have traditionally relied for the production and circulation of books.

Scholars of book history, media studies and law have questioned the desirability of Google's project by pointing to some of its anticipated adverse effects on the global information economy and the modern institution of copyright. In Robert Darnton's view, as prescribed by the terms of the initial settlement agreement, Google Books unduly consolidated power in one company, leaving open the possibility of Google's prioritisation of its own private interests over the public good in the long run.[19] Notwithstanding the non-exclusivity of the agreements between Google and its partner libraries, Google would enjoy a de facto monopoly of access to information in the absence of real competitors. The company could favour profitability over access in the future, for instance, not only by charging for the use of its services but

[12] Ibid.
[13] Ibid.
[14] John Updike, 'The End of Authorship', *The New York Times*, 25 June 2006.
[15] Ibid.
[16] Ibid.
[17] Ibid.
[18] Ibid.
[19] Robert Darnton, 'Google & the Future of Books', *The New York Review of Books*, 12 February 2009.

further by setting high prices for institutional and consumer subscription licences. Siva Vaidhyanathan agreed with Darnton that public and university libraries were better suited for the mass digitisation and facilitation of public access to books.[20] Instead of letting Google secure an inordinate amount of competitive advantage in the global information economy, the public should finance and support libraries to accomplish the task of building the digital archive. For Maurizio Borghi and Stavroula Karapapa, the most troubling aspect of the project concerns not so much its colossal empowerment of a profit-seeking entity as its effective inversion of the copyright system.[21] In dispensing with the need to seek prior authorial consent for the copying and use of copyrighted works through licencing agreements with its partner libraries, Google has transformed copyright from an opt-in system of permissions into an opt-out system, where authors now have to ask for the exclusion of their works from digitisation and display. Google Books has, so to speak, 'turned copyright on its head'.[22] As suggested by Borghi and other commentators, if the case had been tried in other jurisdictions without any exception as broad as the US doctrine of fair use, it would have been unlikely that Google would succeed.[23] That Google Books has now been judicially legitimated in one regime only accentuates a basic tension between mass digitisation and modern copyright: analogue modes of copyright protection might not be as effective in, nor even suited to, the digital environment.

As suggested by the contemporary debate surrounding Google Books, digital technology is in the midst of transforming our dominant cultural–legal understanding of authorship and copyright. It was not too long ago when the legal fiction of the proprietary author, emergent from the historical conditions of late seventeenth- to early nineteenth-century Europe, was criticised for ignoring the manifold social realities of literary production.[24] The outcome of *Authors Guild v Google, Inc* might seem to reflect a further sidelining of the authorial figure, whose work can now be electronically duplicated, diced, displayed and subjected to the mostly hidden

[20] Siva Vaidhyanathan, *The Googlization of Everything (And Why We Should Worry)* (Berkeley: University of California Press, 2011), 169. Other than the antitrust problem, Vaidhyanathan raised a series of objections to the project surrounding user privacy issues, its de facto compulsory licensing system, the further commercialisation of the library space and the inadequacies of Google's search algorithms in regard to books: see Ibid., 149–73.

[21] Maurizio Borghi and Stavroula Karapapa, *Copyright and Mass Digitization* (Oxford: Oxford University Press, 2013), 1–18.

[22] Ibid., 5.

[23] Ibid., 8. See also Paul Ganley, 'Google Book Search: Fair Use, Fair Dealing and the Case for Intermediary Copying' (Working Paper, 13 January 2006), https://papers.ssrn.com/sol3/papers.cfm?abstract_id=875384 (accessed 9 September 2024).

[24] See, for instance, Martha Woodmansee, 'The Genius and the Copyright: Economic and Legal Conditions of the Emergence of the "Author"', *Eighteenth-Century Studies* 17, no. 4 (1984): 425–48; Mark Rose, *Authors and Owners: The Invention of Copyright* (Cambridge, MA: Harvard University Press, 1993); Peter Jaszi, 'Toward a Theory of Copyright: Metamorphoses of "Authorship"', *Duke Law Journal*, 40, no. 2 (1991): 455–502; Martha Woodmansee and Peter Jaszi, eds., *The Construction of Authorship: Textual Appropriation in Law and Literature* (Durham, NC: Duke University Press, 1994).

practices of data mining and computation without consent. Updike's hostility towards the liquefaction of formerly distinct works palpably extends from the writer's close attachment to the practices surrounding the more traditional media of writing and print. Instead of the innovative technology company offering its services to users via the shiny interfaces of digital screens, booksellers still manning the 'lonely forts'[25] of stores filled with material books are the intermediaries lauded at the start and finish of Updike's essay. Google Books is but an exemplary instance of mass digitisation projects launched since the turn of the new millennium to have destabilised our received notions of author, work and copyright.[26] By converting printed works into electronic format through digital photographic scanning and their processing by optical character recognition software, these projects have sought to preserve, enhance access to and compute those works which are, to say the least, not undesirable ends in themselves.[27] And yet, the phenomenon of mass digitisation also attests to a massive disruption in the history of books, contributing to what Borghi and Karapapa have theorised as a threefold paradigm shift.[28] To begin with, books are increasingly viewed not so much as 'works' or expressions of the author addressed to the public as 'data' to be mined and processed in order to achieve distinctive ends of the digital-corporate environment such as '[improving] web services, including advertisement and content personalization'.[29] The suggestion here is that books are now read not so much by human readers as by automatic computing machines programmed by adaptive algorithms. Put strongly, Roland Barthes's well-known provocation about 'the death of the author'[30] in postmodernity must now be qualified as implying the death of the reader in mass digitisation, the human having been replaced by artificial intelligence, which alone can process the massive amounts of data in the 40 million books digitised by Google.[31] Further, as already discussed, copyright seems to be transforming from a regime of '*ex ante* authorizations'[32] into an 'opt-out system'[33] that significantly undercuts the intellectual–proprietary interests of authors. Broadened and emboldened by the Second Circuit Court of Appeals' decision, the doctrine of fair use has become a sturdier legal defence against claims of copyright infringement, anticipating further

[25] Updike, 'The End of Authorship'.

[26] Other projects include the Internet Archive, the Open Library, the Carnegie Mellon Million Book project, the HathiTrust, Europeana, and the Digital Public Library of America: see Borghi and Karapapa, *Copyright and Mass Digitization*, 3–8.

[27] See Karen Coyle, 'Managing Technology: Mass Digitization of Books', *The Journal of Academic Librarianship* 32, no. 6 (3 November 2006): 642–43; Borghi and Karapapa, *Copyright and Mass Digitization*, 11.

[28] Borghi and Karapapa, *Copyright and Mass Digitization*, 15–18.

[29] Ibid., 15.

[30] Roland Barthes, 'The Death of the Author', in *Image Music Text*, trans. Stephen Heath (London: Fontana, 1977), 142–48.

[31] Haimin Lee, '15 Years of Google Books', *Google Blog* (blog), 17 October 2019.

[32] Borghi and Karapapa, *Copyright and Mass Digitization*, 16.

[33] Ibid.

incursions into the so-called exclusive control of authors over their creations. Thirdly, the centrality of powerful intermediaries maintaining the relevant digital databases such as Google is renewed and reasserted. The promise of 'decentralized interaction'[34] amongst users of digital technologies of direct transfer such as peer-to-peer file sharing is, in the context of mass digitisation, threatened by potential de facto monopolies or oligarchies of access to information and culture. Amply borne out by the observations surrounding the controversy of Google Books, these three '"head-turning" traits of mass digitization'[35] urgently necessitate our rethinking of authorship, copyright and their profound co-evolution with media technologies.

This chapter seeks to contribute to our present rethinking of authorship and copyright by revisiting another recent debate that raises very similar questions. The debate surrounds the dominant utilitarian–proprietary approach to copyright, particularly its limits as suggested by three readers of Immanuel Kant's 1785 essay, *Von der Unrechtmäßigkeit des Büchernachdrucks* ('On the Wrongfulness of Reprinting').[36] Through principal recourse to Kant's concept of the book as communicative act, Abraham Drassinower, Maurizio Borghi and Anne Barron have sought to rethink authorship and copyright along non-proprietary lines.[37] I argue that although these leading Kantian voices have demonstrated the power of Kant's essay to reshape our understanding of the thematic conjuncture, they have also underestimated the material dimension of the text that affords the production of its meaning. To generate a more adequate understanding of Kant's text and how it might illuminate the present digital transformation of authorship and copyright, we should look closely at the medial–material specificities of the literary work.

UTILITARIAN COPYRIGHT

Authors Guild v Google, Inc happened despite, and in a sense also because of, the fairly recent global expansion of copyright and intellectual property rights, which has been much discussed and criticised.[38] For example, as Neil Netanel has argued,

34 Ibid., 17.

35 Ibid., 15.

36 Kant, 'On the Wrongfulness of Unauthorized Publication of Books' (1785). For a digitised version of the fifth volume of the *Berlinische Monatsschrift* with Kant's essay stored in the Bavarian State Library, see www.digitale-sammlungen.de/en/view/bsb10926844?q = %28berlinische+monatsschrift+1785%29&page = ,1 (accessed 9 September 2024).

37 The main referenced works include Abraham Drassinower, *What's Wrong with Copying?* (Cambridge, MA: Harvard University Press, 2015); Maurizio Borghi, 'Copyright and Truth', *Theoretical Inquiries in Law* 12, no. 1 (2010): 1–27; Anne Barron, 'Kant, Copyright and Communicative Freedom', *Law and Philosophy* 31, no. 1 (2012): 1–48.

38 For example, see Mark A. Lemley, 'Property, Intellectual Property, and Free Riding', *Texas Law Review* 83 (2005): 1031–1076; Neil W. Netanel, 'Why Has Copyright Expanded? Analysis and Critique', in *New Directions in Copyright Law*, ed. Fiona Macmillan, vol. 6 (Cheltenham: Edward Elgar, 2007), 3–34; Barron, 'Copyright Infringement: "Free-Riding" and the Lifeworld', in *Copyright and Piracy: An Interdisciplinary Critique*, eds. Lionel Bently et al.

copyright expansion in the United States is substantially owed to the high levels of involvement of copyright industries and trade associations in the periodic revisions of copyright legislation.[39] Extensive lobbying by the copyright interest groups and their negotiations with the US Congress have led to 'an ever-expanding set of copyright holder rights, riddled with narrow exceptions for various interested parties present at the bargaining table'.[40] The history of legislative amendments relating to the term of copyright protection alone evidences such an industry-driven expansion of copyright. Mark Lemley has pointed to the eleven-time extension of the copyright term between 1963 and 1998, leading up to the present longest term of seventy years in addition to the author's lifetime for works created after 1 January 1978.[41] For Lemley, the rapid growth of intellectual property is accompanied – and legitimated – by the ascendancy of an 'absolute protection'[42] or a 'full-value'[43] paradigm of intellectual property in both legal scholarship and juridical discourse. On this view, intellectual property is rightly seen as a species of private property and, indeed, real property rights, which entails fortifying the exclusionary rights of owners. In economic-theoretical terms, strong intellectual property rights are said to be needed to internalise the 'externalities'[44] associated with the uses of intellectual property and to minimise 'free riding'[45] on the investments of owners. Allowing owners to gain the 'full social value'[46] of their intellectual property – for instance, by charging for any use – is the best means of incentivising their production. In the context of copyright, any unauthorised copying or use of the author's work that enriches the user would constitute free riding.[47] The lawsuit against Google could have been driven not so much by any potential loss in profits suffered by authors and publishers as by the possibility of Google free riding on their products.[48] Indeed, it has been argued that the increased visibility of the books indexed by Google would not only add to their sales but also spare them from the more ignominious fate of

(Cambridge: Cambridge University Press, 2010), 93–127. As succinctly noted by Anne Barron, in the last few decades, copyright has expanded in scope along four main axes: 'the range of acts restricted to the copyright owner has widened, the range of circumstances in which secondary liability will be found has also widened, the likelihood that courts will find partial or non-literal takings "substantial" (and so infringing) has increased, and the reach of defences and exceptions has narrowed': Barron, 'Copyright Infringement', 98.

39 Netanel, 'Why Has Copyright Expanded? Analysis and Critique', 3–10.

40 Ibid., 5.

41 Lemley, 'Property, Intellectual Property, and Free Riding', 1042. See Title 17 of the United States Code, section 302(a).

42 Lemley, 'Property, Intellectual Property, and Free Riding', 1031.

43 Ibid.

44 Ibid., 1032.

45 Ibid.

46 Ibid., 1031.

47 Ibid., 1043.

48 For a similar observation, see Vaidhyanathan, *The Googlization of Everything*, 59.

cultural oblivion.[49] The authors' persistent action against Google in spite of their foreseeable gains, then, might well evidence the absolute protection paradigm of intellectual property noted in the literature.

By ruling in favour of Google and what was assessed to be in the public's interest, the Second Circuit Court of Appeals would seem to have rejected the emergent absolute protection perspective in intellectual property and reaffirmed the more traditional utilitarian model of copyright as about striking the right balance between two pertinent sets of considerations. In the critical literature, the traditional copyright balance has been theorised in two principal and closely related ways. The first approach is the 'clash-and-balance paradigm',[50] which, as interpreted by Abraham Drassinower and Maurizio Borghi, is reflected in the case law of Canada and the United States. On this view, the two broad considerations on either end of the balance are cast as the putatively competing interests of authors and users, or, more specifically, 'the incentive to create and the imperative to disseminate the works of authorship'.[51] On the one hand, the copyright system accords proprietary rights to authors over their creations as rewards and incentives for the production of original works. On the other hand, the law affirms the public as the ultimate beneficiaries of the system and those works, beneficiaries whose interests extend to consuming those works and, possibly, using them to generate new works. The task of the copyright system is to address the tension between both sides in particular situations and achieve the optimal production and distribution of works that serves society at large.

The other closely related approach is the 'incentives-access paradigm'[52] discussed by Glynn S. Lunney, Jr and Anne Barron, which is a perspective fundamentally shaped by neoclassical economic theory and the calculus of cost–benefit analysis. On this view, copyright imposes two sorts of social costs against which the benefits of granting these rights of exclusion to authors in their creations are to be balanced.[53] First, higher prices can be charged for copyrighted works than for non-copyrighted works in the marketplace, which yields a consumer loss. Second, the creation of new works may be inhibited by the costs of licences for the use of copyrighted works on which those new works are built. These costs are, in sum, the loss of public access to works resultant of any system of copyright. However, similar to the other, this approach assumes that there would be the incentive to invest in the production of

[49] See Cory Doctorow, 'Why Publishing Should Send Fruit-Baskets to Google', *Boing Boing* (blog), 14 February 2006.

[50] Borghi, 'Copyright and Truth', 2. See also Drassinower, *What's Wrong with Copying?*, 17–53. Specifically, Drassinower's account draws on the US Supreme Court decision of *Feist Publications Inc v Rural Telephone Service Co Inc* 499 U.S. 340 (1991) and the Canada Supreme Court decision of *CCH Canadian Ltd v Law Society of Upper Canada* 2004 SCC 13: Drassinower, *What's Wrong with Copying?*, 23–30.

[51] Drassinower, *What's Wrong with Copying?*, 21.

[52] Lunney, 'Reexamining Copyright's Incentives-Access Paradigm'; Barron, 'Copyright Infringement: "Free-Riding" and the Lifeworld', 103.

[53] See Barron, 'Copyright Infringement: "Free-Riding" and the Lifeworld', 103–7.

new works only if the potential to profit from those works is to some extent assured by the law. The challenge for any copyright institution is to '[balance] the benefits of broader protection, in the form of increased incentive to produce such works, against its costs, in the form of lost access to such works'.[54] As Barron clarifies, the incentives-access paradigm is inherently resistant to the sort of maximal copyright protection advanced by absolute protectionists, for the latter is seen as having insufficiently accounted for the social costs of copyright.[55]

Both the justification and outcome of *Authors Guild v Google, Inc* reflect a preference for the public interest to be served not by way of copyright maximalism but through a calibrated balance between incentivising work production via copyright protection and enhancing public access to knowledge. The Second Circuit Court of Appeals' discussion of the law of fair use opens by subordinating the interests of authors to those of the public whom the system ultimately serves: 'Thus, while authors are undoubtedly important intended beneficiaries of copyright, the ultimate, primary intended beneficiary is the public, whose access to knowledge copyright seeks to advance by providing rewards for authorship.'[56] The very development of the doctrine of fair use, which afforded the unauthorised copying of copyrighted works in certain situations that advanced public knowledge, was cited as the law's recognition that 'giving authors *absolute* control over all copying from their works would tend in some circumstances to limit, rather than expand, public knowledge'.[57] Indeed, the four statutory factors for determining fair use reflect the judiciary's need to strike the copyright balance, that is, 'to define the boundary limit of the original author's exclusive rights in order to best serve the overall objectives of the copyright law to expand public learning while protecting the incentives of authors to create for the public good'.[58] That Google Books was eventually legitimated – despite the project's 'commercial motivation'[59] and 'copying of the totality of the original'[60] – evidences the Second Circuit Court of Appeals' willingness to assess the appropriate balance and their commitment to the traditional utilitarian model of copyright.

For Lemley and other supporters of the utilitarian model of copyright, the Second Circuit Court of Appeals' decision might instantiate a kind of triumph over the absolute protection paradigm and a counterpoint to the recent expansion of intellectual property rights. But for Drassinower, Borghi, and Barron, who reject the frame of neoclassical economics, the decision could simply reflect how deeply

54 Lunney, 'Reexamining Copyright's Incentives-Access Paradigm', 485.

55 Barron, 'Copyright Infringement: "Free-Riding" and the Lifeworld', 12–13.

56 *Authors Guild v Google, Inc*, 13.

57 Ibid.

58 Ibid., 15. The four factors are listed in Title 17 of the United States Code, section 107, and extensively discussed in *Campbell v Acuff-Rose Music, Inc*.

59 *Authors Guild v Google, Inc*, 26.

60 Ibid., 30. As noted in the judgment, these two facts are typically assessed as operating against the finding of fair use: see Ibid., 27–33.

entrenched the economic paradigm of copyright is. From the three critical standpoints, the utilitarian model of copyright does not provide any satisfactory account of the proper subject matter of copyright law. It also misconstrues the nature of authorship, the relationship between authors and users, and society at large. Drassinower problematises the utilitarian model or 'value paradigm'[61] of copyright by way of an extended critique of the metaphor of balance as deployed to construe the originality requirement of copyright by the Supreme Courts of the United States and Canada in two landmark cases.[62] One of Drassinower's basic suggestions is that the balance model of copyright fails to account for its adoption of 'value'[63] (specifically, 'economic value'[64]) – as the master category by which to render commensurable the pertinent interests of authors and users. His critique of 'the poverty of value'[65] consists of a series of provocations: Why should copyright law be construed merely as a 'distributive mechanism'[66] that regulates the creation and dissemination of value in a market of authors and users? Does construing the act of authorship as the origination of value, an interest that could be offset by the ultimately weightier alternative of so distributing value as to advance public knowledge, not obscure something specific about authorship?[67] Does the judicial act of balancing the incentive to create works and the imperative to distribute them not fail to account for the originality requirement that more fundamentally determines what falls within the remit of the copyright system in the first place?[68] And does the metaphor of balance not risk mischaracterising the relationship between authors and users as essentially oppositional rather than complementary?[69] Borghi elegantly reframes Drassinower's critique of the copyright balance as relating to the model's failure to afford any serious investigation into the proper subject matter of copyright. In Borghi's words, 'the copyright debate of recent years has focused almost exclusively on the *scope* of copyright ... as if ... the question of the *subject matter* of copyright was not the preliminary and most important one in this debate'.[70] For Borghi and Drassinower alike, the calculative idiom of 'balance', 'value' and 'interest' forecloses any meaningful discussion of what copyright is really about.

61 Drassinower, *What's Wrong with Copying?*, 51.
62 See n. 51. Drassinower also refers to the classic United Kingdom cases of *Walter v Lane* [1900] AC 539 and *University of London Press v University Tutorial Press Ltd* [1916] 2 Ch 601, whose emphasis on labour or the 'sweat of brow' standard of originality forms the background against which the new standards of 'creativity' and 'skills and judgement' advanced in the North American Courts are assessed: see Drassinower, 30–41.
63 Drassinower, 18.
64 Ibid.
65 Ibid., 17.
66 Ibid., 51.
67 Ibid., 55.
68 Ibid., 17.
69 Ibid., 55.
70 Borghi, 'Copyright and Truth', 2.

Similarly, Barron rejects the traditional utilitarian justification of copyright for failing to provide any adequate account of copyright and society. Barron is deeply critical of both the incentives-access and absolute protection paradigms of copyright because of their fundamental grounding in economic theory, which she denounces as a worldview of 'incurable deficiencies'[71] that denies the full significance of the institution in the wider social order. Specifically, she takes issue with the economic model of society as comprised of self-interested, utility-maximising individuals acting in competition with one another, and the concomitant model of copyright law as about the optimal regulation of relationships of exchange between information producers and consumers.[72] For Barron, neither account adequately captures the significance of law, society and the relationship between them.[73] Animated by a shared logic of economic analysis that reductively prioritises the matrices of 'utility' and 'efficiency', both the incentives-access and absolute protection paradigms fail to provide 'a comprehensive analysis of the social significance of copyright'.[74] Thus, the utilitarian reasoning behind the decision of *Authors Guild v Google, Inc* is unlikely to receive Barron's unmitigated support.

Against the prevailing utilitarian model of copyright, Drassinower, Borghi and Barron advance alternative accounts that depart from the orthodox construal of copyright as a form of intellectual property. For their fundamental rethinking of copyright, these scholars draw on Kant's 1785 essay on the book and author's rights. As we shall see, Kant's essay foregrounded the communicative situation between authors and readers that Updike more recently understood as assailed by the mass digitisation of books.

LITERARY COMMUNICATION

Presently, in both common law systems of copyright and civil law regimes of *Urheberrecht* or *droit d'auteur*, the literary works in which authors hold so-called exclusive rights of copying are treated as forms of intellectual property.[75] Unless otherwise specified in the relevant statutes, the author is generally recognised as the rightful owner of the abstract work that has been fixed in some perceptible medium of expression.[76] This means that property in the literary work could be held by its author even as property in the physical book is held by its lawful purchaser. The authority to grant someone permission to copy the work is but one of the

[71] Barron, 'Kant, Copyright and Communicative Freedom', 9.

[72] Ibid., 7.

[73] In that article, Barron cites Jürgen Habermas's social theory as a potential framework with which to rethink copyright law and society: see Ibid., 28–31.

[74] Ibid., 28.

[75] On the relationship between the common law and civil law models, see Bently et al., *Intellectual Property Law*, 35–36.

[76] See, e.g., Title 17 of the United States Code, section 102.

distinguishing rights that extend from the author's literary proprietorship.[77] In *Authors Guild v Google, Inc* it was undisputed that the three author-plaintiffs owned copyrights in works that Google had scanned, indexed, and made searchable and available for snippet view. Their works fulfilled the requirement of originality under section 102 of Title 17 of the United States Code, which, as interpreted by the courts, prescribed a standard of minimal creativity: each was 'independently created by the author (as opposed to copied from other works), and ... [possessed] at least some minimal degree of creativity'.[78] As clarified in the same statutory section, the author's proprietorship extends not to the ideas of the work per se, but to the expression of those ideas: it is the embodiment of those ideas in some 'tangible medium of expression'[79] that forms the object of literary property. This basic distinction between the non-copyrighted idea and the copyrighted expression, also known as the 'idea/expression dichotomy',[80] is one of the key conceptual bases on which copyright systems at national, regional and international levels identify the subject matter of protection.

Contrary to some suggestions in the legal literature, Kant was not a proponent of intellectual property.[81] Kant did not regard the author as the owner of any intangible work materially expressed in the book that warranted protection under any system of property rights. Instead, Kant's case for author's rights was based on a concept of the book as a communicative medium that relayed to the public a *speech* necessarily spoken in its author's name: 'In a book, as a writing, the author *speaks* to his reader; and the one who has printed the book *speaks*, by his copy, not for himself but simply and solely in the author's name. He presents the author as speaking publicly and only mediates delivery of his speech to the public.'[82] The publisher, no less than the book, was the channel through which the author communicated with the reading public. Further, rather than the idiom of property, it was the language of

[77] For instance, under Title 17 of the United States Code, section 106, other rights include preparing derivative works based on the work, distributing copies of the work to the public by sale, and performing the work publicly.

[78] *Feist Publications Inc v Rural Telephone Service Co. Inc*, 345.

[79] Title 17 of the United States Code, section 102.

[80] 'Over the next 200 years, the so-called idea/expression dichotomy became an integral part of US jurisprudence and found its way into the 1991 European software directive (91/250/EEC; Art. 1 (2)), the 1994 WTO TRIPS Agreement and the 1996 WIPO Copyright Treaty': Friedemann Kawohl and Martin Kretschmer, 'Johann Gottlieb Fichte, and the Trap of Inhalt (Content) and Form: An Information Perspective on Music Copyright', *Information, Communication & Society* 12, no. 2 (2009): 214. See also Mario Biagioli, 'Genius against Copyright: Revisiting Fichte's Proof of the Illegality of Reprinting', *Notre Dame Law Review* 86, no. 5 (2011): 1854.

[81] See, for instance, Robert P. Merges, *Justifying Intellectual Property* (Cambridge, MA: Harvard University Press, 2011); William Fisher, 'Theories of Intellectual Property', in *New Essays in the Legal and Political Theory of Property*, ed. Stephen R. Munzer (Cambridge: Cambridge University Press, 2001). For a persuasive critique of these representations of Kant, see Maria Chiara Pievatolo, 'Freedom, Ownership and Copyright: Why Does Kant Reject the Concept of Intellectual Property?', *Società Italiana Di Filosofia Politica*, 2010, 1–10.

[82] Kant, 'On the Wrongfulness of Unauthorized Publication of Books (1785)', 30.

personhood that defined Kant's account of author's rights. In Kant's view, the author had an 'inalienable right (*ius personalissimum*)'[83] for the speech printed in the book to be communicated in his own name. Under this 'most personal right',[84] it was ultimately the author who spoke through the book printed by the publisher. Pursuant to the same fundamental right, the author granted the publisher the right to publish the book by means of a contract.[85] To reprint the book without such a right was to wrong both the legitimate publisher and the author: doing so not only subtracted the profits of the former[86] but further, in so relaying the speech without his permission, violated the latter's 'innate right in his own person'[87] – that is, to speak only as he willed.

Kant's concept of the book as communication or literary speech act is adopted by Drassinower, Borghi and Barron to advance alternative accounts of authorship and copyright that, in their own ways, resist both the utilitarian model of copyright and its basic concept of intellectual property. Reviewing and comparing their respective positions would help us to appreciate the productive ways in which Kant's essay has afforded the critical rethinking of authorship and copyright. It would also prepare us for another way of approaching Kant's text, one already pointed to by the text itself, that could further illuminate the thematic conjuncture. Drassinower's rethinking of copyright proceeds by way of an anti-proprietary rehabilitation of basic copyright categories relating to the subject matter of protection – especially the originality requirement and the related idea/expression dichotomy – that broadly aligns with Kant's concept of the book as communicative act. As we may recall, in the United States (and indeed other Western legal systems), copyright protection extends only to original expressions. 'The idea/expression dichotomy is inseparable from the doctrine of originality. It provides that not originality per se but rather original *expression* is at stake in copyright law.'[88] This means not only that the work must not be copied but also that the work itself refers to the very form in which ideas are expressed. As presently institutionalised, the literary work is treated as an object of property – that is, as a thing in which the owner (often the author) exercises certain proprietary rights of exclusion and control, including and especially the exclusive right of copying. Drassinower rejects the proprietary view of the literary work while retaining the threshold copyright condition that it be the original expression of its author. For Drassinower, the work is not 'an object of ownership'[89] but rather 'a communicative act'.[90] Consistent with the requirement that the work not be copied,

83 Ibid., 35.
84 Ibid.
85 Ibid., 33.
86 Ibid., 29
87 Ibid., 35.
88 Drassinower, *What's Wrong with Copying?*, 56.
89 Ibid., 62.
90 Ibid.

the 'originality' of this act is understood as extending from 'its being a speaking of one's own, a speaking in one's own words'.[91] Under this renewed Kantian understanding of authorship, copyright infringement is understood not as 'some kind of conversion, whether of the tangible book or of the intangible work . . . [but rather as] compelling another to speak'.[92] As Drassinower acknowledges, his proposed substitution of 'speech', 'communication' and 'action' for the reified object of literary property as the proper subject matter of copyright is substantially indebted to Kant .[93]

Kant's concept of the book as speech act also facilitates Drassinower's construal of copyright as a juridical structure that affirms the equality of authors rather than as a distributive mechanism made to achieve a balance between the competing interests of authors and users. Again, the idea/expression dichotomy is key to Drassinower's renewal of copyright from a Kantian perspective.[94] Under utilitarian copyright and the cost–benefit calculus, the idea/expression dichotomy is broadly justified on the grounds that the social costs of granting copyright protection to ideas per se are outweighed by its benefits. Protecting the original expressions of ideas reflects the optimal balance between incentivising the creation of works and disseminating them. Against such an instrumentalist mode of justification, Drassinower re-reads the dichotomy as copyright's affirmation of an egalitarian ethic of authorship: 'The free availability of ideas is but the rubric under which copyright law affirms and recognizes my equality as an author at the very moment at which it affirms and recognizes yours.'[95] Under the renewed dichotomy, the subjects of copyright law are no longer bifurcated as authors and users whose interests in producing and consuming works are opposed. Instead, both are recognised as author-users who are equally entitled to draw on the ideas embodied in one another's works for the making of their own. As sharply put in a preceding article, Drassinower recognises the communicative acts of authors to be premised on the 'intertextuality of creation'.[96] Other communicative acts provide the ideas on which the authors rely to generate their own. In so protecting original expressions while permitting the free flow of ideas, copyright law affirms the necessary mutual indebtedness of communicative acts and, by the same token, the equality of authors as users.

While Drassinower attempts to salvage parts of the copyright institution from its utilitarian and proprietary foundations, which necessarily risks the account's absorption into the paradigm it opposes,[97] Borghi and Barron take Kant's 1785 essay as the basis on which to imagine almost from scratch non-proprietary systems of copyright.

[91] Ibid., 73.

[92] Ibid., 178.

[93] See Ibid., 112–13.

[94] See Ibid., 66–73.

[95] Ibid 7.

[96] Abraham Drassinower, 'Authorship as Public Address: On the Specificity of Copyright vis-a-vis Patent and Trade-Mark', *Michigan State Law Review* 1 (2008): 211.

[97] For a similar critique of Drassinower, see Barron, 'Kant, Copyright and Communicative Freedom', 36–41.

They further turn to Kant's wider philosophical oeuvre, drawing on ethico-political ideas articulated 'outside' Kant's essay and its succinct reprisal in *Die Metaphysik der Sitten* ('The Metaphysics of Morals'),[98] and even to other thinkers' theories. Similar to Drassinower, Borghi uses Kant's concept of the book as public address to redefine the copyright subject matter as an act of speaking to the public in the author's name. Borghi accepts Kant's premise that even as the book might, in one sense, be a speech spoken by the publisher who has printed it, such speech is, in another more fundamental respect, necessarily spoken in the author's name. Because of the non-severable link between the speech and its author, a book may be lawfully printed only if the permission (or 'mandate'[99]) to do so has been granted by the author. Under the publishing contract, what passes from the author is not any right in or extending from any object of property, but instead 'a duty (and a faculty) to retell'[100] – that is, a personal obligation to recommunicate the author's speech to the public. Conducted in the absence of any such permission, the act of reprinting books doubly wrongs the authorised publisher and the non-consenting author.[101] For Borghi, then, there is no intellectual property in the work embodied by the book: nothing ideal is owned by the author. There are only actions in and by means of books, which are the true subject matter of copyright.

Revising the copyright subject matter from 'work' to 'action' is significant to Borghi because it paves the way to a new fundamental justification of copyright as a domain grounded in the same *telos* to which such action is directed, namely the furtherance and maintenance of the pursuit of truth.[102] To be sure, in the 1785 essay, Kant did not provide any general theory of action, nor did he specify any orientation to truth in the copyright speech act. An account of the book as an action necessarily coupled to the author-actor in whose name it was enacted had been sufficient for Kant to establish a case for the unlawfulness of reprinting that extended from a personal right of publishing granted by the author, rather than one ultimately rooted in the author's ownership of any abstract thing.[103] But as Borghi sets out to account

98 See Kant's discussion, 'What Is a Book?' in Immanuel Kant, 'The Metaphysics of Morals (1797)', in *Practical Philosophy*, ed. Paul Guyer and Allen W. Wood, trans. Mary J. Gregor (Cambridge: Cambridge University Press, 1996), 437–38.

99 As Borghi notes, the mandate (*mandatum*) is 'an institution of Roman contract law [that] regulates the relationship between individuals as far as actions to be carried out … are concerned': Borghi, 'Copyright and Truth', 5. The crucial point is that the primary subject matter is not a tangible book or nor a so-called intangible work, but rather an action.

100 Ibid., 7.

101 Ibid., 5.

102 Borghi clarifies that such telos is 'presumptive' rather than actual: it is 'an end which can be reasonably expected in advance, prior to any contingent embodiment of the fact': Ibid., 18. This seems to be his attempt to address the foreseeable problem of differences in motivation between individual authors in particular instances.

103 See Pievatolo, 'Freedom, Ownership and Copyright: Why Does Kant Reject the Concept of Intellectual Property?', 3: 'Kant, by conceiving the book as an action, adopts a strategy based on the *ius personale* only. By using such a strategy, he concludes that the unauthorized printer has

for the rightful *end* that the copyright speech act (and copyright law more generally) serves, he develops a teleological account of actions that draws on an Aristotelian idea of action proposed by Hannah Arendt: 'actions, unlike things, cannot be divorced from the aim and purpose they are directed to and for which they have been entrusted to others. Actions have necessarily a purpose or an end [citing an excerpt from Arendt's *The Life of the Mind* (1978)].'[104] Having supposed that any action, including the copyright speech act, cannot be severed from the *telos* to which it is necessarily oriented, he proceeds to claim that the *telos* of the copyright speech act had already been suggested by Kant in the two elements that constituted the act, namely that the act involved speaking publicly and doing so in one's own name. To suggest what these two elements might mean beyond what was briefly stated in the essay, Borghi turns to some of Kant's other philosophical writings on thinking and publicity.[105] From this ensemble of texts bearing Kant's name, Borghi suggests that speaking publicly is the act by which rational human beings think and ascertain the validity of their own judgements: it is 'the way in which humans can distinguish truth from error'.[106] Public communication is conceived as an intersubjective and dialogical process that facilitates the interlocutors' arrival at a commonly agreed judgement that is true insofar as it accords with the nature of the matter in question.

As regards the requirement for the copyright speech act to be spoken in the author's own name, Borghi grounds this in Kant's idiosyncratic perspective on the public use of reason. As Jürgen Habermas once noted, in 1784, the Prussian King Frederick II had declared that private persons were not allowed to pass judgements on the public actions of political and legal officials because the former lacked the knowledge and expertise to do so.[107] The prohibition reproduced the commonplace understanding of 'private reason' as reason exercised by persons in their personal capacity, and 'public reason' as that which underpinned official actions. But in the same year, through another essay published in the *Berlinische Monatsschrift*, Kant

to be compared to an unauthorized spokesperson rather than to a thief. Therefore, it is not necessary to go beyond the Roman law tradition, by inventing a new *ius reale* on immaterial things.'

[104] See Borghi, 'Copyright and Truth', 7, fn 21.

[105] In their order of reference, these writings include Kant, *Was heißt, sich im Denken orientieren?* ('What Does It Mean, to Orient One's Self in Thinking?') in 8 *Werkausgabe Immanuel Kant* (1968); Kant, *Kritik der reinen Vernunft* ('Critique of Pure Reason') in 3 *Werkausgabe Immanuel Kant* (1968); Kant, *Anthropologie in pragmatischer Hinsicht* ('Anthropology from a Pragmatic Point of View') in 12 *Werkausgabe Immanuel Kant* (1968); Kant, *Beantwortung der Frage: Was ist Aufklärung?* ('Answer to the Question: What Is Enlightenment?') in 11 *Werkausgabe Immanuel Kant* (1968). For his account of truth, Borghi also draws on Hannah Arendt, 'Truth and Politics' in *Between Past and Future* (London: Penguin Books, 2006): see Borghi, 14–17.

[106] Borghi, 11.

[107] Jürgen Habermas, *The Structural Transformation of the Public Sphere: An Inquiry into a Category of Bourgeois Society*, trans. Thomas Burger (London: Polity Press, 1962), 25.

subverted the sovereign prohibition by inverting its distinction between the public and private uses of reason: 'But by the public use of one's own reason I understand that use which someone makes of it *as a scholar* before the entire public of the *world of readers*. What I call the private use of reason is that which one may make of it in a certain *civil* post or office with which he is entrusted.'[108] Kant saw the public use of reason as 'an unrestricted freedom to make use of own reason and to speak in his own person'.[109] Previously degraded as beneath the expertise of officials, the individual's exercise of his own reason to critique official actions became a 'public use of reason' that was infinitely freer and more valuable than its 'private use' by political and legal actors. For the purposes of the 1784 essay, Kant had seen the public use of reason as that which furthered mankind's emergence from immaturity, which was his interpretation of enlightenment. Borghi does not call attention to the collective emancipatory function that Kant had ascribed to the public use of reason. Instead, Kant's definition of public reason as speech spoken 'in his own person' serves as the basis for Borghi's interpretation of the second requirement of the copyright speech act. To speak in the author's own name is for the author to act in a way that is unencumbered by official obligations. This freedom to speak in one's own person helps the author to communicate with the public and test one's own judgements with a view to reaching the *telos* of truth together. To speak publicly and in one's own name is for the author to think in common or 'coalesce'[110] with the public in the service of truth. The copyright speech act is thus reimagined by Borghi as that which allows the author and the public to come together and achieve 'the common end of being in the truth'.[111]

As we have suggested, identifying truth as the *telos* of the copyright speech act allows Borghi to unify the interests of authors and the public that utilitarian copyright tends to assume as divided and in competition. Instead of regarding them as merely engaging in 'an exchange of information values',[112] Borghi sees authors and the public as '*coalescing* parties to a common act of thinking'.[113] Under this reconciliation of authors and the public under the rubric of action and truth, the copyright system itself is transfigured into a relational sphere that facilitates the thinking-in-common oriented towards truth. Copyright becomes 'neither (just) about "the author" as such nor (just) about "the public" as such), but is primarily about the author-public coalescence'.[114] Not so much the striking of an optimal balance between the incentive to create works and the imperative to distribute them,

108 Kant, 'An Answer to the Question: What Is Enlightenment? (1784)', 18.

109 Ibid., 19.

110 For Borghi's discussion of the etymology of 'coalesce' and how it fits his account of copyright as about being in truth with others, see Borghi, 'Copyright and Truth', 18, fn 49.

111 Ibid., 18.

112 Ibid.

113 Ibid.

114 Ibid., 20.

the dialogical endeavour of truth is that which fundamentally concerns and justifies copyright law.

The ethos of resisting utilitarian copyright and copyright expansionism demonstrated in Borghi's and Drassinower's transpositions of Kant to the present is similarly enacted in Barron's scholarship. For Barron, the attraction of Kant's philosophy extends from its power not only to contribute to these critical contemporary efforts but also to do so in way that makes up for a major deficit in their thinking. Barron explicitly distinguishes her position from three clusters of critiques that, in her view, suffer from the same limitation of failing to provide any rich understanding of what is truly at stake in the growth of copyright restrictions and intellectual property rights in particular.[115] These include not only liberal accounts that have relied on the categories of the public domain, free culture and individual freedom of expression to oppose the privatisation of information[116] but also Kantian interventions such as Drassinower's.[117] Whilst sympathetic to Drassinower's proposal of ensuring reciprocal equality amongst authors through the copyright system, Barron notes that Drassinower does not clarify why the egalitarian ethic of authorship warrants protection beyond alluding to its affirmation of the inherent dignity of authorship.[118] This limitation, Barron suggests, extends from Drassinower's exclusive focus on Kant's 1785 essay.[119] To understand what is truly advanced by a dialogical sphere of authorship unfettered by proprietary rights, Barron argues that it is necessary to situate the essay within Kant's ethical, legal and political thought.[120]

Specifically, Barron suggests that the regime of author's rights proposed by Kant in the 1785 essay is only intelligible within the project of collective emancipation

[115] See, especially, Barron, 'Kant, Copyright and Communicative Freedom', 3–6.

[116] The two main referenced works on the public domain are: Pamela Samuelson, 'Challenges in Mapping the Public Domain', in *The Future of the Public Domain: Identifying the Commons in Information Law*, ed. Lucie Guibault and P. Bernt Hugenholtz (Alphen aan den Rijn: Wolters Kluwer Law & Business, 2006), 7–25; James Boyle, 'The Second Enclosure Movement and the Construction of the Public Domain', *Law and Contemporary Problems* 66 (2003): 33–74. Those on free culture and freedom of expression are: Lawrence Lessig, *Free Culture: How Big Media Uses Technology and the Law to Lock Down Culture and Control Creativity* (New York: The Penguin Press, 2004); Neil W. Netanel, *Copyright's Paradox* (New York: Oxford University Press, 2008).

[117] Barron also cites Leslie Kim Treiger-Bar-Am, 'Kant on Copyright: Rights of Transformative Authorship', *Cardozo Arts & Entertainment Law Journal* 25, no. 3 (2008): 1059–1103.

[118] See Barron, 'Kant, Copyright and Communicative Freedom', 8.

[119] Ibid.

[120] In their order of reference, these texts include: Kant, 'Groundwork for the Metaphysics of Morals (1785)'; Kant, 'Critique of Practical Reason (1788)'; Kant, 'The Metaphysics of Morals'; Kant, 'On the Common Saying: That May Be Correct in Theory, But It Is No Use in Practice (1793)'; Kant, 'Toward Perpetual Peace (1795)' all in Immanuel Kant, *Practical Philosophy*, ed. and trans. Mary J. Gregor, *The Cambridge Edition of the Works of Immanuel Kant* (Cambridge: Cambridge University Press, 1996); Kant, *Critique of Judgment (1790)* (Indianapolis, IN: Hackett, 1997).

involving the public use of reason that Kant referred to as 'enlightenment' (*Aufklärung*) in the essay published a year before. Like Borghi, Barron retrieves from the earlier essay the principle of publicity or 'open public debate'[121] as the critical dialogical process of relying on one's own reason to contest and displace traditional forms of authority like ecclesiastical or state authorities. The latter are but secondary to reason, which alone must guide our actions. However, rather than designate 'truth' as the *telos* of publicity, Barron prioritises its character as 'an emancipatory process that ... moves humanity as a whole towards a situation in which "everything submits" to criticism'.[122] The freedom to speak publicly (or what Barron calls 'communicative freedom'[123]) is the key to a collective freedom that is achieved by humankind only when reason has become the definitive authority in the world at large. Communicative freedom and the practice of enlightenment on a global scale would nonetheless require certain legal arrangements as part of its empirical conditions of possibility. As a preliminary move, Barron notes that Kant's philosophy of law or doctrine of right (the *Rechtslehre*) provides a moral justification for imposing a coercive system of laws that is based on the recognition of 'the inevitability of conflict between beings in a context of finitude'.[124] A system of rights has to be enforced so as to secure the empirically conflictual freedoms of persons, though the contents of these rights could and must be subject to public scrutiny.[125] For Barron, the concept of author's rights that Kant introduced in the 1785 essay to address the problem of unauthorised reprinting in eighteenth-century Germany was precisely the legal arrangement proposed to protect communicative freedom in the situation.

More so than Drassinower and Borghi, Barron demonstrates an awareness of some of the historical specificities of Kant's 1785 proposal. As noted in greater detail by Martha Woodmansee, in eighteenth-century Germany, professional writers like Gotthold Ephraim Lessing and Friedrich Gottlob Klopstock were facing a particular problem relating to the burgeoning book trade that occurred in the absence of effective legal mechanisms to restrict the unauthorised reprinting of books.[126] Writers were reliant on publishers and the printing press to publish their books and, from Kant's perspective, relay their speech to the public. Kant himself recognised the importance and value of the printing press and the industry of publishers to mediate the delivery of speech spoken in the author's name: 'Now, publication is speech to the public (through printing) in the name of the author and hence an

[121] Barron, 'Kant, Copyright and Communicative Freedom', 18.
[122] Ibid., 27.
[123] Ibid., 39.
[124] Ibid., 13.
[125] See Ibid., 19: 'In a nutshell, Kant's message is this: subjects must obey the laws in force, but as citizens they should also argue publicly about their rightness.'
[126] See Martha Woodmansee, 'The Genius and the Copyright: Economic and Legal Conditions of the Emergence of the "Author"', *Eighteenth-Century Studies* 17, no. 4 (1984): 431–48.

affair carried on in another's name."[127] However, print technology also afforded the reprinting of already published books by unauthorised publishers and their sale for a higher profit because there was no need to pay for the author's manuscript. The book privilege system allowed individual states to grant publishers protection against reprinting within their respective borders. But given the proximity of the three hundred or so German states and their differential treatments of book piracy, it was not possible for publishers to obtain a privilege in every state. The profitability of book piracy limited the profits of publishers, which in turn affected the livelihood of authors and their communicative freedom. As Barron puts it strongly, 'in the absence of a right to control unauthorized publication, no publisher would purchase a manuscript from an author in the first place'.[128] The author's freedom to speak publicly depended on the willingness of publishers to print their books. If collective emancipation depended on the use of public reason through the medium of print, then the reluctance of publishers to print the books of authors and adequately pay them for their efforts would have affected the very practice of enlightenment that Kant advocated. In the 1785 essay, Kant pushed for a regime of author's rights that saw unauthorised reprinting as a wrong against the publisher, who had been granted an exclusive right to speak in the author's name via a contract with the author. The right to grant this personal right to the publisher, in turn, extended from the author's 'innate right in his own person, namely, to prevent another from having him speak to the public without his consent, which consent certainly cannot be presumed because he has already given it exclusively to someone else'.[129] Without extending the concept of property to any immaterial thing in the book, Kant advanced a legal arrangement that protected the practice of authorised publication and the communicative freedom of authors in eighteenth-century Germany.

For Barron, though Kant's idea of author's rights proposed a solution to a specific problem in eighteenth-century Germany, it nonetheless necessitates a re-evaluation of today's utilitarian and proprietary systems of copyright. How far can utilitarian copyright protect communicative freedom and affirm the practice of enlightenment on a global scale? Does the expansion of copyright and intellectual property rights not constitute an obstacle or 'impediment'[130] to the collective emancipation of

[127] Kant, 'On the Wrongfulness of Unauthorized Publication of Books (1785)', 32. See also Barron, 'Kant, Copyright and Communicative Freedom', 40, fn 29: 'the 1785 Essay on unauthorized reprinting reflects Kant's recognition that communication between speakers in modern conditions is inevitably *channelled* – by technologies and media of communication (print and books in Kant's day; software and networks in ours), by commercial intermediaries (Prussian publishers in Kant's context; global information and entertainment corporations in ours), and by institutional structures (book markets then; information markets generally now) – in ways that may shape the form and content of communication and so the nature of the communication community itself'.

[128] Barron, 'Kant, Copyright and Communicative Freedom', 34.

[129] Kant, 'On the Wrongfulness of Unauthorized Publication of Books (1785)', 35.

[130] Barron, 'Kant, Copyright and Communicative Freedom', 45.

humanity at large? Rather than reproducing these dominant economic frames of copyright, Barron argues for the necessity of considering Kant's alternative of author's rights and the culture of public communication that it promises to secure.

MEDIUM OF LITERATURE

We have recalled three distinctive positions on the question of authorship and copyright that adopt differing interpretations of Kant's 1785 essay and its significance to copyright law today. These readings of Kant call attention to different junctures in the essay and, at times, seek to illuminate them by selectively referring to other parts of Kant's philosophical oeuvre. Emphasising the verbal and dialogical nature of the book as suggested in the essay, Drassinower sees authorship as an author's invitation to the public to engage in a dialogue through new communicative acts that draw on the ideas expressed in others. As rethought by Drassinower, the idea/expression dichotomy evidences the law's affirmation of an egalitarian ethic of authorship that sees authors as equally entitled to be inspired by one another's acts. For Borghi and Barron, on the other hand, the dichotomy and the concept of intellectual property it implies are fundamentally incompatible with Kant's notion of author's rights. Moving beyond Kant's essay to consider his reflections on thinking and publicity, Borghi conceives of authorship as the author–public coalescence that affords our common being in truth. The copyright speech act warrants legal protection precisely by virtue of its necessary orientation towards truth. Similarly referring to these 'external' texts but also to Kant's ethical and legal-political philosophy, Barron grounds authorship in Kant's notions of right, communicative freedom and enlightenment. Authorship is an exercise of the freedom to participate in open public debate, which advances the global project of collective emancipation where reason alone governs human actions. For Barron, Kant's regime of author's rights was the rightful legal arrangement to protect communicative freedom in eighteenth-century Germany, and ought to be considered as a corrective to the proprietary notion of copyright that now prevails.

In so constructing their own positions on authorship and copyright through a close engagement with the philosophical meaning of Kant's essay and other writings, the three contemporary intellectual property scholars seem to demonstrate a shared acceptance of what they understand as a central premise of Kant's essay: the book is a speech spoken in the name of its author addressed to the public, who are in turn invited to reply, likewise with speech spoken in their own name. The structural coupling of the speech to the name of the author, which is non-severable by virtue of what Kant understood as the innate right of the author in one's own person, is what justifies each of the contemporary scholars' recourse to the writings bearing the author's name to illuminate the meaning of Kant's speech of 1785. Each scholar's 'speech' could also be understood as assenting to their respective – and even one another's – Kantian perspectives on authorship. From within Drassinower's position, the three scholars have drawn on the ideas in Kant's essay to articulate their own original ways of rethinking authorship and copyright. For the purposes of Borghi's truth-oriented theory, the speech acts of the scholars evidence the coming-together in truth of their authors' being, which is their necessary end. Lastly, from Barron's perspective, the affinities and differences in their positions reflect and emanate from the process of critical debate that is the motor of progress in the global project of collective emancipation in reason. All three scholars have approached Kant's essay as a speech addressed to themselves as members of public, to which they have responded with their own speech that could, in turn, be seen as invitations to other members of the public (like ourselves) to interpret and critique their positions. Authorship as a recursive dialogue of interventions is one way of reading Kant's essay and the scholarship it has inspired that appears to have been authorised by Kant himself.

And yet, as Barron shows some awareness of, the 'speech' of 1785 already registers in its philosophical meaning a dimension of authorship that exceeds such emphasis on the acts of interpretation and critique surrounding it.[131] Kant recognised that publishing in eighteenth-century Germany was an activity of relaying a speech coupled to the author that specifically relied on the medium of print. 'He presents the author as speaking publicly and only mediates delivery of his speech to the public ... He indeed provides in his own name the *mute instrument for delivering the author's speech to the public* [reference mark]; but to *bring his speech to the public* by printing it, and so to show himself as the one *through whom the author* speaks to the public, is something he can do only in the name of another.'[132] In the accompanying footnote (see Figure 1.1), Kant explained that the printed book was 'mute' because it relayed the author's speech not by means of sound as in the instances of the 'megaphone' or 'mouth', but rather by means of the letter: 'This is what is essential here: that what is thereby delivered is not a *thing* but an *opera*, namely *speech*, and indeed by letters. By calling it a mute instrument I distinguish it from one that delivers speech by sounds, such as a megaphone or even the *mouth* of another.'[133] Kant not only understood the speech of authors in his day to be '*channelled*'[134] by the technology of print, but also saw such a mode of relay as being an optical one that relied on the visual perception of the reader. Print was – and continues to be – an optical medium: it can relay the 'speech' of the author only by means of the visible letters imprinted on the page. The opticality of print is reaffirmed by Kant in the passage on the nature and legal status of the book in *The*

[131] See n. 127 for Barron's important observation of the technological, economic and institutional bases of modern communication that Kant had apprehended.

[132] Kant, 'On the Wrongfulness of Unauthorized Publication of Books (1785)'. See also Kant's ventriloquism of the publisher: 'Through me a writer will by means of his letters have informed you of this or that, instruct you, and so forth. I am not responsible for anything, not even for the freedom which the author assumes to speak publicly through me: I am only the medium by which it reaches you.': Ibid.

[133] Ibid.

[134] See n. 127.

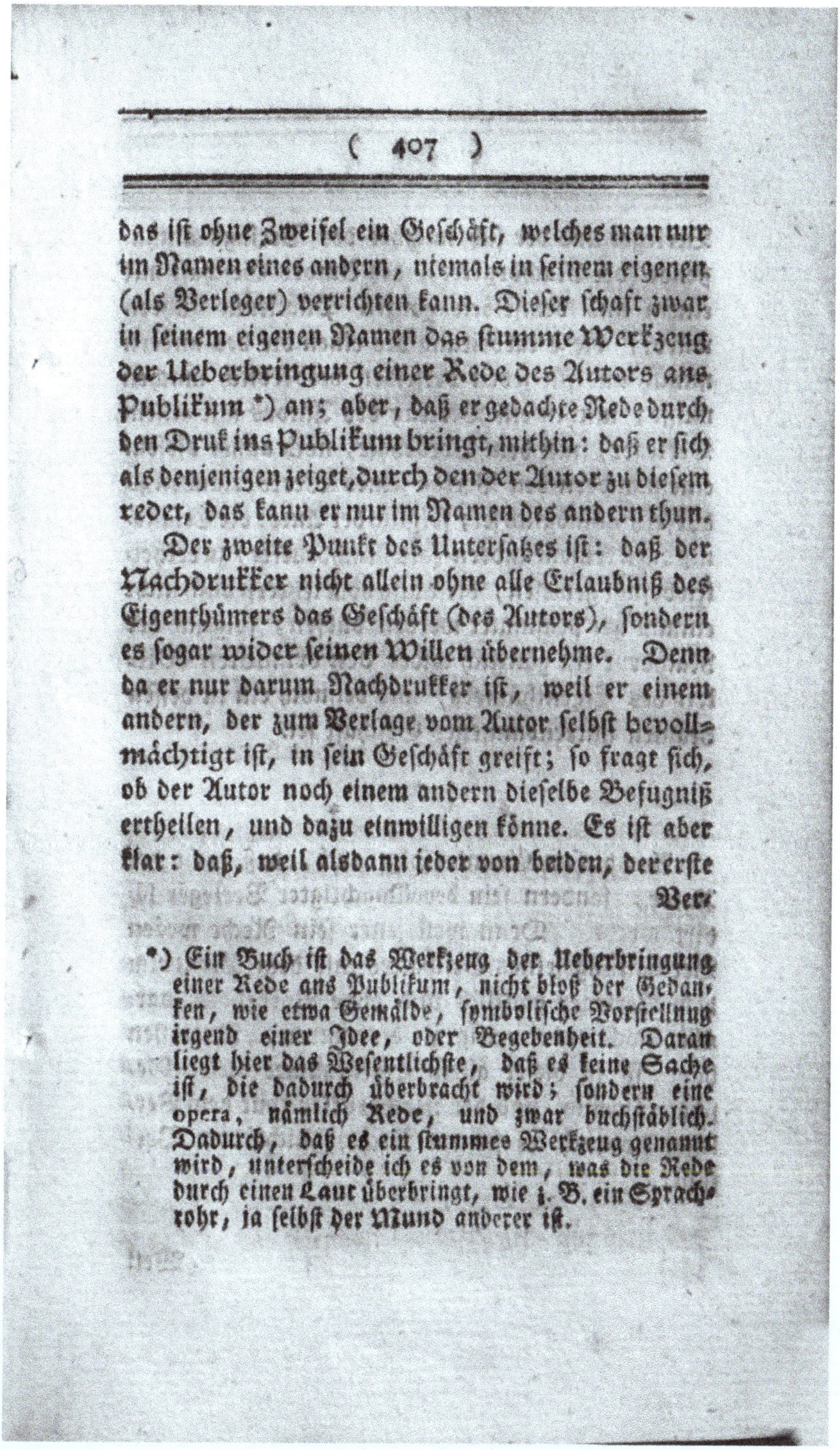

(407)

das ist ohne Zweifel ein Geschäft, welches man nur im Namen eines andern, niemals in seinem eigenen (als Verleger) verrichten kann. Dieser schaft zwar in seinem eigenen Namen das stumme Werkzeug der Ueberbringung einer Rede des Autors ans Publikum *) an; aber, daß er gedachte Rede durch den Druk ins Publikum bringt, mithin: daß er sich als denjenigen zeiget, durch den der Autor zu diesem redet, das kann er nur im Namen des andern thun.

Der zweite Punkt des Untersatzes ist: daß der Nachdrukker nicht allein ohne alle Erlaubniß des Eigenthümers das Geschäft (des Autors), sondern es sogar wider seinen Willen übernehme. Denn da er nur darum Nachdrukker ist, weil er einem andern, der zum Verlage vom Autor selbst bevoll= mächtigt ist, in sein Geschäft greift; so fragt sich, ob der Autor noch einem andern dieselbe Befugniß ertheilen, und dazu einwilligen könne. Es ist aber klar: daß, weil alsdann jeder von beiden, der erste

Ver=

*) Ein Buch ist das Werkzeug der Ueberbringung einer Rede ans Publikum, nicht bloß der Gedanken, wie etwa Gemälde, symbolische Vorstellung irgend einer Idee, oder Begebenheit. Daran liegt hier das Wesentlichste, daß es keine Sache ist, die dadurch überbracht wird; sondern eine opera, nämlich Rede, und zwar buchstäblich. Dadurch, daß es ein stummes Werkzeug genannt wird, unterscheide ich es von dem, was die Rede durch einen Laut überbringt, wie z. B. ein Sprachrohr, ja selbst der Mund anderer ist.

FIGURE 1.1 Footnote on the opticality of books in Kant's 1785 essay.

Metaphysics of Morals: 'A book is a writing (it does not matter here, whether it is written by hand or set in type, whether it has few or many pages) which represents a discourse that someone delivers to the public by visible signs.'[135]

Why might the mediality and opticality of the book matter? In line with the emphasis on the authorial speech that is shared with the public through publication, there is the possibility of understanding the medium of print as being that which simply facilitates the transmission of the author's discourse to the public. In the previously cited passage from *The Metaphysics of Morals*, Kant did not seem to think there was any significant difference between handwritten and printed texts that might affect our understanding of authorship. A book that has been printed is no less the speech of its author than the handwritten manuscript is. The nature of a book as speech is defined not so much by print as by language. As a broadcast medium, print may help to facilitate the public use of reason that is the collective emancipatory practice of enlightenment. But it is the linguistic nature of the book that first affords the communication of its speech and what the author understands about the world.[136] In so focusing on interpreting Kant's essay in the light of contemporary issues in copyright law and/or Kant's wider philosophical system, the three legal scholars, too, seem to regard as their priority the meaningful content of the speech. The fact that their interpretations of Kant rely on different versions of the text, including the printed translation in *The Cambridge Edition of the Works of Immanuel Kant* (as cited by Drassinower and Barron) and the digital translation in the archive of *Primary Sources on Copyright (1450-1900)* (as cited by Borghi), is apparently immaterial. The materiality of Kant's essay as it was originally published in the *Berlinische Monatsschrift* matters only inasmuch as it affords its translation into a form that permits scholarly interpretation and debate. The perspective here is that the medium is only secondary to the meaningful speech it conveys and incites. The medium matters only inasmuch as it is the vehicle for the message.

But if we were to turn to other traditions of scholarship that take the medium more seriously, we would find that the very technical specificity of a book as a printed text could be the key to its historical significance, which exceeds what is typically understood as its meaningful or philosophical content. Indeed, the latter could be seen as quite derivative of the former, not only in the sense that any meaningful act of interpretation is advanced only on the basis of the material letters perceived but also in the sense that the resultant meaning often entails a forgetting of those medial conditions of possibility that supplement, or even subvert, it. Taking as their methodological starting point Marshall McLuhan's provocation that 'the

[135] Immanuel Kant, 'The Metaphysics of Morals (1797)', in *Practical Philosophy*, ed. Paul Guyer and Allen W. Wood, trans. Mary J. Gregor (Cambridge: Cambridge University Press, 1996), 437.

[136] On the equation of transmission channels with language by John Locke and other Enlightenment philosophers, see Bernhard Siegert, *Relays: Literature as an Epoch of the Postal System*, trans. Kevin Repp (Stanford, CA: Stanford University Press, 1999), 1.

medium is the message',[137] the media-historical studies of Friedrich Kittler have suggested some specific ways in which the mediality and opticality of printed books contributed to the emergence of the Romantic fiction of authorship as the creation of an original work by a sovereign author or poetic genius in Germany circa 1800.[138] Kittler recalls that literary production in eighteenth-century Germany was premised on techno-institutional conditions of possibility (i.e. a 'discourse network'[139]), which included for instance the pedagogical practices of German mothers reading to their children from printed vernacular primers like Ernest Tillich's *Erstes Lesebuch für Kinder* ('First Reader for Children').[140] The elementary operation of alphabetising children and preparing them to be future German authors was administered by mothers through ABC books of the like, which attests to the subjectivating function of print media and their ancillary techniques.

Even though it was by means of print that alphabetised authors wrote and created the meaningful works in which they claimed ownership, they tended not to see those material conditions of possibility, which, in the case of the printed page, were ironically visible. Consider, for instance, the scenes involving a hallucinating young poet in E. T. A. Hoffmann's *Der goldne Topf* ('The Golden Flower Pot'),[141] which Kittler reads as emblematic of German Romanticism's blindness to the optical medium that first afforded the construction of meaning. As the young student Anselmus sat in the azure chamber of Archivarius Lindhorst's house copying the latter's manuscripts, he heard whispers from Serpentina ('I am near, near, near! I help you: be bold, be steadfast, dear Anselmus! I toil with you so that you may be mine!'[142]) that facilitated his completion of the task almost without having to refer to the manuscript ('he scarcely needed to look at the original at all'[143]). The materiality of the letter, otherwise visible to any reader, was ceded to a speech that was of infinitely greater significance to the writer himself: 'Whereas the caffeine-drunk bureaucrat Heerbrand beheld dancing Fraktur letters and the insane Klockenbring hallucinated the syllables and images of absent books, the Poet Anselmus hears only a single Voice whose flow makes his roman letters rounded, individualized,

[137] Marshall McLuhan, *Understanding Media: The Extensions of Man* (Cambridge, MA: The MIT Press, 1994), 7.

[138] See Friedrich Kittler, 'Authorship and Love', *Theory, Culture & Society* 32, no. 3 (2015): 15–47; Kittler, *Discourse Networks 1800/1900*; Friedrich Kittler, *Optical Media: Berlin Lectures 1999*, trans. Anthony Enns (Cambridge: Polity Press, 2010). See also Friedrich Kittler, 'Unpublished Preface to Discourse Networks', trans. Geoffrey Winthrop-Young, *Grey Room* 63 (2016): 90–107; Friedrich Kittler, 'The Perspective of Print', trans. Geoffrey Winthrop-Young and Michael Wutz, *Configurations* 10, no. 1 (2002): 37–50.

[139] See Kittler, *Discourse Networks 1800/1900*, 369.

[140] See the section on 'Learning to Read': Ibid., 27–53.

[141] E. T. A. Hoffmann, 'The Golden Flower Pot', in *The Best Tales of Hoffmann*, ed. E. F. Bleiler (New York: Dover Publications, Inc., 1967), 1–70.

[142] Ibid., 34.

[143] Ibid., 35.

and – the distinguishing feature – unconscious.'[144] Only belatedly – that is, after the deed had been accomplished – did Anselmus see what he had written in a state of alphabetised intoxication: 'authorship arises in rereading what had been unconsciously written in the delirium'.[145] From an alphabetised culture extended the work, whose 'ownership' was belatedly ascribed to the author. But the author did not even notice the letters he transcribed, much less see the wider technical infrastructure to which he and the work were coupled. As we have suggested, such an instance of the denial of the materiality of the letter and other nodes of the discourse network is not an exclusive privilege of the Romantic poet. In so centring their reading of Kant's text on its philosophical content (that is, Kant's 'speech'), so too have the contemporary legal scholars slipped into the position of Anselmus. The medial-materialities of Kant's 1785 essay as a printed text that forms part of the German periodical have ceded visibility to its ideal propositions.

The printed book of eighteenth-century Germany responded to the public's desire for images at a time before images could be physically stored and transmitted by means of photography.[146] In technical and scientific volumes we find realistic illustrations and pictures that claim to represent the world as it is, which further the Enlightenment's search for objective knowledge. In Romantic novels, on the other hand, we see phantasmal scenes like those of Anselmus's hallucinations, which are not unlike the projections of the *lanterna magica*. Be they the images of 'fiction' or 'non-fiction', of 'real' or 'imagined' perception, of the *camera obscura* or its ghostly successor, the book's imagery relies on the printed page with its arrangement of graphic marks that affords reading. '[S]ince everything depended on putting individual letters in their place, Gutenberg's print technology required a spatial geometry. Each lead letter was located in relation to its neighbour to the right, left, top and bottom; in other words, each letter filled an empty space that was already waiting for it.'[147] The printed page is that visible layer of the book that enables the book to perform its imaginary and meaningful functions.

Other than in media theory, the printed page has been studied in the overlapping fields of bibliography, book history, print culture, literary studies, typography and graphic design for its interplay with the sphere of meaning to which legal scholarship has largely restricted itself when approaching a text like Kant's 1785 essay.[148] To

[144] Kittler, *Discourse Networks 1800/1900*, 100.

[145] Ibid., 109.

[146] See Kittler, *Optical Media: Berlin Lectures 1999*, 89–117.

[147] Kittler, 'The Perspective of Print', 38.

[148] See, e.g., Genette, *Paratexts*; Jerome J. McGann, *The Textual Condition* (Princeton, NJ: Princeton University Press, 1991); George Bornstein, *Material Modernism: The Politics of the Page* (Cambridge: Cambridge University Press, 2001); Alberto Manguel, 'A Brief History of the Page', in *A Reader on Reading* (New Haven, CT: Yale University Press, 2010), 120–27; Peter Stoicheff and Andrew Taylor, eds., *The Future of the Page* (Toronto: University of Toronto Press, 2004); John Trimbur, 'Delivering the Message: Typography and the Materiality of Writing', in *Rhetoric and Composition as Intellectual Work*, ed. Gary A. Olson (Carbondale:

cite a recent example, in *How the Page Matters* (2011), Bonnie Mak traced the evolution of the page as a material interface between the designer and the reader across the communicative-medial epochs of scribal, print and digital culture by comparing three corresponding versions of a fifteenth-century treatise, Buonaccorso da Montemagno's *Controversia de nobilitat* (1428). In so juxtaposing the manuscript, print and digital copies of the text, she showed how different editorial decisions relating to textual presentation (or what she called the 'architectures of the page'[149]), ranging from the materials out of which the pages were made to their layout of distributed letters, blank spaces and images, affected the message it transmitted. The choice of typeface at a particular moment in history that afforded different options, for instance, could evidence some relations between the text and various traditions that were then operative – consolidating, inflecting or perhaps diverging from them. Our interpretations of textual meaning could be determined by the media-materialities of the page that communicates it. Indeed, we may suggest that the optical page could be read as an index of its historical significance – or what Walter Benjamin called the 'aura'[150] of the work of art – which necessarily exceeds its interpretive content. To ask not so much what the printed page 'means' (a hermeneutic question) as what it 'evidences' (a techno-historical question) could be the starting point in an attempt to correct the bias against the materiality of the text in question. But, of course, as we may already have seen in our review of the contemporary takes on Kant's essay, the two questions relating to the two slopes of the printed book are necessarily intertwined: as we try to grasp the 'meaning' of the text, we already find ourselves operating within a field circumscribed by the material text. And an inquiry into the media-historical specificities of Kant's original text could well affect what is understood as its proper 'message'.

How might we re-read Kant's 1785 essay such that due regard is given to the printed text as an optical medium and to the material page as a spatio-temporal index? In Brad Pasanek and Chad Wellmon's 'Enlightenment, Some Assembly Required' (2016), we find an exemplary reading of Kant's *Beantwortung der Frage. Was ist Aufklärung?* ('An Answer to the Question: What Is Enlightenment?') (1784) essay that may serve as our model for an alternative way of looking at a printed book.

Southern Illinois University Press, 2002), 188–202. See also Daniel Berkeley Updike, *Printing Types: Their History, Forms, and Use; A Study in Survivals* (Cambridge, MA: Harvard University Press, 1922); Lucien Febvre and Henri-Jean Martin, *The Coming of the Book: The Impact of Printing 1450–1800*, ed. Geoffrey Nowell-Smith and David Wootton, trans. David Gerard (London: NLB, 1976); Elizabeth L. Eisenstein, *The Printing Press as an Agent of Change: Communications and Cultural Transformations in Early-Modern Europe, Volumes I and II* (Cambridge: Cambridge University Press, 1979); Elizabeth L. Eisenstein, *The Printing Revolution in Early Modern Europe* (Cambridge: Cambridge University Press, 1983).

149 See Bonnie Mak, *How the Page Matters* (Toronto: University of Toronto Press, 2011), 9–21.

150 Walter Benjamin, 'The Work of Art in the Age of Mechanical Reproduction', in *Illuminations*, ed. Hannah Arendt, trans. Harry Zohn (London: Fontana Press, 1992). For this interpretation of Benjamin's aura as relating to the presence of a work in time and space as evidenced by the material features of the text, see Bornstein, *Material Modernism*, 30–31.

Let us consider their treatment of the title of Kant's earlier essay. As it had originally appeared in the lead essay of the December 1784 issue of the German periodical (see Figure 1.2), the essay title did not consist only of the words. According to the bibliographic norm that was operative at the time of Kant's writing, the parenthesis was a citation that directed readers to a page of an essay in the December 1783 issue of the same periodical, namely Johann Friedrich Zöllner's *Ist es rathsam, das Ehebündniß nicht ferner durch die Religion zu sancieren?* ('Is it wise to no longer sanction marriage through religion?'). If we were to turn to page 516, we would find the question *Was ist Aufklärung?* in the footnote, accompanied by Zöllner's complaint about the absence of any satisfactory answer to the question despite its importance.[151] By thus citing Zöllner's own essay in his essay title promising 'an answer to the question' Kant directs the readers to a network of references – in which his essay is located – as the reply. The public use of reason that Kant had suggested in his 'speech' as essential to the practice of enlightenment was, thus, fundamentally dependent on the system of print (or 'bibliographic system'[152]) that the title foregrounded. The 'entire public of the *world of readers*'[153] before whom one's own reason was to be exercised did not precede the printed books with which one was engaging. There was no 'public sphere' of rational subjects before the subjectivating practices of reading and writing that extended from the infrastructure of print. Rather, books, authors and readers had co-evolved as a culture mediated by the technology of print and the techniques surrounding it.

In the title of Kant's original essay of 1784, we find a visible trace of the bibliographic system in eighteenth-century Germany that conditioned its articulation. But in its subsequent reprints, the parenthetical cross-reference was excised, which contributed to the de-historicisation and de-mediatisation of Kant's reflections on the practice of enlightenment. The English translation in *The Cambridge Edition of the Works of Immanuel Kant* is only one recent participant in this continual erasure of Kant's own awareness of some of the technical a priori on which his articulation of authorship as speech act depended. The editorial and/or translational decision is symptomatic of a wider tendency to neglect the medial-materialities of the text in contemporary interpretations of Kant. 'Despite this linking of essay to essay, scholars have long read Kant's essay in isolation, as *Kant's* essay, an autonomous piece of thinking [citing James Schmidt, 'Misunderstanding the Question: What Is Enlightenment' (2011)]. Dislocated from its position in the Enlightenment network of citation, it has been reduced to its ostensible *philosophical* content and arguments.'[154] Though referring to posterior treatments of Kant's

[151] See 'J. F. W. Zöllner: Ist es rathsam, das Ehebündniß nicht ferner durch die Religion zu sancieren? (1783)', Universität Bielefeld: Universitätsbibilothek, accessed 9 September 2024, http://ds.ub.uni-bielefeld.de/viewer/image/2239816_002/535/LOG_0076/.

[152] Pasanek and Wellmon, 'Enlightenment, Some Assembly Required'.

[153] Kant, 'An Answer to the Question: What Is Enlightenment? (1784)', 18.

[154] Pasanek and Wellmon, 'Enlightenment, Some Assembly Required'.

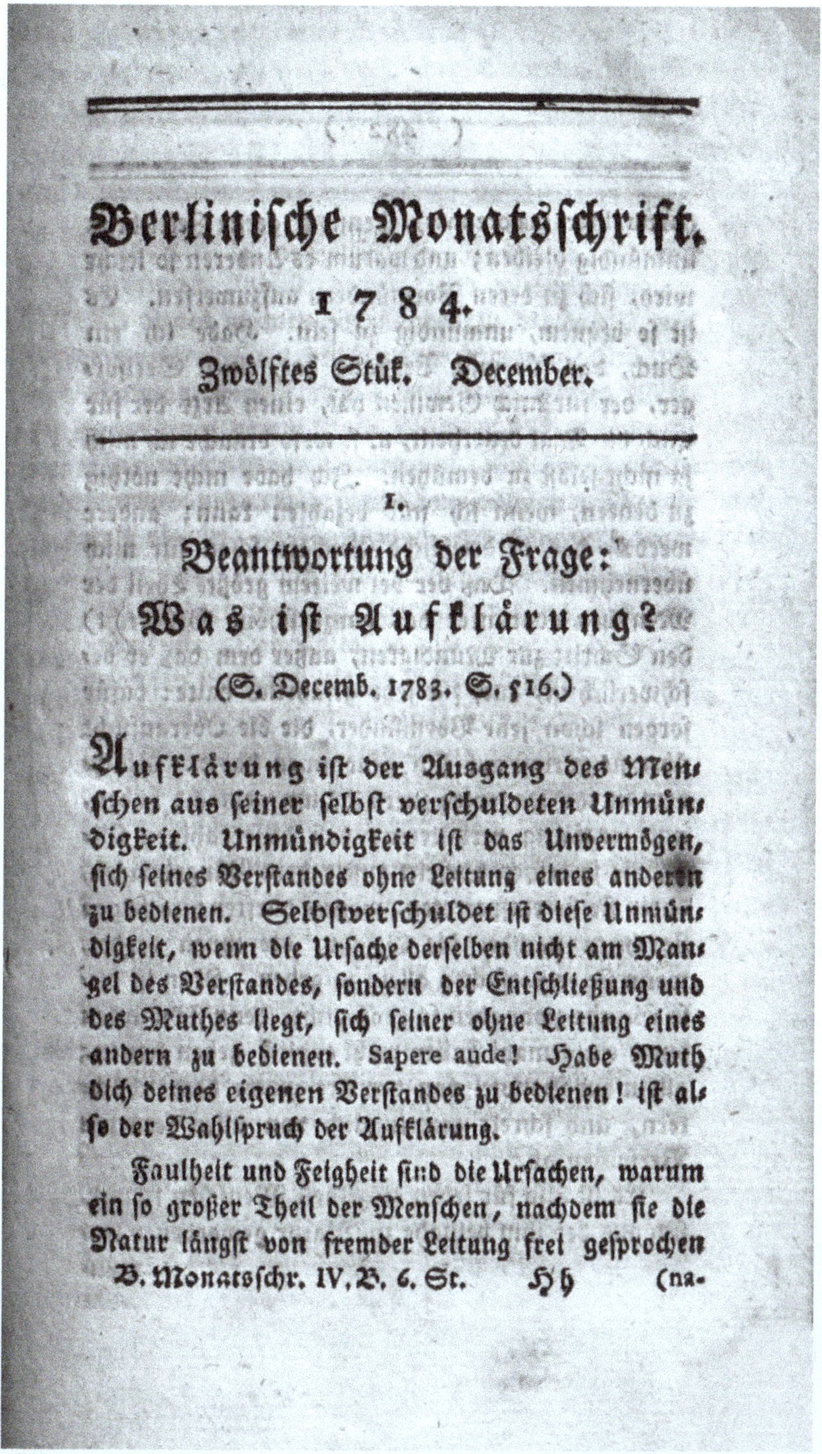

Berlinische Monatsschrift.

1784.

Zwölftes Stük. December.

1.

Beantwortung der Frage:

Was ist Aufklärung?

(S. Decemb. 1783. S. 516.)

Aufklärung ist der Ausgang des Menschen aus seiner selbst verschuldeten Unmündigkeit. Unmündigkeit ist das Unvermögen, sich seines Verstandes ohne Leitung eines anderen zu bedienen. Selbstverschuldet ist diese Unmündigkeit, wenn die Ursache derselben nicht am Mangel des Verstandes, sondern der Entschließung und des Muthes liegt, sich seiner ohne Leitung eines andern zu bedienen. Sapere aude! Habe Muth dich deines eigenen Verstandes zu bedienen! ist also der Wahlspruch der Aufklärung.

Faulheit und Feigheit sind die Ursachen, warum ein so großer Theil der Menschen, nachdem sie die Natur längst von fremder Leitung frei gesprochen

B. Monatsschr. IV. B. 6. St. Hh (na-

FIGURE 1.2 Title page of Kant's 1784 essay on enlightenment.

1784 essay, this critique by Pasanek and Wellmon could just as well apply to those of Kant's later essay.

To be sure, none of the three Kantian scholars has been oblivious to the medial-materialities of the cultural works whose production, distribution and use copyright law purports to regulate. For instance, reflecting on the decision of *Authors Guild v Google, Inc*, Drassinower has suggested that Google's mass digitisation project involves a 'merely technical, noncommunicative reproduction incidental to the operations of digital technology'[155] rather than any act of recommunicating authorial speech to the public. On Drassinower's view, rather than instantiating any fair use of copyrighted works, the scanning and indexing of these works to be made searchable on Google's website could be more adequately understood and legitimated as a 'nonuse'[156] of works, which does not involve compelling authors to speak. As noted from the outset, Borghi and his co-author Karapapa have assessed the phenomenon of mass digitisation as involving a threefold paradigmatic shift relating to the transformation of works to data, the inversion of copyright into an opt-out system, and the recentralisation of informational power in digital intermediaries such as Google. This latest phase in the digital revolution is thus seen as radically disruptive to our received notions of authorship and copyright. Other than literature, Barron has studied other cultural works of music, film, the visual arts and the distinctive places they occupy within copyright law and other disciplinary discourses, recognising their generic differences.[157] In their own ways, these moments in their scholarship evidence some attentiveness to the technological (re)mediation of cultural works.

And yet, in interpreting Kant's 1785 essay for the purposes of rethinking copyright and authorship, these scholars have largely prioritised its 'message' over the 'medium'. In so doing they have obscured the dependence of the meaningful work on its material body, and the possible transactions between them. This tendency to underestimate what Hans Ulrich Gumbrecht and Karl Ludwig Pfeiffer have called the 'materialities of communication'[158] is not at all distinctive to the legal academy. Shortly before his death, Kittler suggested that until recently, Western philosophy had devoted itself to preserving Aristotle's distinction between form (*eîdos*) and matter (*húle*).[159] Whereas the ideal aspects of beings were regarded as their essence, their material or corporeal bases were deemed inconsequential and irrelevant to

155 Drassinower, *What's Wrong with Copying?*, 225.

156 Ibid.

157 See, for instance, Anne Barron, 'Copyright Law and the Claims of Art', *Intellectual Property Quarterly* 4 (2002): 368–401; Anne Barron, 'The Legal Properties of Film', *Modern Law Review* 67, no. 2 (2004): 177–208; Anne Barron, 'Copyright Law's Musical Work', *Social & Legal Studies* 15, no. 1 (2006): 101–27.

158 Hans Ulrich Gumbrecht and Karl Ludwig Pfeiffer, eds., *Materialities of Communication* (Stanford, CA: Stanford University Press, 1994).

159 Friedrich Kittler, 'Towards an Ontology of Media', *Theory, Culture & Society* 26, no. 2–3 (2009): 23–31.

ontological inquiry. To undo the characteristically philosophical violence of privileging form over matter, it is arguably necessary for copyright scholars to attend closely to the medial-materialities of literature and other cultural works. Doing so could help to clarify our understanding of the present digital transformation of authorship and copyright. With respect to Kant's 1785 essay, what remains to be done is to revisit it in the light of media theory and restore to sight its printed pages.

2

From Paratexts to Print Machinery

COPYRIGHT QUA PROPRIETARY AUTHORSHIP

Where books and other textual forms are concerned, the terms 'work' and 'literary work' in particular are often used to designate the main subject matter of copyright protection, both nationally and internationally.[1] The Berne Convention 1886 not only foregrounds in the title its overarching interest in the 'protection of literary and artistic works' but further identifies 'books, pamphlets, and other writings'[2] as some of the tangible forms that literary works may take. In copyright scholarship, it has been suggested that the Berne Convention's adoption of 'literary work' as its final term of reference was substantially owed to the German delegation's objection to the French delegation's proposed use of 'literary property', which the former regarded as being at odds with the concept of *Urheberrecht* in German law.[3] The absence of reference to 'property' or 'property right' in the Convention might seem to support the suggestion that the treaty evinced, and continues to do so in its latest revision, a non-proprietary understanding of author's rights.[4] Nonetheless, it is also apparent from the more recent copyright directives issued by the European Union that literary works are now understood as objects of 'intellectual property' in European and international copyright law.[5] In the United Kingdom, the Copyright, Designs

[1] Chapter 3 addresses copyright in the typographical arrangement of published editions, a more recent doctrine that presents a more materialist, though still limited, perspective on the literary artefact.

[2] Berne Convention for the Protection of Literary and Artistic Works, article 2.

[3] See Sam Ricketson, *The Berne Convention for the Protection of Literary and Artistic Works: 1886-1986* (London: Centre for Commercial Law Studies, Queen Mary College and Kluwer, 1987), 154–55.

[4] For this suggestion in the literature, see Sam Ricketson and Jane Ginsburg, 'The Berne Convention: Historical and Institutional Aspects', in *International Intellectual Property: A Handbook of Contemporary Research*, ed. Daniel J. Gervais (Cheltenham: Edward Elgar Publishing Limited, 2015), 13.

[5] See, especially, the Information Society Directive of 2001 ('Directive 2001/29/EC of the European Parliament and of the Council of 22 May 2001 on the Harmonisation of Certain

and Patents Act 1988 ('CDPA 1988') expressly conceives of copyright as 'a property right which subsists ... in ... original literary, dramatic, musical or artistic works',[6] likewise reflecting the synonymity between 'literary work' and 'literary property' in contemporary copyright systems. Under the present legal orthodoxy, when books are nominated as literary works, they are at once understood to be objects of intellectual property, that is, so-called intangible objects created and owned by persons, referred to as 'authors'.[7]

The intangible nature of the literary work tends to be simply assumed in contemporary copyright law and scholarship.[8] The very differentiation between the fields of property law and intellectual property law is premised on a categorical distinction between 'physical' and 'non-physical' forms susceptible to ownership. Where an asset is non-physical, as in the instance of the literary work, the law provides that it has first to be embodied in some perceptible form so as to be disposed to regulation. For instance, under section 102 of Title 17 of the United States Code, copyright protection 'subsists ... in works of original authorship fixed in any tangible form of medium of expression ... from which they can be perceived, reproduced or otherwise communicated'. Though distinguished from tangible forms, the copyright work nonetheless requires a material form to be protected as such. The printed book comprised of inked paper bound between covers is but one of the substantial forms in which the work appears. Effectively situated at the threshold of the physical and the non-physical, the concept of 'work' affords the law's movement between the domains of the perceptible and the imperceptible so as to enforce a system of rights and obligations in which the 'author' stands as a key beneficiary.[9]

The significance of authorship in copyright law has been much discussed in copyright scholarship, initially often in critical projects aimed at disclosing its contingency and limits,[10] but more recently also as part of proposed correctives to the utilitarian-proprietary paradigm of copyright.[11] To be sure, it is possible to

Aspects of Copyright and Related Rights in the Information Society'). The latest directive similarly affirming copyright as a species of intellectual property rights is the Directive on Copyright in the Digital Single Market of 2019 ('Directive (EU) 2019/790 of the European Parliament and of the Council of 17 April 2019 on Copyright and Related Rights in the Digital Single Market and Amending Directives 96/9/EC and 2001/29/EC').

6 Copyright, Designs and Patents Act 1988, section 1(a).

7 See, for instance, section 9 of the CDPA 1988, which defines the author of the literary work as 'the person who creates it'.

8 Exceptionally, see Sherman and Bently's (2003) history of the 'mentality of intangible property' (pp. 9–59) in eighteenth- and nineteenth-century Britain.

9 Brad Sherman has sharply suggested that 'the copyright work is better seen as a quasi-object or hybrid that is both tangible and intangible at the same time': see Brad Sherman, 'What Is a Copyright Work?', *Theoretical Inquiries in Law* 12, no. 1 (2011): 120.

10 See, for instance, Woodmansee, 'The Genius and the Copyright: Economic and Legal Conditions of the Emergence of the "Author"'; Jaszi, 'Toward a Theory of Copyright: Metamorphoses of "Authorship"'; Woodmansee and Jaszi, *The Construction of Authorship*; Rose, *Authors and Owners*.

11 On Kantian copyright scholarship, see Chapter 1.

identify modulations in the understanding of authorship adopted in different copyright regimes. A brief comparison between what are often accepted as the prevailing standards of originality in the United States and the United Kingdom, for instance, would suggest that there are multiple ways of conceiving the contribution to the literary work a person must make to be recognised as its author in copyright law. Simply put, whereas the US Supreme Court has clarified that authorship presupposes originality in the sense of 'independent creation plus a modicum of creativity'[12] (*Feist Publications Inc. v Rural Telephone Service Co. Inc.* 111 S.Ct. 1282 (1991), p. 1288), the British courts still largely affirm the traditional view that origination simply entails some requisite amount of 'skill, labour, and expense'.[13] Yet, as Jane Ginsburg has noted in a comparative study of seven contemporary copyright regimes,[14] the varying notions of authorship across jurisdictions do coincide in a shared understanding of the author as the personal creator of the work: 'Despite these variations [in originality standards], I nonetheless conclude that in copyright law, an author is (or should be) a human creator who, notwithstanding the constraints of her task, succeeds in exercising minimal personal autonomy in her fashioning of the work'[15] (p. 1064). For Ginsburg, a proper understanding of copyright law necessitates our recognition of authors as the central subjects whose creative endeavours copyright law seeks to stimulate so as to advance public knowledge.[16] Such a claim about the centrality of authors to copyright law is backed by the Constitution of the United States, which recognises 'securing for limited Times to Authors . . . the exclusive Right to their . . . Writings'[17] to be a means of promoting scientific progress. Though lacking equivalent constitutional support, the United Kingdom expressly defines in its copyright statute the author of the work as 'the person who creates it',[18] similarly stressing the notion of personal intellectual creation as the touchstone of authorship. Such continuities between common law and civil law systems, and across national and international copyright regimes, suggest a commonly ingrained approach to the work as an intellectual creation of its personal author. On this view, the book is regarded as embodying an intangible object created by an author, whose proprietary rights are granted and protected under the prevailing copyright system. The threshold requirement of 'originality' collaborates with the operative terms 'work' and 'author' to re-entrench the modern

[12] *Feist Publications Inc. v Rural Telephone Service Co. Inc.* 111 S.Ct. 1282 (1991), p. 1288.

[13] *Walter v Lane* [1900] AC 539, p. 552; *Ladbroke (Football) v William Hill (Football)* [1964] 1 WLR 273.

[14] These include both common law jurisdictions (the United States, Canada, the United Kingdom, and Australia) and civil law systems (France, Belgium, and the Netherlands).

[15] Jane Ginsburg, 'The Concept of Authorship in Comparative Copyright Law', *Depaul Law Review* 52 (2003): 1064.

[16] Ibid., 1063.

[17] Constitution of the United States, article 1, section 8, clause 8.

[18] Copyright, Designs and Patents Act 1988, section 9.

myth of the author as personal creator and owner of literature (and other cultural forms).

This chapter seeks to destabilise the central position of the proprietary author in copyright law. Following on from Chapter 1's call to study the peripheral matters of Kant's *Von der Unrechtmäßigkeit des Büchernachdrucks* ('On the Wrongfulness of Reprinting') (1785),[19] I now turn to a series of paratexts within and surrounding those printed pages as indices of their medial-material conditions of possibility. We consider not only the epitextual background of the German Enlightenment in which the *Berlinische Monatsschrift* was produced, but also the peritextual specimens of catchwords, signature marks, and various front matter of Kant's periodical essay.[20] This medial reading suggests the periodical to be deeply involved in the operations of a print machinery preceding the authorial figure, the existence of which perturbs copyright law's attachment to original authorship.

PLACE AND GENRE OF THE *BERLINISCHE MONATSSCHRIFT*

In studies of the historical event and period that we now call the German Enlightenment, it is not unusual to note the suggestion that one of its defining practices was, precisely, that of defining what the practices of enlightenment were. As discussed in Chapter 1, the *Berlinische Monatsschrift* had published Kant's perspective on the matter less than a year before his essay on author's rights. In *Beantwortung der Frage: Was Ist Aufklärung?* (1784) ('An Answer to the Question: What is Enlightenment?'), Kant conceived of enlightenment as the use of 'one's own understanding',[21] which released oneself from an immature state of dependence on another. Though it might appear to bear the philosophical form of a universal proposition, Kant's account of enlightenment was deeply political.[22] To valorise the use of one's own reason as an emancipatory practice was to oppose the Prussian King Frederick II's contemporaneous declaration, which forbade laypersons from passing judgements on the actions of public officials because the

[19] See www.digitale-sammlungen.de/en/view/bsb10926844?q = unrechtm&page = 432,433 (accessed 9 September 2024); Immanuel Kant, 'On the Wrongfulness of Unauthorized Publication of Books (1785)', in *Practical Philosophy*, ed. Paul Guyer and Allen W. Wood, trans. Mary J. Gregor, The Cambridge Edition of the Works of Immanuel Kant (Cambridge: Cambridge University Press, 1996), 27–35; 'Kant: On the Unlawfulness of Reprinting, Berlin (1785)', Primary Sources on Copyright (1450-1900), eds L. Bently & M. Kretschmer, accessed 9 September 2024, www.copyrighthistory.org/cam/tools/request/showRepresentation.php?id = representation_d_1785.

[20] On Genette's concept of paratext, see Introduction.

[21] Immanuel Kant, 'An Answer to the Question: What Is Enlightenment? (1784)', in *Practical Philosophy*, ed. and trans. Mary J. Gregor (Cambridge: Cambridge University Press, 1996), 17.

[22] For two competing 'philosophical' and 'political' interpretations of Kant's essay, see Franco Venturi, *Utopia and Reform in the Enlightenment* (Cambridge University Press, 1971), 1–17; James Schmidt, 'Misunderstanding the Question: "What Is Enlightenment?": Venturi, Habermas, and Foucault', *History of European Ideas* 37 (2011): 43–52.

former purportedly lacked the requisite expertise.[23] The declaration had reproduced the commonplace understanding of 'private reason' as that which was exercised by persons in their personal capacity, and 'public reason' as that which extended to official actions. Kant inverted that basic distinction. Formerly debased as being beneath the expertise of officials, the individual's critique of official actions was transfigured into a 'public use of one's reason'[24] that was infinitely freer and more valuable than the execution of bureaucratic and institutional duties. The latter became merely the 'private use of reason'.[25] For Kant, it was the public use of reason, 'an unrestricted freedom to make use of his own reason and to speak in his own person',[26] that facilitated the human being's emergence from immaturity.

Further, Kant clarified that it was principally in the media of writing and print that the public use of reason occurred. The 'public' element of enlightenment related not simply to the critique of state and institutional actions, but also to the broadcasting of such critique to the masses through textual publications: 'But by the public use of one's own reason I understand that use which someone makes of it *as a scholar* before the entire public of the *world of readers*.'[27] For Kant, the public use of reason involved the production, circulation, and reading of printed matter. Enlightenment, it would seem, was a thoroughly literate enterprise that surrounded the focal object of the eighteenth-century book.

This is also where a continuity between Kant's essays on enlightenment and author's rights becomes apparent. Published in less than a year apart from each other, the essays commonly apprehended the book as the communicative interface between the scholar-author and the reading public. The book afforded the practice of enlightenment, that is, the use of one's own reason, because it relayed its author's speech to the reader. Kant's later account of the book as the optical medium that conveyed a speech necessarily spoken in the author's name was consistent with his prior understanding of the use of public reason as a freedom to speak in one's own person. '[The publisher] indeed provides in his own name *the mute instrument for delivering the author's speech to the public*; [footnote inserted] but to *bring his speech to the public* by printing it, and so to show himself as the one through whom the author speaks to the public, is something he can do only in the name of another'.[28]

[23] See Jürgen Habermas, *The Structural Transformation of the Public Sphere: An Inquiry Into a Category of Bourgeois Society*, trans. Thomas Burger (Cambridge: Polity Press, 1962), 25.

[24] Immanuel Kant, 'An Answer to the Question: What Is Enlightenment? (1784)', in *Practical Philosophy*, ed. and trans. Mary J. Gregor (Cambridge: Cambridge University Press, 1996), 18.

[25] Ibid.

[26] Ibid., 19.

[27] Ibid., 18.

[28] Immanuel Kant, 'On the Wrongfulness of Unauthorized Publication of Books (1785)', in *Practical Philosophy*, ed. Paul Guyer and Allen W. Wood, trans. Mary J. Gregor, *The Cambridge Edition of the Works of Immanuel Kant* (Cambridge: Cambridge University Press, 1996), 30. As discussed in Chapter 1, Kant explained in the accompanying footnote that the printed book was 'mute' because it relayed the author's speech not by means of sound as in the instances of the 'megaphone' or 'mouth', but rather by means of the letter.

As Anne Barron has also suggested, the regime of author's rights was proposed by Kant as the legal arrangement to protect the freedom to speak publicly through print in eighteenth-century Germany, which he had situated at the heart of enlightenment practice.[29]

The medium of the book was understood by Kant to be fundamental to the emancipatory practice of enlightenment. And yet, in the 1784 essay, the book was first figured as a threat to individual autonomy and the project of enlightenment that sought to secure it: 'If I have a book that understands for me, a spiritual advisor who has a conscience for, a spiritual advisor who has a conscience for me, a doctor who decides upon a regimen for me, and so forth, I need not trouble myself at all.'[30] Grouped together with the commanding figures of theology and medicine, the epistemic object was recognised as one of the main adversaries of enlightenment: it inhibited the use of one's own understanding. Appearing to be an authoritative record of knowledge, a book threatened to divest its reader of the will to participate in the production of other books that mediated the use of public reason. Thus, for Kant, the societal function of the book in eighteenth-century Germany was markedly ambivalent: it was, at once, the friend and enemy of enlightenment culture.

Kant's suspicion of the book arose alongside the booming print trade of late eighteenth-century Germany. Like many other parts of eighteenth-century Europe, Germany saw the rapid proliferation of printed books and other literary forms such as pamphlets, newspapers, periodical journals, encyclopaedias, lexica, and bibliographies.[31] Especially in the latter half of the century, the German literary market was evidently flourishing. Let us consider some indicative statistics in the literature. As estimated by Eltjo Buringh and Jan Luiten van Zanden, the total number of printed books in Germany rose from 98 million in the seventeenth century to 195 million in the eighteenth century.[32] Relying on another dataset, Eckhart Hellmuth and Wolfgang Piereth suggest that more than two-thirds of the total production of German language books in that century were likely to have been published after 1760.[33] Similarly, Helga Brandes notes that the rapid market

[29] Anne Barron, 'Kant, Copyright and Communicative Freedom', *Law and Philosophy* 31, no. 1 (2012): 22.

[30] Kant, 'An Answer to the Question'. See also Brad Pasanek and Chad Wellmon, 'Enlightenment, Some Assembly Required', in *The Eighteenth Centuries: Global Networks of Enlightenment*, ed. David T. Gies and Cynthia Wall (Charlottesville: University of Virginia Press, 2018).

[31] On the proliferation of printed matter in eighteenth-century Europe, see 'Proliferation', in *Interacting with Print: Elements of Reading in the Era of Print Saturation*, by The Multigraph Collective (Chicago: The University of Chicago Press, 2018), 243–59.

[32] Eltjo Buringh and Jan Luiten van Zanden, 'Charting the "Rise of the West": Manuscripts and Printed Books in Europe, a Long-Term Perspective from the Sixth through the Eighteenth Centuries', *Journal of Economic History* 69 (2009): 417.

[33] Eckhart Hellmuth and Wolfgang Piereth, 'Germany, 1760-1815', in *Press, Politics and the Public Sphere in Europe and North America, 1760-1820*, ed. Hannah Barker and Simon Burrows, trans. Angela Davies (Cambridge: Cambridge University Press, 2002), 71.

expansion was captured in the catalogues of the Leipzig and Frankfurt book fairs: 'In 1763, the number of new titles listed in these catalogues had risen since 1721 by 265; during the next forty years from 1763 to 1805 the rate of new titles grew tenfold (2,821 more books appeared in 1805 than in 1763). Around 1740 about 750 new titles entered the market annually; during the 1780s and 1790s there were about 5,000 each year.'[34] Periodical publishing, too, expanded rapidly: Thomas Broman reminds us that more than 2,000 periodicals were launched between 1765 and 1800.[35] In the 1770s alone, Jeremy D. Popkin observes that there were 718 new periodicals.[36] These statistics on print proliferation reflect the rapidly growing demand for information, which correlated with the rising literacy rates of the German inhabitants and the expansion of the reading public.[37]

From the distance of the twenty-first century, the phenomenon of print proliferation in eighteenth-century Germany and its associated increases in readership and literacy might seem to be of transparent advantage to individual growth and societal development. In its time, however, print proliferation was accompanied by much epistemological, cultural and ethical anxiety amongst scholars and writers.[38] Disease-related metaphors were used to describe, denounce and caution against print saturation and the excesses of reading. German historian Johann Gottfried Hoche compared the 'reading addiction'[39] in Germany to the 'infectious … yellow fever in Philadelphia'[40] of 1793, condemning it as 'the source of moral degeneracy in children'[41] and of intellectual decline. 'The mind is savaged instead of being ennobled. One reads without purpose, enjoys nothing and devours everything.'[42] It was suggested that the indiscriminate, excessive reading habits of the

[34] Helga Brandes, 'The Literary Marketplace and the Journal, Medium of the Enlightenment', in *German Literature of the Eighteenth Century: The Enlightenment and Sensibility*, ed. Barbara Becker-Cantarino (Rochester, NY: Camden House, 2005), 79.

[35] Thomas Broman, 'Periodical Literature', in *Books and the Sciences in History*, ed. Marina Frasca-Spada and Nick Jardine (Cambridge: Cambridge University Press, 2000), 225.

[36] Jeremy D. Popkin, 'Periodical Publication and the Nature of Knowledge in Eighteenth-Century Europe', in *The Shapes of Knowledge from the Renaissance to the Enlightenment*, ed. Donald R. Kelly and Richard H. Popkin (Berlin: Springer Science & Business Media, 1991), 207.

[37] See Hellmuth and Piereth, 'Germany, 1760-1815', 71: 'In the last third of the eighteenth century, a maximum of 15 percent of the 25 million inhabitants of the German Reich could read; by the end of the century this figure had risen to about 25 per cent.'

[38] See Chad Wellmon, *Organizing Enlightenment: Information Overload and the Invention of the Modern Research University* (Baltimore, MD: Johns Hopkins University Press, 2015), 4.

[39] Johann Gottfried Hoche, *Vertraute Briefe über die jetzige Lesesucht und über den Einfluß derselben auf die Verminderung des häuslichen und öffentlichen Glücks*. ('Intimate Letters: The Current Reading Addiction and Its Influence on the Reduction of Domestic and Public Happiness') (Hanover: Ritscher, 1794); translation from 'Proliferation', in *Interacting with Print: Elements of Reading in the Era of Print Saturation*, by The Multigraph Collective (Chicago: The University of Chicago Press, 2018), 252.

[40] Ibid.

[41] Ibid.

[42] Ibid.

German literate public achieved nothing other than self-abasement and civilisational decline. Similarly, German scholar and publisher Johann George Heinzmann condemned the rampant circulation of printed matter (and the incessant chatter about them) as 'the plague of German Literature'.[43] Print proliferation was adversely assessed as involving the virulent fetishisation of books as commodities serving no desirable end.

In so distrusting the book for having displaced its reader as the agent and subject of knowledge, Kant contributed to the growing suspicion amongst his contemporaries that knowledge had been reduced to fungible commodities. His more critical intervention, however, was to call for the reappropriation of print as an enlightenment technology. Rather than continuing to fetishise books and other textual forms as commodities whose indiscriminate consumption merely concealed one's concomitant objectification, Kant argued that persons should reclaim their autonomy over and through the medial object.[44] Apprehended as an optical medium that relayed a speech necessarily spoken in the author's name, the book materially afforded the public use of reason that served the proper *telos* of human emergence from immaturity. Print publishing was the mediated process by which one used one's own reason, spoke in one's own name, and released oneself from a captive state of reliance on another. The apparent surfeit of books and texts was to be addressed neither by condemning nor by abandoning print technology, but by purposefully redirecting it to these human-centred ends.

Recent and contemporary enlightenment scholars such as Franco Venturi have read Kant's essay as advancing a 'philosophical interpretation of the German *Aufklärung*'[45] that proceeded by tracing the idea of enlightenment to its origins in Roman antiquity. As the argument goes, it was from Horace's Epistle II, Book I, *Ad Lollium*, that Kant retrieved the phrase *sapere aude* and transposed it to eighteenth-century Germany as the motto of enlightenment. According to Venturi, Kant's bias towards the history of ideas led to the philosopher's neglect of the political realities in which enlightenment was practised. However, as James Schmidt has rightly pointed out, such a treatment of Kant's essay ironically suppressed those passages and dimensions of Kant's essay that suggest it to be profoundly involved in the politics of its time.[46] For Kant's concept of the public use of reason effectively conveyed the necessity for persons, civil servants included, to make use of their own reason – in their capacity as scholar-authors – to critically assess their socio-political situation. As we have further noted, Kant's concept was premised on an inversion of

[43] Johann Georg Heinzmann, *Appel an Meine Nation: Über die Pest der deutschen Literatur* ('A Plea from My Nation: On the Plague of German Literature') (Bern, 1795).

[44] Kant, 'An Answer to the Question', 18.

[45] Franco Venturi, *Utopia and Reform in the Enlightenment* (Cambridge: Cambridge University Press, 1971), 1.

[46] James Schmidt, 'Misunderstanding the Question: "What Is Enlightenment?": Venturi, Habermas, and Foucault', *History of European Ideas* 37 (2011): 43–44.

the commonplace distinction between private and public reason that King Frederick II had used to justify limiting the freedom of laypersons to critique the actions of public figures. In so opposing the censorious sovereign edict, Kant's essay critically engaged with late eighteenth-century German politics.

Whilst engaged with the political affairs of eighteenth-century Germany, Kant's 1784 essay on enlightenment also responded to the rapidly evolving medial situation, particularly the troubling phenomenon of print proliferation in Germany and Europe at large. To address the glut of printed books and other textual forms, Kant proposed a rehabilitated understanding of the book as the medium of enlightenment. Not so much a fungible commodity, the book was a crucial technology that afforded the public use of reason and the human being's emergence from immaturity. Similarly attentive to the rapidly evolving medial conditions of the European Enlightenment, contemporary media and literary scholars such as Clifford Siskin and William Warner have sought to rethink the Enlightenment as 'an event in the history of mediation'.[47] The singularity of the Enlightenment was to be found in the communicative media, practices and institutions in which it occurred. 'By apprehending Enlightenment as an event in the history of mediation, we are arguing that one cannot disentangle the phenomenon called Enlightenment from the particular forms and genres, the associational practices, and the protocols first developed in the long eighteenth century.'[48] As the scholars further noted, the booming book trade had been widely discussed in eighteenth-century Europe. For Kant, print proliferation was to be critically appropriated and understood as part of the mediated process of 'enlightenment', whose meaning Johann Friedrich Zöllner had – in a footnote – invited other readers of the *Berlinische Monatsschrift* to clarify.[49]

Unlike his more monumental works, Kant's successive interventions in the discourse surrounding print proliferation did not bear the form of a philosophical treatise. Rather, it was in the genre of the periodical essay – particularly essays published in the *Berlinische Monatsschrift* – that Kant advanced his concept of the public use of reason and the legal regime to protect it. For a long time, the fields of book history and print culture had largely focused on the medium of the book and its surrounding practices. But perhaps attesting to the recent emergence of 'periodical studies',[50] there are now multiple histories of the periodical that address the specificities of the genre. Often taken as a starting point in these accounts is a set of analytical differences between the two textual forms, one of which concerns their

[47] Clifford Siskin and William Warner, 'This Is Enlightenment: An Invitation in the Form of an Argument', in *This Is Enlightenment*, ed. Clifford Siskin and William Warner (Chicago: The University of Chicago Press, 2010), 1.

[48] Ibid., 22.

[49] 'J. F. W. Zöllner: Ist es rathsam, das Ehebündniß nicht ferner durch die Religion zu sancieren? (1783)' Universität Bielefeld: Universitätsbibilothek at http://ds.ub.uni-bielefeld.de/viewer/image/2239816_002/535/LOG_0076/ (last accessed on 9 September 2024). See Chapter 1.

[50] Sean Latham and Robert Scholes, 'The Rise of Periodical Studies', *The Modern Language Association of America* 121, no. 2 (2006): 517–31.

respective temporal structures. Whereas the modern book is broadly understood as a relatively self-contained publication that is more or less complete by the time of its appearance before the reader (subject, of course, to qualifications or complications, such as the possibility of new editions), the periodical is known to be published in 'continuing serial form'.[51] Our contemporary understanding of the academic journal as consisting of regularly published issues of articles and other texts, such as letters and book reviews, substantially coheres with the German historian Joachim Kirchner's definition of the modern periodical:

> Seventeenth- and eighteenth-century periodicals were founded as publications, intended to continue for an unlimited period, to be published with more or less regular frequency, each publication meant for a generally limited group of readers, multiplied mechanically and in such a manner that the single issues are recognizable as (periodically) appearing parts of a uniformly edited entity, and striving after varied contents within their own specialized professional or scientific field.[52]

These expectations and features – continuity and regularity in publication, the use of print technology for its mass reproduction and relay to subscribed readers, and the editing of issues that include a variety of contents even as they participate in some whole – typically define the periodical genre. In more recent scholarship, further distinctions have been made between the periodical and other textual forms in terms of authorship and topicality. Thomas Broman notes that while the authored monograph is often presented as dominated by 'a single authorial voice',[53] each periodical issue 'contains a multiplicity of voices that sometimes speak to each other, sometimes to other writings, and sometimes to no one in particular'.[54] And while newspapers are seen as 'wholly topical and transfer their attention to the next matter of interest with every issue',[55] periodicals tend to evidence greater commitment to their selected topics, using each as 'the occasion for more sustained discussion and reflection'.[56]

Notwithstanding these apparent generic differences between books, newspapers and periodicals, a closer look at some critical studies would suggest the historical evolution of these textual forms to be deeply intertwined. Kirchner's history of German periodicals from the late seventeenth century to the turn of the twentieth century privileged as its starting point the 1665 launch of the French *Journal des*

51 Popkin, 'Periodical Publication and the Nature of Knowledge in Eighteenth-Century Europe', 203.

52 Joachim Kirchner, *Das deutsche Zeitschriftenwesen: seine Geschichte und seine Probleme*, vol. 1 (Wiesbaden: Harrassowitz Verlag, 1958), 32–33; translation from Wilmont Haacke, 'German Periodicals: Their Historiography and Sociography', *International Communication Gazette* 13, no. 3 (1967): 243.

53 Broman, 'Periodical Literature', 226.

54 Ibid.

55 Ibid.

56 Ibid.

Sçavans, which continues to be seen as the first learned journal in Europe.[57] But it is now also acknowledged that the periodical was anticipated by other handwritten and printed texts that similarly embodied its defining characteristics of seriality and periodicity. In pre-histories of the periodical, it is not the codex – and its gradual succession of the two-handed scroll from around the second century AD – that claims priority.[58] Rather, Jeremy Popkin notes that, as early as 1540, a rudimentary form of the periodical – a regularly printed list of commodities traded in the Antwerp market – had been in circulation.[59] Unlike the eighteenth-century periodical, that early price list was not fully printed: the current prices of the printed index of commodities were handwritten.[60] Nonetheless, it bore the salient features of periodicity and publicness in its dissemination of useful knowledge. These features would be re-embodied by the first political newspapers to appear in early seventeenth-century Europe – at least two of them appeared in Germany by 1609.[61] Those fully printed texts organised contemporary events in chronological sequences and were sold to the reading public. More so than the early price lists, the newspapers 'systematized the collection and organization of data about the political world',[62] turning apparently random flows of information into more coherent, more intelligible forms of knowledge about the world in which their readers inhabited. Their regular appearance probably helped to foster a greater sense of order in seventeenth-century Europe than did the sixteenth-century news sheets or broadsides, which appeared far more sporadically.[63] The sense-making enterprise would later be joined by learned journals, such as the *Journal des Sçavans*, the English *Philosophical Transactions* (also from 1666), the Italian *Giornale de' letterati* (from 1668), the Latin *Acta Eruditorum* (from 1682) and the German *Monats-Gespräche* (from 1688), along with entertainment magazines, such as the French *Mercure galant* (from 1672). The periodical genre would continue to diversify in topics of interest and multiply, both in titles and individual output, across the eighteenth century and beyond. Some major categories of eighteenth-century journals include moral weeklies, women's journals and review journals.[64] There were not only general magazines that dealt with a wide range of subjects but also specialist journals that focused on some, including 'theology, philosophy, law, medicine, education, natural sciences,

57 See Wilmont Haacke, 'German Periodicals: Their Historiography and Sociography', *International Communication Gazette* 13, no. 3 (1967): 237.

58 See Cornelia Vismann, *Files: Law and Media Technology*, trans. Geoffrey Winthrop-Young (Stanford, CA: Stanford University Press, 2008), 40–43.

59 Popkin, 'Periodical Publication and the Nature of Knowledge in Eighteenth-Century Europe', 204–05.

60 Ibid., 212.

61 Ibid., 205.

62 Ibid.

63 Broman, 'Periodical Literature', 227.

64 For a study of these periodical genres, see Brandes, 'The Literary Marketplace and the Journal, Medium of the Enlightenment', 79–102.

economics, music, architecture and military science'.[65] As Hellmuth and Piereth have noted, the *Berlinische Monatsschrift* was one of the late eighteenth-century 'historico-political journals'[66] that, notwithstanding their varied contents, engaged closely with political topics such as the question of enlightenment.

Like the glut of books in the eighteenth century, the contemporaneous growth in periodicals evidenced a heightening demand for reading materials. Such an expansion of the literary market has been attributed to a coalescing nexus of historical changes. As we have previously noted, there was a clear rise in the literacy rates of eighteenth-century Germany and other parts of Europe, which translated into a widening of the reading public. 'Around 1700 only 5 percent of the German population or approximately 80,000 to 85,000 people are estimated to have been literate, but by 1800 we count between 350,000 and 550,000 potential readers (or an increase of about 25 percent).'[67] Further, Germany might have experienced a sort of 'reading revolution'[68] or fundamental alteration in reading habits that intensified the demand for a wider variety and larger quantity of materials. As Rolf Engelsing's hypothesis went, the literate public shifted from an intensive reading of a relatively limited selection of texts to an extensive reading of a greater number of varied texts. Engelsing's study has been criticised for exaggerating the extent of the shift.[69] But if such an alteration in reading habits did happen, it would probably have facilitated the popularisation and diversification of the periodical genre.

Though similarly riding on the rising demand for reading materials, the periodical genre has flourished under certain economic conditions that rendered periodical publishing more successful than book publishing in some ways. As commonly noted by Popkin, Broman and Adrian Johns, the successive launches of eighteenth-century journals, however short-lived, were perhaps partly owed to the market assessment that periodical publishing tended to be less risky an enterprise than book publishing. In contrast to the uncertainties surrounding the profitability of publishing a novel or monograph, the qualities of standardisation and repetition in content and format of consecutive issues in any periodical, and the promise of a steady flow of income from subscribers, provided greater assurance of its commercial viability.[70] For printing houses, subscription arrangements ensured a consistent stream of work and payment: unlike in the case of books, master-printers did not have to wait for

[65] Eckhart Hellmuth and Wolfgang Piereth, 'Germany, 1760-1815', in *Press, Politics and the Public Sphere in Europe and North America, 1760-1820*, ed. Hannah Barker and Simon Burrows, trans. Angela Davies (Cambridge: Cambridge University Press, 2002), 72.

[66] Ibid.

[67] Brandes, 'The Literary Marketplace and the Journal, Medium of the Enlightenment', 80.

[68] Rolf Engelsing, *Der Bürger als Leser: Lesergeschichte in Deutschland* 1500-1800 (Stuttgart: J. B. Metzler, 1974); translation from Popkin, 'Periodical Publication and the Nature of Knowledge in Eighteenth-Century Europe', 208.

[69] Popkin, 'Periodical Publication and the Nature of Knowledge in Eighteenth-Century Europe', 208.

[70] Ibid., 209; Broman, 'Periodical Literature', 234.

payments from authors only at the end of long projects, but could rely on more frequent payments based on the periodicity of journal issues to keep the printing houses running.[71] Further, as Johns has suggested, periodicity could have helped to mitigate some consequences of unauthorised reprinting: for instance, the losses suffered by the reprinting of any particular issue could be recouped in later issues.[72] The temporal structure of the periodical genre suited the economic demands of eighteenth-century publishing and printing, making it a promising venture for the participants in the book trade. It might even have inspired the printing and selling of certain books in instalments or by subscription, such as multi-volume encyclopaedias.[73]

In the light of Broman's recent study of the financial records of the Thurn und Taxis Post, which was one of the main postal systems that distributed and sold periodicals to subscribers in eighteenth-century Germany, we can suggest that the expansion of the periodical trade was materially supported by the postal infrastructure that relayed communications across the Holy Roman Empire.[74] The very emergence of newspapers and periodicals depended on the prior establishment of postal routes in Europe during the early sixteenth century. The postal network allowed not only the exchange of personal, commercial and political correspondences but also the production and distribution of handwritten newsletters such as the Fugger newsletters (1568–1604) that anticipated the first fully printed political newspapers of the seventeenth century.[75] Following their invention, printed newspapers and periodicals could not only reach their reader-subscribers by post but also be sold and distributed at local post offices. By the late eighteenth century, German postmasters, such as those of the Thurn und Taxis Post, participated in the lucrative periodical business by contracting with publishers to distribute and sell them at local offices.[76] For example, with respect to the 1783 launch of a new periodical, *Wöchentliche Nachrichten vom Handel* ('Weekly Trade News'), the post office in Gotha received about a quarter of the revenues for contributing towards the periodical's subscription and distribution.[77] Hence, the expansion of the periodical trade could be traced to the postal systems that operated as the intermediaries and channels between publishers and readers.

[71] Adrian Johns, 'Miscellaneous Methods: Authors, Societies and Journals in Early Modern England', *The British Journal for the History of Science* 33, no. 2 (2000): 162.

[72] Ibid., 164.

[73] Popkin, 'Periodical Publication and the Nature of Knowledge in Eighteenth-Century Europe', 209.

[74] Thomas Broman, 'The Profits and Perils of Publicity: Allgemeine Literatur-Zeitung, the Thurn Und Taxis Post, and the Periodical Trade at the End of the Eighteenth Century', *Notes and Records: The Royal Society Journal of the History of Science* 69, no. 3 (2015): 261–76.

[75] Ibid., 227.

[76] Ibid., 266–67.

[77] Ibid.

Whereas eighteenth-century books substantially relied on the less mobile spaces of bookshops and book fairs for their trade, the *Berlinische Monatsschrift* and other periodicals could be more readily circulated through the same postal infrastructure that afforded the emergence of the preceding lightweight forms – the handwritten newsletters and printed newspapers. In so identifying this closer proximity of the periodical to the newspaper than the book, we move closer to seeing the periodical's distinctive place in the German Enlightenment. Recall that, for Kant, it was based on printed matter that the public use of reason proceeded. Based on the prominence of the book in Kant's writings on enlightenment and author's rights, we suggested that he might have considered the book to be the privileged medium of enlightenment. And yet, it was in the form of the periodical essay – an essay in the *Berlinische Monatsschrift* – that Kant advanced his perspective on enlightenment. Given its continuous, regular appearance before the public – a periodic rhythm prescribed by its temporal structure, and materially enabled by the postal infrastructure of postal routes, local post offices and postmen – could the periodical not, in fact, be the 'medium of the Enlightenment *par excellence*'?[78]

There is much in the literature suggesting the critical contributions of periodicals, especially the *Berlinische Monatsschrift*, to Kant's understanding of enlightenment. As Popkin has suggested, in its tendency to reach out to the broader reading public and beyond a narrow circle of intellectuals, the periodical genre suited the enlightenment ethos of subjecting knowledge to public scrutiny espoused by Kant (and, later, by Habermas): 'Even more than the book, which might languish unread, the journal was the chosen vehicle for this public debate.'[79] The avoidance of philosophical jargon in Kant's essay contributions to the *Berlinische Monatsschrift*, as prescribed by its format as a popular journal, would have facilitated its reading by scholars and non-scholars alike. From its inception, the *Berlinische Monatsschrift* was envisioned by its editors, Friedrich Gedike and Johann Erich Biester, as an enlightenment medium – that is, as the means by which 'to spread useful enlightenment and to banish pernicious errors and enterprises of unmeritorious conviction'.[80] As observed by John Christian Laursen, Biester frequently reiterated the journal's role in critical publicity: '"Candidness was ever its character; the spread of freedom of thought ... was its goal; the undoing of the chains of untruth, the recovery of the right to one's own investigations and one's own thinking were often in different

78 Eckhart Hellmuth and Wolfgang Piereth, 'Germany, 1760-1815', in *Press, Politics and the Public Sphere in Europe and North America, 1760-1820*, ed. Hannah Barker and Simon Burrows, trans. Angela Davies (Cambridge: Cambridge University Press, 2002), 72.

79 Popkin, 'Periodical Publication and the Nature of Knowledge in Eighteenth-Century Europe', 211.

80 See Friedrich Gedike and Johann Erich Biester, 'Vorrede', www.digitale-sammlungen.de/de/view/bsb10926840?q=%28Berlinische+Monatsschrift.+1&page=9,10 (accessed 9 September 2024); my translation.

disguises, its object."'[81] Further, as James Schmidt and others have demonstrated, the journal was closely affiliated with the *Berliner Mittwochsgesellschaft* ('Berlin Wednesday Society'), a secret society committed to enlightening the public, in which the editors participated as members.[82] Though strategically concealing their weekly meetings from the public, the Society relied on the journal to broadcast their findings.[83] As noted by Brad Pasanek and Chad Wellmon, many of the lectures that opened those meetings were later published in the *Berlinische Monatsschrift.*[84] One of these reworked pieces was Moses Mendelssohn's response to the question of enlightenment in the September 1784 issue, which was based on the lecture delivered at a meeting in May earlier that year.[85] Relayed to the subscribers across late eighteenth-century Germany, the monthly periodical based in Berlin worked to inform and structure 'the entire public of the *world of readers*',[86] directing them towards a print-based culture of public debate.

The postal infrastructure materially enabled periodicals to operationalise the principle of publicity, that is, the public use of reason that Kant theorised as the practice of enlightenment. Through the December 1784 issue of the *Berlinische Monatsschrift*, Kant could address the phenomenon of print proliferation – which arose amidst convergent historical changes such as the increase in literacy rates and shift in reading habits. The glut of books and other printed matter, which threatened to dispossess readers of their agency, was to be managed through the exercise of public use. The periodical essay and the *Berlinische Monatsschrift* at large were a technology by which to regulate what Chad Wellmon has called the 'information overload'[87] of late eighteenth-century Germany. Enlightenment periodicals of the

[81] Norbert Hinske and Michael Albrecht, *Was ist Aufklärung? Breiträge aus der Berlinischen Monatsschrift* (Darmstadt: Wissenschaftliche Buchgesellschaft, 1977), 318; translated and cited in John Christian Laursen, 'The Subversive Kant: The Vocabulary of "Public" and "Publicity"', in *What Is Enlightenment? Eighteenth-Century Answers and Twentieth-Century Questions*, ed. James Schmidt (Berkeley: University of California Press, 1996), 263.

[82] James Schmidt, 'Introduction: What Is Enlightenment? A Question, Its Context, and Some Consequences', in *What Is Enlightenment? Eighteenth-Century Answers and Twentieth-Century Questions*, ed. James Schmidt (Berkeley: University of California Press, 1996), 3; Brad Pasanek and Chad Wellmon, 'Enlightenment, Some Assembly Required', in *The Eighteenth Centuries: Global Networks of Enlightenment*, ed. David T. Gies and Cynthia Wall (Charlottesville: University of Virginia Press, 2018).

[83] See James Schmidt, 'The Question of Enlightenment: Kant, Mendelssohn, and the Mittwochgesellschaft', *Journal of the History of Ideas* 50, no. 2 (1989): 272.

[84] Brad Pasanek and Chad Wellmon, 'Enlightenment, Some Assembly Required', in *The Eighteenth Centuries: Global Networks of Enlightenment*, ed. David T. Gies and Cynthia Wall (University of Virginia Press, 2018).

[85] Moses Mendelssohn, 'On the Question: What Is Enlightenment? (1784)', in *What Is Enlightenment? Eighteenth-Century Answers and Twentieth-Century Questions*, ed. and trans. James Schmidt (Berkeley: University of California Press, 1996), 53–57; see Schmidt, 'Introduction: What Is Enlightenment? A Question, Its Context, and Some Consequences', 3.

[86] Kant, 'An Answer to the Question: What Is Enlightenment? (1784)', 18.

[87] Chad Wellmon, *Organizing Enlightenment: Information Overload and the Invention of the Modern Research University* (Baltimore, MD: John Hopkins University Press, 2015), 4.

sort served to critique and control the saturation of books. Other types of periodicals, such as review journals, also acted as critical tools for readers to differentiate between books of varying qualities.[88] Yet these periodicals could have performed their regulatory functions only by adding to the vast quantity of printed matter and exacerbating the phenomenon of print proliferation. A version of this paradox was noted in the editors' preface to the first issue of the *Berlinische Monatsschrift*: 'Among the excellent, good, mediocre, and bad periodicals with which our fatherland is enriched, endowed, flooded, and afflicted, our Berlinische Monatsschrift now also appears.'[89] Nonetheless, as the editors recognised, the paradox did not necessarily announce the failure of their enlightenment goal. Rather, it pointed to the preceding historical conditions – political, economic and medial-material – in which the periodical arose, and which it sought to reconfigure.

HOW THE PERIODICAL TURNED INTO BOOKS

If we juxtapose the first pages of Kant's original 1785 essay with those of its translation in *The Cambridge Edition of the Works of Immanuel Kant*, we shall see some of the past paratextual features that were not carried over into the contemporary English text (see Figure 2.1). In the German essay, between the main textual body and the footnote, we can identify a couple of apparently displaced markings along an invisible line that bibliographers call the 'direction line'.[90] At the far-right of the direction line we find the last word of the page's main text, *wie* ('how'), which has been dropped to that corner from the line above it. If we turn to the next page, we shall find a repetition of the word *wie*, from which the main text continues. The pattern continues across all fifteen pages of Kant's essay, with the solitary last word of each page in the direction line mirroring the first word of the subsequent page, as if anticipating the latter's arrival. Indeed, Kant's essay was, in this sense, foreseen in and by the periodical contribution before it: *1. An einen jungen Dichte* ('To a Young Poet') by Justus Möser. In the May 1785 issue of the *Berlinische Monatsschrift*, Kant's essay bore not only its German title, but also its assigned number within the ten publications in the issue: 2. *Von der Unrechtmäßigkeit des Büchernachdrucks*. On the last page of Möser's letter, which is the verso of the leaf before the first of Kant's, we find the marking 2. *Von*. In the same way, the last page of Kant's essay is marked 3. *Der*, which is the first word and serial number of the following contribu-

88 Broman, 'Periodical Literature', 230–36.

89 See Friedrich Gedike and Johann Erich Biester, 'Vorrede', Münchener DigitalisierungsZentrum Digitale Bibliothek, 1783, www.digitale-sammlungen.de/de/view/bsb10926840?q = %28Berlinische+Monatsschrift.+1.+1781%29&page = 8,9.

90 'The Hand-Printed Book', in *A New Introduction to Bibliography*, by Philip Gaskell (New Castle, DE: Oak Knoll Press, 2000), 7.

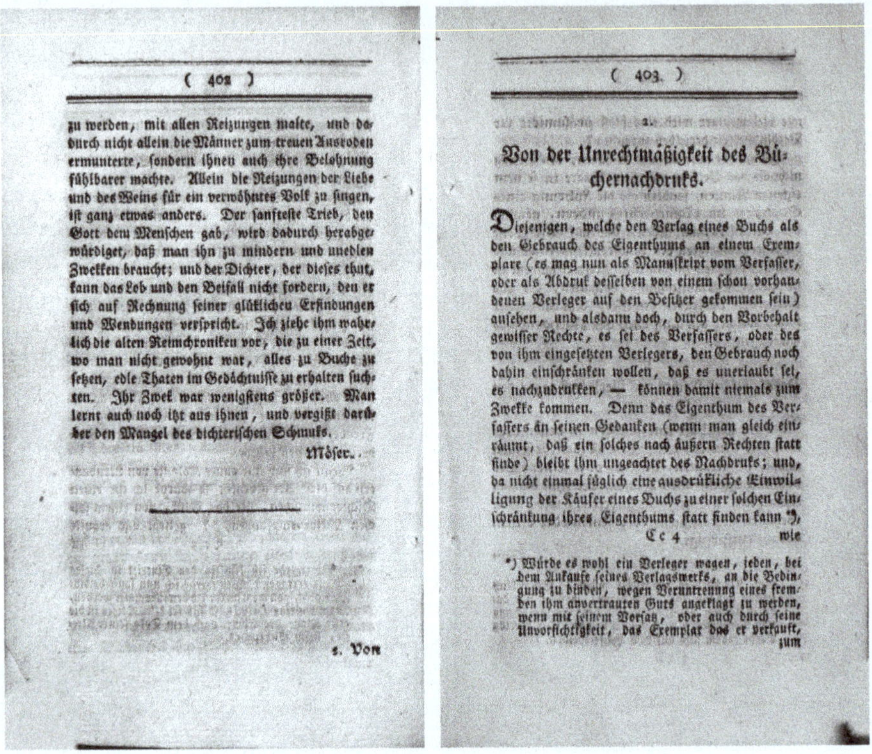

(402)

zu werden, mit allen Reizungen malte, und dadurch nicht allein die Männer zum treuen Ausroden ermunterte, sondern ihnen auch ihre Belohnung fühlbarer machte. Allein die Reizungen der Liebe und des Weins für ein verwöhntes Volk zu singen, ist ganz etwas anders. Der sanfteste Trieb, den Gott dem Menschen gab, wird dadurch herabgewürdiget, daß man ihn zu mindern und unedlen Zwekken braucht; und der Dichter, der dieses thut, kann das Lob und den Beifall nicht fordern, den er sich auf Rechnung seiner glüklichen Erfindungen und Wendungen verspricht. Ich ziehe ihm wahrlich die alten Reimchroniken vor, die zu einer Zeit, wo man nicht gewohnt war, alles zu Buche zu setzen, edle Thaten im Gedächtnisse zu erhalten suchten. Ihr Zwek war wenigstens größer. Man lernt auch noch itzt aus ihnen, und vergißt darüber den Mangel des dichterischen Schmuks.

Möser.

2. Von

(403.)

2.

Von der Unrechtmäßigkeit des Büchernachdruks.

Diejenigen, welche den Verlag eines Buchs als den Gebrauch des Eigenthums an einem Exemplare (es mag nun als Manuskript vom Verfasser, oder als Abdruk desselben von einem schon vorhandenen Verleger auf den Besitzer gekommen sein) ansehen, und alsdann doch, durch den Vorbehalt gewisser Rechte, es sei des Verfassers, oder des von ihm eingesetzten Verlegers, den Gebrauch noch dahin einschränken wollen, daß es unerlaubt sei, es nachzudrukken, — können damit niemals zum Zwekke kommen. Denn das Eigenthum des Verfassers an seinen Gedanken (wenn man gleich einräumt, daß ein solches nach äußern Rechten statt finde) bleibt ihm ungeachtet des Nachdruks; und, da nicht einmal füglich eine ausdrükliche Einwilligung der Käufer eines Buchs zu einer solchen Einschränkung ihres Eigenthums statt finden kann *),

Cc 4 wie

*) Würde es wohl ein Verleger wagen, jeden, bei dem Ankaufe seines Verlagswerks, an die Bedingung zu binden, wegen Veruntreuung eines fremden ihm anvertrauten Guts angeklagt zu werden, wenn mit seinem Vorsatz, oder auch durch seine Unvorsichtigkeit, das Exemplar das er verkauft, zum

FIGURE 2.1 First page of Kant's 1785 essay and the verso facing it.

tion: a poem entitled 3. *Der Gefange* ('The Prisoner'). This series of paratexts, which point to and beyond Kant's essay, are called 'catchwords'.[91]

'Page-by-page catchwords'[92] of the sort used in the *Berlinische Monatsschrift* were one of the systems that had emerged in Western Europe during the early days of print for book producers to prescribe and track the physical structures of the books into which manuscripts were made. Books as codices, that is, 'pairs of leaves folded into gatherings or quires',[93] were produced pursuant to these types of functional systems. Even before Johann Gutenberg's mid-fifteenth-century invention of the printing press, earlier practices of writing in the direction line of the verso of the final leaf of a gathering the first word of the recto of the first leaf of the subsequent gathering had been adopted in early medieval Latin books circa 1000.[94] Those early 'gathering catchwords'[95] mostly worked to ensure the gatherings were bound in

[91] Daniel Sawyer, 'Page Numbers, Signatures, and Catchwords', in *Book Parts*, ed. Dennis Duncan and Adam Smyth (Oxford: Oxford University Press, 2019), 142.

[92] Ibid., 143.

[93] Ibid., 139.

[94] Ibid., 142.

[95] Ibid.

order. By the time that page-by-page catchwords became more or less standardised as a printing convention around the mid-sixteenth century, the system served at least two functions in addition to its contribution to bookbinding. Before book production arrived at the binding phase, the pages of the text had first to be arranged for printing in a particular sequence on large sheets of paper, after which the printed sheets could be cut and folded into gatherings. This activity of 'imposition'[96] was undertaken by a workman in the printing house, the 'compositor',[97] whose responsibilities also included assembling the requisite printing types. Imposing catchwords helped the compositor to ensure the pages were in order. During bookbinding, the catchwords, assisted the binder also by ensuring the pages were correctly arranged. Further, as Daniel Sawyer has suggested, during the reading of the book, these catchwords, by virtue of their repetitive and anticipatory character, would have eased the reader's transition from page to page, especially if the book was read aloud.[98]

The catchword *wie* is hardly the only paratext that indexed the making of the *Berlinische Monatsschrift*, registering 'how' the manuscripts submitted by Kant and other authors to the editors became the printed pages enclosed between covers. To its left, centred within the same direction line, is another marking that reads 'Cc4'. Unlike the catchword, this paratextual feature does not appear on every page of Kant's essay, but only on the first two rectos and last three rectos of the leaves that comprise it. The recto of the leaf that comes after that of the first page is marked 'Cc5'. In the following three leaves, each direction line simply contains a catchword. Only on the rectos of the sixth, seventh and eighth leaves do we find 'Dd', 'Dd2' and 'Dd3', respectively. But like catchwords, this series of markings both precede and succeed Kant's essay. 'Cc', 'Cc2' and 'Cc3' appear in the opening and closing leaves of Möser's letter, while 'Dd4' and 'Dd5' would appear in the third poem and the fourth essay. In the May 1785 periodical issue, catchwords begin from its first contributions and end with its last. There is no *1. An* anticipating Möser's letter, nor does final page of the issue include any catchword that heralds the June 1785 issue. Catchwords appear within individual issues of the *Berlinische Monatsschrift*, grouping them as relatively self-contained wholes. This second set of serial markings, however, cuts across the six issues that form the first volume of the *Berlinische Monatsschrift* in 1785. For instance, 'Bb5' is found in the last contribution to the April issue, and the June issue begins with 'Ii', continuing from the last markings of May's. The volume begins with 'A'– 'A5' in the first pieces in the January issue and ends with 'Oo'–'Oo5' from the last few in the June issue. In bibliography, these markings are called 'signatures' or 'signature marks'.[99]

96 'The Hand-Printed Book', in *A New Introduction to Bibliography*, by Philip Gaskell (New Castle, DE: Oak Knoll Press, 2000), 5.

97 Ibid.

98 Sawyer, 'Page Numbers, Signatures, and Catchwords', 143.

99 Ibid., 140.

These signature marks in the German periodical were a hybrid system in which two older modes of sorting the leaves and gatherings of texts met. As Sawyer reminds us, the antecedents date back to well before print culture, the earliest evidence of which arose in late antiquity.[100] 'Leaf signatures',[101] usually comprised of numbers (e.g. 1–5), were used to mark every leaf of the first half of each gathering. On the other hand, 'gathering signatures'[102] often appeared as a letter (e.g. A–O) or number marked on the recto of the first leaf of each gathering, or on the verso of the last leaf of the gathering. It was in late medieval times that leaf and gathering signatures became combined, marking not just the first and last leaves of a gathering but also the gathering as part of a codex. The combined form in the *Berlinische Monatsschrift* – identifying gatherings by serial letters from A to O, and from Aa to Oo, and marking leaves from 1 to 5 – dates back to others that were rapidly adopted by print producers during the incunable period. Like the system of catchwords, the signature series guided the work of binders by prescribing the text's intended binding order. These systems were all the more significant at a time when texts, be they eighteenth-century novels or periodicals, were usually sent for binding only some-time after they had been purchased.[103] Eighteenth-century publishers, readers and binders could rely on these systems to have gatherings of leaves assembled into bound codices.

Like other periodicals, the *Berlinische Monatsschrift* did not reach its subscribers as bound volumes comprised of multiple issues. As its name indicates, the *Berlinische Monatsschrift* was published only once a month, each issue of which would usually have been delivered through the post as stitched gatherings of leaves. Though not yet enclosed in front and back paper boards, these issues would have, to some extent, resembled books in their printed matter. For instance, the May 1785 issue contained not just Kant's essay and nine other contributions but also the front matter of a title page – including, in chronological sequence, the names of the periodical and editors, its month of issue, an imprint identifying the place of publication and the printing house, and a table of contents – followed by an advertising page. These opening paratexts, along with the internal serial markings of catchwords, signature marks and page numbers, would have lent some sense of unity to the periodical issue. Indeed, to collate these printed matter as a unit for sale already constitutes an act of binding, inasmuch as doing so defines the issue's boundaries and ascribes value to it.[104] To assemble this issue and the other five from the first half of 1785 into a bound volume, then, is to engage in an act of rebinding: to unravel the 'whole' that it was and form another.

[100] Ibid.
[101] Ibid.
[102] Ibid.
[103] See 'Binding', in *Interacting with Print: Elements of Reading in the Era of Print Saturation*, by The Multigraph Collective (Chicago: The University of Chicago Press, 2018), 49–65.
[104] Ibid., 51.

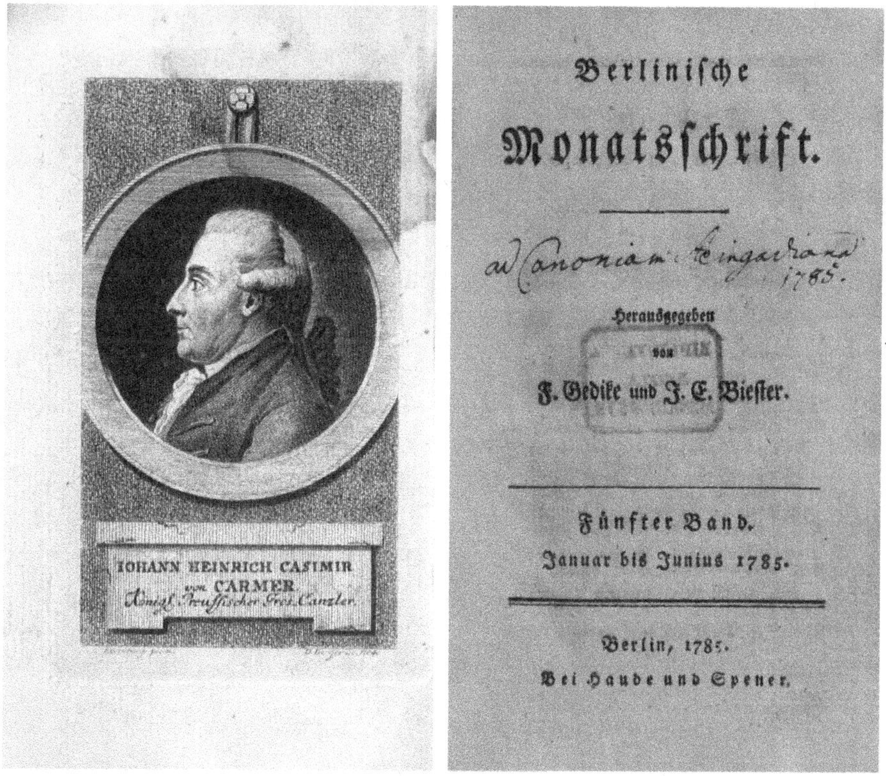

FIGURE 2.2 Frontispiece and title page of the fifth volume of the *Berlinische Monatsschrift*.

But if we return to the front matter of the volume comprised of the January–June 1785 issues of the periodical, it would seem that the subscribers needed more than the usual contents represented in the May issue to build the book as a whole (see Figure 2.2). After the flyleaf separating the front paper board from the printed pages, we find on the verso of the first leaf of the text block a portrait-style frontispiece of an eighteenth-century Prussian jurist, Johann Heinrich Casimir von Carmer. The copper-plate engraving consists of a circular frame affixed to a wall, which depicts a side profile of the head and upper torso of the jurist as if looking to the reader's left and outside the book. Below the circular frame, engraved in Roman type, are his name and title as King Frederick II's Grand Chancellor. Facing us, on the recto of the next leaf, we find the volume's title page, again specifying the names of the periodical and its editors, the publishing house and place of publishing, and further identifying it as the fifth volume consisting of the six issues from January to June 1785. Thereafter, we find a consolidated table of contents, entitled *Inhalt des fünften Bandes* (Contents of the Fifth Volume), listing the full contributions of the six issues and their page numbers. Then, instead of the title page, table of contents and advertising page of the January issue, we see the first contribution to the month's issue (another piece by Möser), followed by the others. To form the fifth volume, then, the subscriber-reader must have received the book's own frontispiece, title page, and table of contents.

If we turn to the preface of the very first volume of the *Berlinische Monatsschrift*, we shall learn that these bookmaking materials had been purposefully given at selected times by Gedike and Biester:

> Each month, an issue of six to seven sheets stitched together is published. Six issues make up one volume. With the sixth issue, the main title is given. Our idea as publishers is to occasionally (at least before the first issue of each volume) provide, at no additional price, a clean and faithful copper engraving of a special, deserving man whose image is not yet well known, which would delight us as much as the public.[105]

Based on this key editors' peritext, the frontispiece of Carmer would probably have been received by the January 1785 issue, while the main title and consolidated table of contents should have arrived with the June 1785 issue. From the very beginning of the *Berlinische Monatsschrift*, then, the editors had devised and carried out the plan of encouraging their readers to turn the individual issues into a bound volume by supplying them with these bookmaking materials every half year. The readers were, thereby, mobilised as participants in the making of each lasting volume of the *Berlinische Monatsschrift*. As well put by Pasanek and Wellmon, 'The readers then participate in the Enlightenment not least by converting their periodicals into bound books; the serialised *Monatsschrift* providing a kind of kit that a reader could use (in cooperation with a book binder) to collect the individual pieces of the journal into a volume (*ein Band*) that would lend the journal the printed book's greater sense of stability and heft.'[106]

In so enlisting its reader-subscribers as bookmakers through these material means, the *Berlinische Monatsschrift* joined other eighteenth-century periodicals in promoting their own survival and longevity during the age of print proliferation. Rather than being a unique stratagem of Gedike and Biester, the distribution of those sorts of front matter was quite a common practice in periodical publishing. As Popkin has noted, 'throughout the eighteenth century, journal publishers assumed that readers would bind and preserve the index numbers of their journals: subscribers regularly received title pages, indexes, and sometimes engraved illustrations that had not been included with the number of the journal when it was first sent out but which were

[105] See Friedrich Gedike and Johann Erich Biester, 'Vorrede', Münchener DigitalisierungsZentrum Digitale Bibliothek, 1783, www.digitale-sammlungen.de/de/view/bsb10926840?q=%28Berlinische+Monatsschrift.+1.+1781%29&page=8,9; my translation.

[106] Brad Pasanek and Chad Wellmon, 'Enlightenment, Some Assembly Required', in *The Eighteenth Centuries: Global Networks of Enlightenment*, ed. David T. Gies and Cynthia Wall (Charlottesville: University of Virginia Press, 2018).

intended to be bound with it in its definitive form'.[107] Becoming a book was one of the material methods by which the periodical sought to overcome its own ephemerality: an obsolescent condition where the value of its printed matter was ceded to, or equated with, that of the innumerable others constituting the 'plague of German literature'.[108] To rebind every six issues of the *Berlinische Monatsschrift* into a hard-backed volume that could stand on the shelf for a long time and pulled out for re-reading at any future point was to value it as worthy of storage and retrieval. Gedike and Biester provided the instructions and materials for the individual reader's revaluation of the received issues and, in so doing, improved its odds against the very phenomenon of print proliferation that the editors and Kant had identified as the medial-material conditions for their respective interventions.

Catchwords, signature marks, page numbers, title pages, imprints, tables of contents, advertising pages, frontispiece – none of these paratexts were inherited by the English translation of Kant's essay in *The Cambridge Edition of the Works of Immanuel Kant*. Their excision reflects not so much editorial neglect as the loss of their historical functions. As Gérard Genette has noted, paratexts are developed to fulfil particular functions that allow them to present the text as a book. Thus, their lifespans are intimately related to how far they are needed to fulfil these functions: 'a paratextual element may . . . disappear, definitively or not, by authorial decision or outside intervention or by virtue of the eroding effect of time'.[109] As books were increasingly sold in bound copies by publishers, and the processes of book production became more standardised and reliable (especially in the age of electronic publishing), catchwords and signature marks were no longer seen as necessary to guide the assembly of books. 'Their disappearance is a marker of increasing predictability in the book and of the shift of the responsibility for binding from owners to producers.'[110] Having been transposed from the *Berlinische Monatsschrift* to an Anglophone edition comprising 'all of Kant's writings on moral and political philosophy',[111] Kant's essay now bears its own page numbers, title and intertitle pages, imprints and table of contents. Instead of the frontispiece of an unfamiliar but important jurist the editors sought to introduce to the public, we now find another portrait on the book cover – the illuminated head of Kant the author, peering at the dark grounds on which he stood. Following the nineteenth- and twentieth-century development of other mass media such as radio, television and the

[107] Popkin, 'Periodical Publication and the Nature of Knowledge in Eighteenth-Century Europe', 206.

[108] Heinzmann, *Appel an Meine Nation*.

[109] Gérard Genette, *Paratexts: Thresholds of Interpretation*, trans. Jane E. Lewin (Cambridge: Cambridge University Press, 1997), 1.

[110] Daniel Sawyer, 'Page Numbers, Signatures, and Catchwords', in *Book Parts*, ed. Dennis Duncan and Adam Smyth (Oxford: Oxford University Press, 2019), 142.

[111] This is stated in the preface to Immanuel Kant, *Practical Philosophy*, ed. and trans. Mary J. Gregor, The Cambridge Edition of the Works of Immanuel Kant (Cambridge: Cambridge University Press, 1996).

internet, print has long ceased to be the preferred medium for advertising. Many of the 'prior' and 'original paratexts'[112] – those which had appeared before, within or alongside Kant's essay at the time of its publication – were probably excluded from the contemporary edition because of their perceived obsolescence.

And yet, as I have suggested, these discarded paratexts are valuable in their continuing indexical functions: they point to the print machinery of the German Enlightenment that produced the *Berlinische Monatsschrift*, and which the enlightenment periodical sought to steer. As long recognised in the fields of book history and print culture, books are not the exclusive creations of their authors, but the effects of larger assemblages of technologies, techniques, objects, institutions and other persons. Robert Darnton has diagrammatised a 'communications circuit'[113] through which printed books had tended to pass. In that circuit, authors were located within a series of other industry actors including publishers, printers, shippers, booksellers, readers and binders. The actions of those involved persons were, in turn, defined and delimited by particular historical conditions variously called 'intellectual', 'economic', 'social', 'political' and 'legal'. This study of Kant's essay in the fifth volume of the *Berlinische Monatsschrift* has similarly suggested a decentring of the figure of the author: instead of being simply the material embodiment of an author's 'own intellectual creation', Kant's essay was deeply involved in the historical processes that produced it and other printed matter in eighteenth-century Germany. Its material paratexts evidence the technologically mediated labour of compositors, printers, binders, advertisers, editors, readers, authors, etc. Together with the postal system, these text- and bookmaking processes participated in the gargantuan print apparatus that mediated the German Enlightenment. It was through the very medium of print that Kant, Gedike, Biester and others sought to clarify and advance public enlightenment and to intervene strategically in the phenomenon of print proliferation. Authorship in the German Enlightenment was intimately bound up with a broader medial-material assemblage without which essays, periodicals and books would not have been possible.

THE PRINT MACHINERY OF THE GERMAN ENLIGHTENMENT

In their history of modern intellectual property law, Brad Sherman and Lionel Bently suggested that the now trite treatment of literary works as forms of intangible property (in short, the 'mentality of intangible property'[114]) arose during the premodern debate over literary property leading up to the decision of *Donaldson v*

[112] Gérard Genette, *Paratexts: Thresholds of Interpretation*, trans. Jane E. Lewin (Cambridge: Cambridge University Press, 1997), 5.

[113] Robert Darnton, 'What Is the History of Books?', *Daedalus* 111, no. 3 (1982): 68.

[114] Brad Sherman and Lionel Bently, *The Making of Modern Intellectual Property Law* (Cambridge: Cambridge University Press, 2003), 10.

Becket (1774).[115] Faced with the pressing issue of whether authors retained a perpetual property right in their labours at common law that surpassed the fourteen-year term of copyright protection conferred by the Statute of Anne 1710,[116] participants in the debate took opposing positions on the threshold question of the ontological status of literary property. For some who were against the very recognition of literary property, the supposedly incorporeal or intangible nature of authorial labour was cited as preventing any requisite occupancy or possession of the object amounting to the acquisition of title.[117] By contrast, those in favour of perpetual literary property claimed that the mental labour invested in authorial creation was, à la Locke's notion of possessive individualism, sufficient to found the author's property right. Occupancy was but an alternative to, if not a subsidiary of, labour as a category that justified the recognition of proprietary rights.[118] This question regarding the basis on which literary property could or could not be acquired, along with others pertaining to its identification and relation to the public,[119] dealt with the nature of the subject matter of literature and the (im)possibility of literary ownership. Despite their differing takes on whether and how far property may subsist in literature, both positions assume the distinction between mental and manual labour, between the exertions of the mind and body, which similarly defines their understanding of the pertinent subject matter.[120] In the premodern and modern phases of intellectual property law alike, literature tends to be understood as consisting in the intellectual efforts of the originating author, which are protected as forms of intangible property.

This study of Kant's 1785 essay and some of its constitutive paratexts has suggested that literature need not be viewed in intangible or in proprietary terms. Despite the prevailing emphasis placed on the notion of the authorial speech act in Kantian copyright scholarship,[121] the essay also understood the book to be a printed artefact whose visible marks facilitated its reception by readers. Instead of viewing the book as a material embodiment of an intangible literary work created and owned by its

[115] 4 Burr. 2408, 98 ER 257; 2 Bro PC 129, 1 ER 837. To be clear, for Sherman and Bently, the distinction between 'modern' and 'premodern' intellectual property law concerned not so much the socio-historical period in which the law developed as the doctrinal shift from a 'subject-specific and reactive' mode of treating and regulating the subject matter of protection to one that was more 'abstract and forward-looking': see, especially, Sherman and Bently, *The Making of Modern Intellectual Property Law*, 3–5. For a critique of this periodisation, see Kathy Bowrey, 'Law, Aesthetics and Copyright Historiography: A Critical Reading of the Genealogies of Martha Woodmansee and Mark Rose', in *Research Handbook on the History of Copyright Law*, ed. Isabella Alexander and H. Tomás Gómez-Arostegui (Cheltenham: Edward Elgar Publishing, 2016), 43–44.

[116] The full title: 'An Act for the Encouragement of Learning, by Vesting the Copies of Printed Books in the Authors or Purchasers of such Copies, during the Times therein mentioned'.

[117] Brad Sherman and Lionel Bently, *The Making of Modern Intellectual Property Law* (Cambridge: Cambridge University Press, 2003), 21–24.

[118] Ibid.

[119] Ibid., 24–25.

[120] Ibid., 15–18.

[121] See Chapter 1.

author, Kant perceived it to be an optical medium that operated within a communicative situation, one that recognised authors as persons who relied on the technology to communicate with the public and perform the emancipatory practice of enlightenment. In line with his personal understanding of the author and medial account of the book, Kant's proposed regulatory regime for book publishing eschewed the idiom of property rights and instead recognised legitimate publishers as agents contractually empowered by personal authors.[122] Kant's prioritisation of authors and publishers as the main actors and controllers of book production is both deepened and problematised by this study of the essay's paratexts. Both the epitextual background of the German Enlightenment and peritextual features of the periodical essay have directed us to the print machinery of eighteenth-century Germany. The indexed assemblage of print technologies, practices, infrastructures, and actors was the medial-material a priori that afforded the very production and circulation of Kant's essay. Connecting but also preceding authors, publishers and books, this print machinery suggests the terms and doctrines of copyright law to be insufficient to deal with the complexities of the book's emergence. As the myth of the proprietary author is reproduced through the triadic terms of 'work, 'author' and 'originality', copyright law continues to suppress the deep historicity of literary production. Renewed attention to the medial-materialities of the print artefact is, arguably, necessary to counteract this.

[122] Alain Pottage, 'Literary Materiality', in *Routledge Handbook of Law and Theory*, ed. Andreas Philippopoulos-Mihalopoulos (London: Routledge, 2019), 409–29.

3

Materialities of Type

PUBLISHERS AS AUTHORS

Though foundational to copyright law, authors are not its only proprietary beneficiaries. Publishers, too, are recognised as holding ownership rights in books. In the United Kingdom, section 1(1) of the Copyright, Designs and Patents Act 1988 ('CDPA 1988') defines copyright as a 'property right'[1] that subsists not only in 'original literary, dramatic, musical or artistic works'[2] but also in 'the typographical arrangement of published editions'.[3] Under section 8(1) of the same Act, a 'published edition' means that of 'the whole or any part of one or more literary, dramatic, or musical works', though the House of Lords has clarified that the published edition of a newspaper referred to the publication as whole rather than to any of its constitutive articles.[4] This category of copyright is primarily intended to protect the publisher's interests rather than the contributing authors'. Yet, the Act also defines the publisher as the 'author' of the typographical arrangement of any published edition, 'the person who creates it',[5] as if copyright in published editions were grounded in authorship as the fundamental basis on which the law proceeds.

Compared with copyright in the literary work, copyright in typographical arrangement is of fairly recent origin, first recognised only in the Copyright Act 1956.[6] As noted in some legal authorities, typographical copyright (also known as 'published edition copyright') arose partly in response to contemporaneous technological developments, particularly improvements in optical lithography that eased the

1 Copyright, Designs and Patents Act 1988, section 1(1).

2 Ibid., section 1(1)(a).

3 Ibid., section 1(1)(c).

4 See *Newspaper Licensing Agency Ltd v Marks & Spencer Plc* [2001] UKHL 38 (discussed later in the chapter).

5 Copyright, Designs and Patents Act 1988, sections 9(1) and 9(2)(d).

6 See Copyright Act 1956, section 15.

reproduction of printed editions.[7] In the 1952 Report of the Copyright Committee, it is recorded that the Publishers Association had proposed the inclusion of copyright in typographical arrangement in the Copyright Act 1956 so as to prevent any 'unscrupulous competitor'[8] from reproducing the printed edition of any literary or musical work 'by photolithography or similar means'.[9] Having made the production of reprints faster and cheaper than traditional typesetting, photographic technology was exploited to reap the benefits of the publisher's investments in the original edition. Photolithography was referenced in section 15(3) of the Copyright Act 1956, which defined the infringing act of the publisher's copyright as 'the making, by any photographic or similar process, of a reproduction of the typographical arrangement of the edition'.[10] Though the Publishers Association had pushed for a fifty-year term of protection, the Copyright Committee decided that a twenty-five-year term, which corresponded to that of copyright in gramophone records, films and photographs, would be sufficient.[11] The perspective on publishers as authors of typographical work anticipated the present approach adopted in the CDPA 1988. Under the English copyright system of today, the publisher is recognised to be an author inasmuch as it is to this individual that the creation of the typography is attributed. The existence of such a causal relationship between author and work is the factual basis on which a property right in typographical arrangement is granted to the publisher.

The co-subsistence of literary and typographical copyright in any printed publication under this expanded rubric of authorship was discussed in *Newspaper Licensing Agency Ltd v Marks & Spencer Plc*.[12] Tasked to clarify the boundaries of typographical copyright, the House of Lords addressed two main issues: the first being whether a 'published edition' referred to the individual articles of a newspaper or to the newspaper as whole; and the second, whether there was any substantial reproduction of the pertinent typographical arrangement that amounted to copyright infringement. In what follows, I review Lord Hoffmann's response to both questions so as to generate a working understanding of copyright's treatment of the literary artefact and its material form.[13] Doing so paves the way for this chapter's analysis of how the materialities of Breitkopf Frakur, the typeface in which Kant's 1785 essay

7 See, for example, *Newspaper Licensing Agency Ltd v Marks & Spencer Plc* [2001] UKHL 38, paragraph 5.

8 The Copyright Committee of Great Britain, *Report of the Copyright Committee* (Her Majesty's Stationery Office, 1952), 110, paragraph 306.

9 Ibid.

10 Copyright Act 1956, section 15(3). In section 17(5) of the CDPA 1988, a more general definition of 'making a facsimile copy of the arrangement' is adopted, suggesting the updated Act's recognition of more recent technologies such as digital scanning that now facilitate typographical reproduction.

11 See *Report of the Copyright Committee*, 111, paragraph 309. This accords with the present term of protection: see Copyright, Designs and Patents Act 1988, section 15.

12 [2001] UKHL 38.

13 The other four Lords agreed with Lord Hoffmann's reasoning and ruled with it.

was set, disclose the limits of the law's account of literature as objects of intellectual property.

In *Newspaper Licensing Agency Ltd v Marks & Spencer Plc*, the relevant genre of publication was that of newspapers, particularly national and regional newspapers.[14] As Lord Hoffmann noted, each newspaper was understood as comprised of multiple objects in which different categories of copyright could subsist at the same time.[15] The individual articles were 'literary works' that, if 'original', were protected under section 1(1)(a) of the CDPA 1988. The same section provides for the protection of original 'artistic works', which would have covered any original drawings and photographs in the newspaper. Regarding the dispute at hand, however, the pertinent aspect of the newspaper was its typographical layout, the protection of which was prescribed under section 1(1)(c) of the same Act. Typographical copyright in newspapers had been assigned by their publishers to the plaintiff-appellant, a company that dealt with copyright licensing on their behalf. The plaintiff-appellant had issued a licence to a press cutting agency for the copying of portions of those newspapers, the latter service of which had been contractually obtained by defendant-respondent. However, the defendant-respondent had made further copies of those cuttings and distributed them to its employees without any license to do so. The plaintiff-appellants claimed that copyright in the typographical arrangement of the newspapers, specifically the typographical arrangement of each individual article, had been infringed. The first issue was whether the notion of 'published edition' whose typographical arrangement was protected under the CDPA 1988 referred to the newspaper as a whole or to the individual articles. Did the publisher hold copyright in the typographical arrangement of each article of the newspaper or only in the layout of the entire publication? If the former was true, any photocopy of a press cutting would likely mean a 'facsimile copy' of the typographical arrangement of the article that constitutes copyright infringement under section 17(5) of the CDPA 1988; if the latter, there would arise the further question of whether the replicated typography was a 'substantial part' of the layout of the entire newspaper, the substantiality requirement for infringement being referenced in section 16(3)(a) of the same Act.[16]

Lord Hoffmann's decision may be understood in reference to two positions advanced by the lower court judges that he would overrule. For both the High Court judge, Lightman J, and the dissenting judge in the Court of Appeal decision, Chadwick LJ, typographical copyright materially aligned with literary copyright in that the former subsisted in the layout of each literary work.[17] Insofar as each article

[14] The High Court judgment provides more details about the newspapers: see *Newspaper Licensing Agency Ltd v Marks & Spencer Plc* [1999] RPC 536, 539, paragraph 5.

[15] See *Newspaper Licensing Agency Ltd v Marks & Spencer Plc* [2001], paragraph 4.

[16] Ibid., paragraph 8.

[17] *Newspaper Licensing Agency Ltd v Marks & Spencer Plc* [1999] RPC 536, 539–40, paragraph 6; *Newspaper Licensing Agency Ltd v Marks & Spencer Plc* [2001] Ch 257, 273–78, paragraphs 50–68.

of the newspaper constituted a 'literary work', it also constituted a distinct 'published edition' whose typographical arrangement was protected under the CDPA 1988. In support of this position, Lightman J cited Walton J's decision in *Machinery Market Ltd v Sheen Publishing Ltd*[18] as an agreeing precedent. The earlier case concerned advertisements in a trade magazine published by the plaintiff that had been photographically reproduced without permission in another rival magazine published by the defendant. In addressing the question of whether the defendant had infringed any typographical copyright provided under section 15 of the Copyright Act 1956, Walton J held that each advertisement was a 'literary work' whose printing in the magazine constituted a 'published edition' within the meaning of that section. Since only the head and foot of the original advertisements had been altered in their reproduced forms, there was a substantial copying of the typographical arrangement of each advertisement that amounted to copyright infringement. Affirming the precedent, Lightman J held in the present case that copyright subsisted in the typographical arrangement of each newspaper article, and the typographical arrangements were substantially reproduced by the defendant in the photocopies distributed to its employees.

When the case reached the Court of Appeal, Chadwick LJ diverged from the majority reversal of Lightman J's decision, agreeing instead with the latter's construction of typographical copyright as being attached to the individual literary work within the newspaper. Nonetheless, less reliance was placed on *Machinery Market Ltd v Sheen Publishing Ltd*, which Chadwick LJ found to lack evidence of the Court's substantial engagement with the possibility that the pertinent layout might be that of the entire publication rather than that of the individual contribution.[19] According to the majority opinions by Gibson LJ and Mance LJ, the intended legislative meaning of 'published edition' was that of its 'natural'[20] and 'commercial'[21] meaning, which they understood to be the entire product made and sold by the publishers. As the latter put it, 'What is on this basis protected corresponds with the commercial product which the publisher creates, publishes and sells, that is the whole edition.'[22] Opposing their interpretation, Chadwick LJ based his interpretation of section 8(1) of the CDPA 1988 on a definition of 'edition' in the *Oxford English Dictionary*: just as 'edition' was defined as '[one] of the differing forms in which a literary work ... was published',[23] so too did 'published edition', in its reference to 'one or more literary ... works', extend to the entire publication *and* to

[18] [1983] FSR 431. See *Newspaper Licensing Agency Ltd v Marks & Spencer Plc* [1999] RPC 536, 542, paragraph 13.
[19] *Newspaper Licensing Agency Ltd v Marks & Spencer Plc* [2001] Ch 257, 277, paragraph 64.
[20] Ibid., paragraph 19.
[21] Ibid., paragraph 85.
[22] Ibid.
[23] Ibid., paragraph 50.

each of the constituent works. For Chadwick LJ, it would be 'artificial'[24] to hold that each of the literary works of a newspaper did not constitute a 'published edition'. For instance, where a musical score and lyrics were published as a single choral work, there would be three published editions with their respective typographical arrangements: the published edition of the score as a musical work, that of the lyrics as a literary work, and that of the combined work.[25] By analogy, the multiple literary and artistic works published as part of any newspaper would imply multiple typographical copyrights, with those of the individual articles subsisting alongside that of the newspaper as a whole.

Departing from the interpretations of the two lower court judges, Lord Hoffmann delinked the concept of published edition from that of the literary work, arguing that the statutory definition evidenced the lack of any 'necessary congruence'[26] (nor any 'necessary correlation'[27]) between the two concepts. Unlike Chadwick LJ, Lord Hoffmann did not think that the phrase 'one or more literary ... works' in the definition of published edition implied any legislative recognition of the constituent work as an object in which typographic copyright subsisted. Rather, the same phrase was read to affirm that the published edition could well comprise multiple works, which meant that it exceeded the proportions of the individual work and referred to the published product as a whole. Echoing the majority judges of the Court of Appeal, Lord Hoffmann adopted what he understood to be the meaning of the term as used in the publishing industry: 'The edition is the product, generally between covers, which the publisher offers to the public.'[28] Parliament intended for 'published edition' to mean 'what a publisher would understand by an edition',[29] which was not that of a literary work within a larger publication. With respect to each newspaper whose parts had been photocopied by the defendant-respondent, then, only one typographical copyright (namely, typographical arrangement of the publication in its entirety) had been vested in the publisher and later assigned to the plaintiff-appellant.[30]

Before commenting on what Lord Hoffmann's reply to the first definitional issue reveals about copyright's treatment of the literary artefact and its material form, let us note his no-less-illuminating response to the second issue concerning the substantiality requirement of typographical copyright infringement. Having decided that the

[24] Ibid., paragraph 62.
[25] Ibid., paragraph 61.
[26] *Newspaper Licensing Agency Ltd v Marks & Spencer Plc* [2001] UKHL 38, paragraph 11.
[27] Ibid., paragraph 14.
[28] Ibid.
[29] Ibid., paragraph 16.
[30] In so arriving at this interpretation of 'published edition', Lord Hoffmann followed Wilcox J's decision in *Nationwide News Pty Ltd v Copyright Agency Ltd* (1995) 128 ALR 285, a case before the Federal Court of Australia that had adopted the same 'holistic' interpretation of newspapers as 'published editions'. Wilcox J's decision was subsequently affirmed on appeal: see *Nationwide News Pty Ltd v Copyright Agency Ltd* [1996] FCA 257.

pertinent typographical arrangement was that of each newspaper in its entirety, Lord Hoffmann then considered whether the partial photocopies made by the defendant-respondent amounted to substantial parts of each arrangement. The starting point was that the substantiality requirement for copyright infringement involved a qualitative, rather than a quantitative, assessment of that which had been copied.[31] This meant that it was not a question of how much had been reproduced, but whether the reproduced matter sufficiently reflected the sort of underlying 'interest'[32] protected by the particular category of copyright. In the instance of a literary or an artistic work, the protected interest was reflected in the standard of originality based on which copyright protection was granted, namely in the 'skill and labour'[33] that the author had invested in the work's creation. Similarly, with respect to typographical copyright, the substantial copying of any typographical arrangement was to be determined in reference to the skill and labour involved in its original production. As Lord Hoffmann put it, 'one must ask whether there has been copying of sufficient of the relevant skill and labour to constitute a substantial part of the edition's typographical arrangement'.[34]

In Lord Hoffmann's brief account of the nature of the skill and labour involved in producing the typographical arrangement of a modern newspaper, we find an instance of copyright law's attempt to find a vocabulary with which to describe the visual materiality of the printed text and the processes that produced it:

> In the case of a modern newspaper, I think that the skill and labour devoted to typographical arrangement is principally expressed in the overall design. It is not the choice of a particular typeface, the precise number or width of the columns, the breadth of margins and the relationship of headlines and strap lines to the other text, the number of articles on a page and the distribution of photographs and advertisements but the combination of all of these into pages which give the newspaper as a whole its distinctive appearance. In some cases that appearance will depend upon the relationship between the pages; for example, having headlines rather than small advertisements on the front page. Usually, however, it will depend upon the appearance of any given page. But I find it difficult to think of the

[31] See *Ladbroke (Football) Ltd v William Hill (Football) Ltd* [1964] 1 WLR 273, which was the locus classicus of the qualitative approach that Lord Hoffmann cited.

[32] *Newspaper Licensing Agency Ltd v Marks & Spencer Plc* [2001] UKHL 38, paragraph 24. Lord Hoffmann was citing from Sackville J's appellate opinion affirming Wilcox J's decision, which deployed the language of interest to elucidate the substantiality requirement of published edition copyright. Lord Hoffmann's reasoning very much resembles Sackville J's, suggesting that his decision on the second issue substantially relied on the appellate decision, no less than his reply to the first issue depended on Wilcox J's: compare *Nationwide News Pty Ltd v Copyright Agency Ltd* [1996] FCA 257 and *Newspaper Licensing Agency Ltd v Marks & Spencer Plc* [2001] UKHL, paragraphs 19–24.

[33] *Newspaper Licensing Agency Ltd v Marks & Spencer Plc* [2001] UKHL 38, paragraph 19. Here, Lord Hoffmann cited the case of *Designers Guild Ltd v Russell Williams (Textiles) Ltd (trading as Washington DC)* [2000] 1 WLR 2416, which dealt with artistic copyright in fabric designs.

[34] *Newspaper Licensing Agency Ltd v Marks & Spencer Plc* [2001] UKHL 38, paragraph 20.

> skill and labour which has gone into the typographical arrangement of a newspaper being expressed in anything less than a full page. The particular fonts, columns, margins and so forth are only, so to speak, the typographical vocabulary in which the arrangement is expressed.[35]

Lord Hoffmann analytically divided the visible form or 'appearance' of the newspaper as a whole into different types of content, ranging from its 'typeface', 'fonts', 'columns' and 'margins' to various examples of its textual ('headlines', 'strap lines' and 'articles') and visual images ('photographs' and 'advertisements'). Further, he recognised these typographic components to be spatially interrelated, their 'arrangement' evidenced in the relationship between different types of pages (e.g. the 'front page' of headlines and other pages with advertisements) and in the combination of elements that constitute a single page.[36] For Lord Hoffmann, it was the making of these various aspects of the newspaper's presentation, described in terms of a 'typographical vocabulary', that instantiated the 'skill and labour' protected by typographical copyright. Since copyright law recognises the publisher to be the proprietary author of the published edition under copyright law, the publisher is the very subject to whom the law attributes the exercise of such protected skill and labour.

Taking the newspaper page to be the basic evidential unit by which the publisher's typographical labour was expressed, Lord Hoffmann agreed with the Court of Appeal decision that none of the photocopied press cuttings sufficiently replicated a substantial part of the presentation of each newspaper. Because many of these photocopies entailed items that were refitted to appear on A4-sized sheets, they did not even reproduce the full article itself. Accordingly, the House of Lords unanimously held that there was no infringement of typographical copyright.

Lord Hoffmann's reply to these two issues in typographical copyright suggests that copyright law is no stranger to the visual materiality of the text. To begin with, the very recognition of a property right in the *typographical arrangement* of a newspaper, as opposed to only those in the *literary and artistic* works comprising it, evidences the copyright system's understanding that the book consists of more than what are typically regarded as its interpretable or semantic 'contents'. Rather, the very optical conditions that make these contents legible to the reader, variously called the newspaper 'design', 'layout' and 'presentation', are registered in copyright law as useful products of skill and labour deserving of protection. Already in the High Court decision there was a dual recognition of the pertinent subject matter of protection as 'the image on the page'[37] and of its basic significance to the reading experience: 'The typographical arrangement of a newspaper is of importance to the

[35] Ibid., paragraph 23.

[36] See, also, Ibid., paragraph 26: 'The presence of other material on the page and the spatial relationship of the articles to each other are important parts of its typographical arrangement.'

[37] *Newspaper Licensing Agency Ltd v Marks & Spencer Plc* [1999] RPC 536, 541, paragraph 9.

general reader, for it affects how reader friendly are the newspapers and the articles in it and the impact of the contents on the reader.'[38] Those instances of the 'typographical vocabulary' cited by Lord Hoffmann would suggest the law's recognition of some of those tangible means by which its contents are relayed to the readers.

Yet, this remains a quite specific, and parochial, understanding of the visual materiality of the printed text. By virtue of its operation as a problem-solving institution with its own substantive doctrines and interpretive practices, copyright law apprehends the visible surface of the publication only in a way that accords with the norms and rationality of the system. For instance, Lord Hoffmann only enumerated the typographical components of 'typeface', 'columns', 'margins' and so forth because these were understood as comprising the product of the publisher's 'skill and labour'. It was by reference to the perceived interest underlying typographical copyright, particularly the interest in protecting the publisher's investments, that the typography of the newspaper was defined. Further, the significance of typographical arrangement is limited to its role in presenting a 'reader-friendly' product, the making of which the utilitarian copyright system regulates and promotes through the granting of intellectual-proprietary rights to publishers and authors. Viewed alongside the system's broad objective of encouraging the production of new works, typographic arrangements matter only in terms of their communicative-commercial function.

Despite recognising the importance of typography to reading and communication, copyright law insists on a strict bifurcation of the literary artefact into its constitutive 'literary and artistic works' on the one hand, and its overall 'typographical arrangement' on the other. This is apparent not only in the statutory ascription of a distinct category of proprietary right with its own mode of infringement to each subject matter but also in Lord Hoffmann's delinking of the concept of published edition from that of the underlying works. Pursuant to his judgment, the pertinent 'typographical arrangement' under section 1(1)(c) of the CDPA 1988 is doubly removed from the literary work: one, consistent with the Act's categorisation of objects and rights, copyright in the 'literary work' is affirmed to be distinct from copyright in the typography of its published form. Whereas the latter can be infringed only with a 'facsimile copy',[39] that is, with an exact reproduction of the visible surface of the work, the former may be infringed with the reproduction of the work 'in any material form', that is, with an inexact copying of its expression that, nonetheless, reproduces something essential to the work. Recognising this difference between the two types of copyright, Lord Hoffmann cited the case of *Designers Guild Ltd v Russell Williams (Textiles) Ltd (trading as Washington DC)*,[40] which had found there to be a substantial reproduction of a fabric design amounting to copyright infringement even though the reproduced fabric lacked any 'photographic

[38] Ibid., 541, paragraph 10.

[39] Copyright, Designs and Patents Act 1988, section 17(5).

[40] [2000] 1 WLR 2416.

fidelity'[41] to the original. Though the case pertained to artistic copyright, it attested to copyright law's protection of something beyond the material surface of the work, which Lord Hoffmann recognised to be no less applicable to literary, dramatic and musical works.[42] Second, in so affirming a 'holistic' understanding of 'published edition', Lord Hoffmann distinguished the typography of the publication as a whole from that of each of the contributing works, thus further separating the spheres of literary works and typographical arrangements.

My claim is that copyright law's bifurcation of the literary artefact into the two aspects of authorial expression and typographical arrangement works to generate and sustain the order of proprietary rights ascribed to the subjects of authors and publishers. On the one hand, the object of the original 'literary work' is recognised to be the creation of its author or authors, whose investment of skill and labour into the work's production is protected through the law's granting of a property right in the work, including the exclusive right of reproduction. On the other, the conceptually distinct object of the entire typographical arrangement of the work's published edition is conceived to be the output of the publisher or publishers, which similarly warrants copyright protection. Both instances converge in their (re)production of an originalist aesthetics of the literary artefact as being divided between the labours of authors and publishers, both of whom are perceived to be the creators of those intangible objects fixed in the medium of the text. As publishers, too, are seen as author-creators, reproduced across the rift between the rightful domains of each of the two subjects is a common myth of authorship: the idea that embodied in literary artefacts are distinct ideal objects with their respective subjects standing over against them as their rightful owner-creators.

This chapter continues to problematise the myth of authorship ratified and entrenched by the doctrines of typographical and literary copyright. I probe the limits of the legal account of literature by attending to the materialities of the Breitkopf Fraktur typeface in which Kant's 1785 essay was set. To sharpen Kant's account of the visual-corporeal dimension of literature, I juxtapose his text with Johann Gottlieb Fichte's 1793 contribution to the *Berlinische Monatsschrift*, the latter of which both anticipates and undermines the contemporary copyright perspective.[43] I then turn to some aspects of the production and perception of the

[41] *Newspaper Licensing Agency Ltd v Marks & Spencer Plc* [2001] UKHL 38, paragraph 19.

[42] Ibid., paragraph 20.

[43] 'Fichte: Proof of the Unlawfulness of Reprinting, Berlin (1793)', Primary Sources on Copyright (1450–1900), eds. L. Bently and M. Kretschmer, accessed 9 September 2024, www.copyrighthistory.org/cam/tools/request/showRecord.php?id=record_d_1793; 'Immanuel Kant: Von der Unrechtmäßigkeit des Büchernachdrucks (1785)', Universität Bielefeld: Universitätsbibilothek, accessed 9 September 2024, http://ds.ub.uni-bielefeld.de/viewer/image/2239816_005/430/LOG_0055/; Immanuel Kant, 'On the Wrongfulness of Unauthorized Publication of Books (1785)', in *Practical Philosophy*, ed. Paul Guyer and Allen W. Wood, trans. Mary J. Gregor, *The Cambridge Edition of the Works of Immanuel Kant* (Cambridge: Cambridge University Press, 1996), 27–35. For an insightful reading of Fichtean genius as copyright's *pharmakon*, see Mario Biagioli, 'Genius against Copyright: Revisiting Fichte's Proof of the Illegality of Reprinting', *Notre Dame Law Review* 86, no. 5 (2011): 1847–68.

Breitkopf Fraktur typeface in which the essays were set, attending to their implications on the question of authorship. In line with Chapter 2's focus on the print machinery of the German Enlightenment, I argue that these materialities of Breitkopf Fraktur direct us to the profound interactions between human actors and print technologies that constitute the printed book, the complexity of which far exceeds copyright's account of literature.

THE EYES AND BODIES OF LITERATURE

More than a century and a half before typographical copyright was first legislated in the United Kingdom, questions about the relationship between the ideal and material dimensions of literature, between the intangible and tangible properties in books, had already surfaced in Germany. The typographical materiality of the printed book was explicitly broached in Kant's 1785 essay, though it also fundamentally informed Fichte's later text. Comparing these two exemplary contributions to the *Berlinische Monatsschrift* would not only sharpen our understanding of the aesthetics of literary property today and its continuities with older modes of thinking dating back to the German Enlightenment but also uncover an alternative way of approaching the literary artefact that displaces the limits of copyright.

Fichte's and Kant's pieces contributed to a long historical debate concerning the wrongfulness of the reprinting of books and other publications, which occurred within the broader context of print proliferation, unauthorised reprinting and the weakly regulated book trade of the Holy Roman Empire during the eighteenth century.[44] As discussed in Chapter 2, amidst the growing demand for reading materials during that time, German authors and publishers were confronting the unauthorised reprinting of their texts. Though dating back to at least the late fifteenth century, the problem of unauthorised reprinting only reached 'epidemic proportions'[45] during the eighteenth century with the heightening profitability of books corresponding to their rising demand amidst higher literacy rates, a shift in reading habits and other contributing historical changes. In the literature on this topic we often find mention of the lack of effective legal mechanisms to regulate the unauthorised copying and sale of publications within the markedly fragmentary political context of the Holy Roman Empire, which was comprised of more than three hundred states unbound by any common government or uniform legal code.[46] Prior to the first German copyright laws[47] it was principally a system of privilege

[44] See Martha Woodmansee, 'The Genius and the Copyright: Economic and Legal Conditions of the Emergence of the "Author"', *Eighteenth-Century Studies* 17, no. 4 (1984): 425–48.

[45] Ibid., 437.

[46] Geographically, the Holy Roman Empire cut across today's territories of Austria, Germany, Hungary and Switzerland: see Ibid., 438.

[47] See, for instance, the Prussian Copyright Act of 1837.

(*privilegium impressorium*) that regulated the book trade.[48] Upon application to the pertaining German state authorities, privileges could be issued to authors, publishers and printers to prohibit the reprinting and sale of particular books in the territory within a specific period of time without the privilege holder's consent.[49] The fragmentary political context, however, frustrated the efforts of privilege holders to take action against pirate publishers and printers. Privilege protection was geographically limited in the sense that it applied only within the borders of the state that had granted it.[50] To seek full protection, then, the author, publisher or printer had to apply for a privilege in every state, which was impractical. Further, the states held divided positions on book piracy, which effectively meant that book pirates could continue with their otherwise prohibited activities in those states that endorsed them. Whereas the Prussian government was willing to negotiate with other states to vindicate the interests of Prussian publishers whose books had been pirated, the government also silently endorsed the pirating activities of its own publishers.[51] Piracy was even actively promoted in Austria and other southern German states, producing the infamously prolific Viennese pirate publisher and bookseller, Johann Thomas von Trattner.[52] Pursuant to the activities of reprinting and sale, legitimate publishers and authors suffered losses that affected their trade and livelihood.[53] The circumstances led to a long debate over the wrongfulness of reprinting, which Woodmansee dated as having happened between 1773 and 1794.[54] Participants in the debate ranged from publishers and jurists to poets and philosophers, amongst whom were Fichte and Kant.[55]

[48] The other main pillar of book regulation was that of censorship: see Pamela E. Selwyn, *Everyday Life in the German Book Trade: Friedrich Nicolai as Bookseller and Publisher in the Age of Enlightenment*, 1750–1810 (University Park: Pennsylvania State University Press, 2000), 183.

[49] According to an eighteenth-century German jurist J. J. Moser, the privilege system forbade 'certain books from being reprinted within a certain period of time against the will and the detriment of the privilege holder, or copies reprinted elsewhere from being sold within the German empire': see Selwyn, *Everyday Life in the German Book Trade*, 182.

[50] Woodmansee, 'The Genius and the Copyright', 438.

[51] Selwyn, *Everyday Life in the German Book Trade*, 185.

[52] See Martha Woodmansee, 'Publishers, Privateers, Pirates: Eighteenth-Century German Book Piracy Revisited', in *Making and Unmaking Intellectual Property: Creative Production in Legal and Cultural Perspective*, ed. Mario Biagioli, Peter Jaszi and Martha Woodmansee (Chicago: University of Chicago Press, 2011), 183.

[53] Woodmansee has commented extensively on the difficulties faced by serious German writers such as Christian Fürchtegott Gellert (1715–69) and Gotthold Ephraim Lessing (1729–81) to receive adequate compensation for their work: see Woodmansee, 'The Genius and the Copyright', 431–40.

[54] Woodmansee, 'The Genius and the Copyright', 440.

[55] See Ibid., footnote 32: 'Among the publishers and legal experts who contributed were Phillip Erasmus Reich, Joachim Heinrich Campe, Johann Stephan Pütter and Johann Jakob Cella; the contributing poets and philosophers included Zacharias Becker, Gottfried August Bürger, Kant, Feder, Ehlers, and Fichte.'

Fichte's essay offers a *Beweis der Unrechtmäßigkeit des Büchernachdrucks* ('proof of the wrongfulness of reprinting'), the focus of which coheres with the author's prioritisation of the moral and legal question raised by the practice over that of its utility (see Figure 3.1). Contrary to preceding voices in the debate that had argued for the permissibility of reprinting based on its public benefits, Fichte thought that no utility could justify a wrongful practice.[56] To prove the wrongfulness of reprinting was to overrule all arguments for the practice grounded in its usefulness. There are two parts to Fichte's case that may seem to cohere with certain aspects of modern copyright and intellectual property law. One, it was from a *proprietary* perspective that Fichte evaluated the practice of unauthorised reprinting, arguing that the author held 'ownership'[57] (*Eigenthum*) of something in the book implying the wrongfulness of the practice. Contrary to the limited terms for copyright protection in today's legal systems, however, Fichte understood literary property as being 'perpetual'[58] or 'enduring'[59] (*fortdaurend*). Two, Fichte advanced a concept of the book premised on a twofold distinction that some copyright scholars have suggested as having anticipated the idea/expression dichotomy of modern copyright law.[60] Fichte distinguished the 'physical aspect'[61] [*das körperliche*] of the book, particularly the 'printed page'[62] [*das bedruckte Papier*], from its 'ideal aspect'[63] [*sein Geistiges*], the division of which resembles our present legal categorisation of literary objects into personal property on the one hand and intellectual property on the other. As Fichte noted, whereas the lawful purchase of a physical book would have granted its buyer absolute ownership of it (including the right of its destruction), the transaction would not have necessarily granted the buyer any property right in its ideal aspect.[64] Yet, Fichte also observed that a book was typically bought to be read, that is, not for its paper per se but for its 'content' [*Inhalt*], suggesting then that a

56 'Fichte: Proof of the Unlawfulness of Reprinting, Berlin (1793)', 445. See, for instance, Reimarus, 'Publishing from the Perspective of the Writer, the Publisher, and the Public, Reconsidered', cited at the start of Fichte's piece (443–45) and satirised in a concluding parable that culminated in the hanging of 'useful' thief (474–83).

57 'Fichte: Proof of the Unlawfulness of Reprinting, Berlin (1793)', 458.

58 Ibid.

59 The word 'enduring' is Borghi's translation, which seems to be closer to the literal sense of the German: see Maurizio Borghi, 'Owning Form, Sharing Content: Natural-Right Copyright and Digital Environment', in *New Directions in Copyright Law*, ed. Fiona MacMillan, vol. 5 (Cheltenham: Edward Elgar Publishing, 2007).

60 See, for example, Kawohl and Kretschmer, 'Johann Gottlieb Fichte, and the Trap of *Inhalt* (Content) and *Form*: An Information Perspective on Music Copyright', 214; Biagioli, 'Genius against Copyright', 1854. It should be noted that these scholars were ultimately interested in pointing to important differences between Fichte's content/form distinction and the idea/expression dichotomy of copyright systems.

61 'Fichte: Proof of the Unlawfulness of Reprinting, Berlin (1793)', 447.

62 Ibid.

63 Ibid.

64 Ibid.

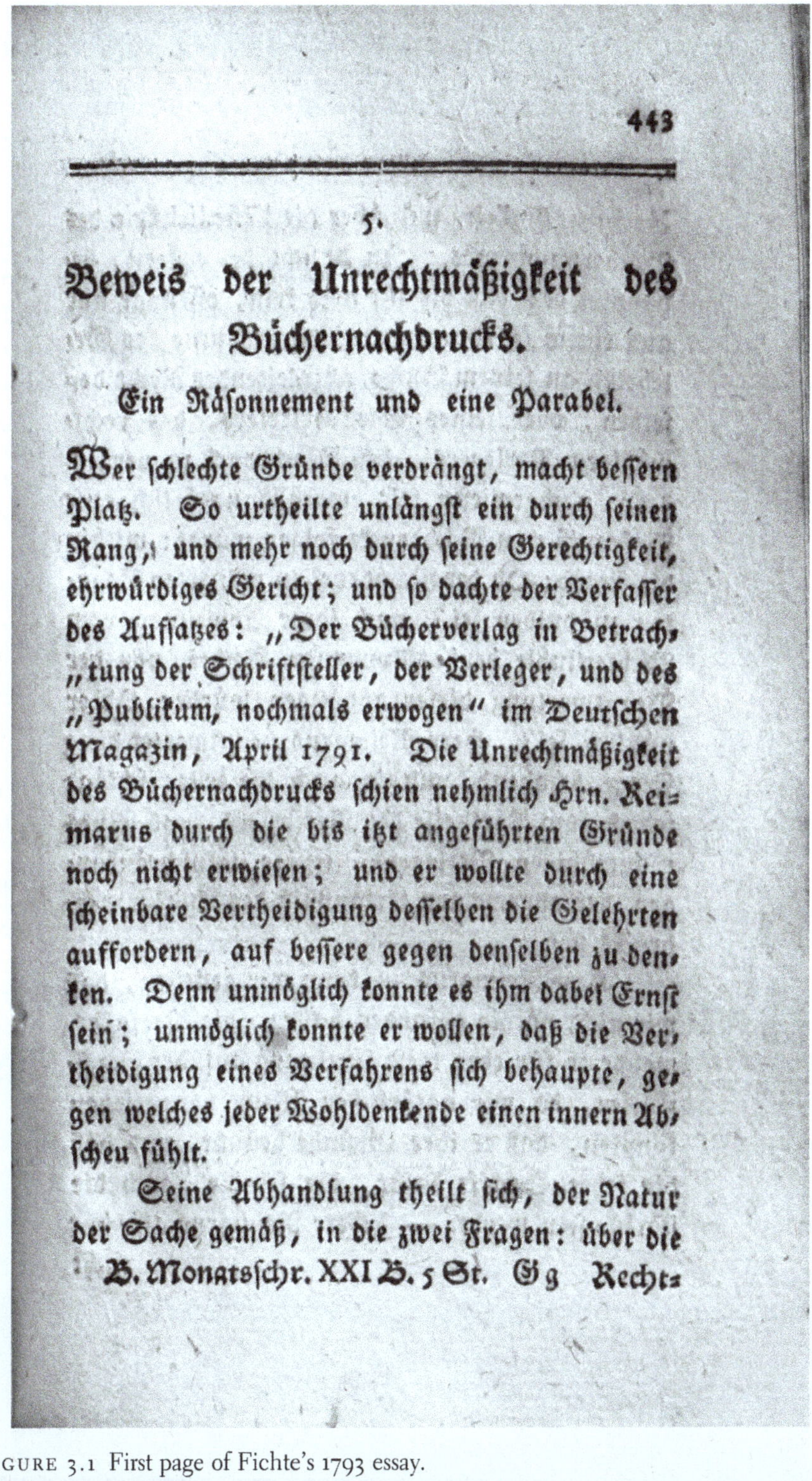
443

5.

Beweis der Unrechtmäßigkeit des Büchernachdrucks.

Ein Räsonnement und eine Parabel.

Wer schlechte Gründe verdrängt, macht bessern Platz. So urtheilte unlängst ein durch seinen Rang, und mehr noch durch seine Gerechtigkeit, ehrwürdiges Gericht; und so dachte der Verfasser des Aufsatzes: „Der Bücherverlag in Betrachtung der Schriftsteller, der Verleger, und des „Publikum, nochmals erwogen" im Deutschen Magazin, April 1791. Die Unrechtmäßigkeit des Büchernachdrucks schien nehmlich Hrn. Reimarus durch die bis itzt angeführten Gründe noch nicht erwiesen; und er wollte durch eine scheinbare Vertheidigung desselben die Gelehrten auffordern, auf bessere gegen denselben zu denken. Denn unmöglich konnte es ihm dabei Ernst sein; unmöglich konnte er wollen, daß die Vertheidigung eines Verfahrens sich behaupte, gegen welches jeder Wohldenkende einen innern Abscheu fühlt.

Seine Abhandlung theilt sich, der Natur der Sache gemäß, in die zwei Fragen: über die

B. Monatsschr. XXI B. 5 St. Gg Recht-

FIGURE 3.1 First page of Fichte's 1793 essay.

right in something relating to its ideal aspect had passed to the purchaser.[65] This was where Fichte drew a second distinction between two parts to the ideal aspect of the book that served as the conceptual basis on which to prove the wrongfulness of reprinting:

> This ideal aspect is in turn divisible into a material aspect [*das Materielle*], the content [*Inhalt*] of the book, the ideas [*Gedanken*] it presents; and the form [*Form*] of these ideas, the way in which, the combination in which, the phrasing and wording in which they are presented.[66]

Having thus differentiated between the 'content' and 'form' of the ideal aspect of the book, Fichte argued that the buyer of the book acquired, along with its printed paper, the right to appropriate its ideal content through the investment of mental labour. Not accidentally, Fichte illustrated the exercise of such an acquired right through the example of an 'assiduous and rational study'[67] of Kant's *Kritik der reinen Vernunft* ('Critique of Pure Reason'). The book's content was potentially 'the common property of many'[68] in the sense that it could at once be held by multiple readers by virtue of its ideal or intangible nature. As regards the 'form' of the ideas in the book, Fichte claimed that it remained 'forever [the author's] exclusive property'.[69] It was on the basis of this perpetual and exclusive property of the author that Fichte both justified the practice of authorised publication and condemned the practice of unauthorised reprinting. Through a publishing contract the publisher acquired from the author a particular property right or 'usufruct',[70] which permitted the publisher to 'sell'[71] the right to appropriate the ideas of the book by printing and marketing it to the public. Reprinting without the author's permission was wrongful because it effectively 'usurped'[72] the usufruct that only the author, as the rightful owner of the 'form' in the book, could have granted.

In Fichte's distinction between form and content, one may find echoes of the modern idea/expression dichotomy. Specifically, Fichte's recognition of the ideas presented in the book as potentially exceeding any individual's exclusive right of possession or control could be compared to the 'idea' limb of the modern dichotomy, which affirms ideas as being unencumbered by intellectual property rights and belonging to the public domain.[73] In *Hollinrake v Truswell*,[74] the English Court of

65 Ibid., 448.
66 Ibid., 447.
67 Ibid., 448. The same page provides the example of Kant's book.
68 Ibid., 450.
69 Ibid., 451.
70 Ibid., 457.
71 Ibid.
72 Ibid.
73 One of the classic formulations of the idea/expression dichotomy arose in Justice Bradley's opinion in the US Supreme Court case of *Baker v Selden*, 101 US 99 (1879).
74 [1894] 3 Ch. 420.

Appeal offered one of the earliest formulations of the dichotomy: 'Copyright . . . does not extend to ideas, or schemes, or systems, or methods; it is confined to their expression; and if their expression is not copied the copyright is not infringed.'[75] Lindley LJ held that the copied method of measuring parts of the arm and elbow for the cutting of a sleeve, which had been printed on a piece of cardboard, was not the subject matter of copyright protection within the meaning of section 2 of the Copyright Act 1842. The dichotomy is often justified on the grounds that ideas should not be monopolised by any private individual, but rather should remain freely available for public use.[76] For instance, in *Baker v Seldon*,[77] which was the precedent cited by the English Court of Appeal in support of the dichotomy, the United States Supreme Court held that an author's copyright in a book describing a system of book-keeping did not extend to the system itself. The latter was seen to be the 'common property of the whole world'[78] that could be used and explained by any author in their own way. As Justice Bradley put it, the object of publishing a book on science or the arts, which was 'to communicate to the world the useful knowledge which it contains',[79] would be 'frustrated if the knowledge could not be used without incurring the guilt of piracy of the book'.[80] The judicial recognition of ideas presented in the book as 'common property' belonging to no single author would seem to resonate with Fichte's concept of content, the latter of which was understood to bear the potential for appropriation by those labouring to read it. Similarly, Fichte's ascription of property rights in the 'form' of the book, described to be the 'phrasing and wording' in which ideas are presented, seems to anticipate copyright law's understanding of original 'expression' in modern copyright law, or the 'way in which ideas are expressed', as the proper subject matter of protection. Copyright scholars such as Friedemann Kawohl and Martin Kretschmer have, accordingly, stressed the 'huge influence'[81] of Fichte's distinction between form and content on the development of national, regional and international copyright law, which have codified the idea/expression dichotomy.

Nonetheless, Fichte's concept of form was based on a theory of the mind as the giver of literary form – a theory that copyright doctrine could, at most, be said to tacitly reflect in its recognition of the author as being the originating source of literary expression. Early in the essay, Fichte foregrounded the central importance of the mind to his proof by noting that the proof was grounded in the 'immediately

75 *Hollinrake v Truswell* [1894] 3 Ch. 420.

76 See Brad Sherman, 'Appropriating the Postmodern: Copyright and the Challenge of the New', *Social and Legal Studies* 4 (1995): 37.

77 101 US 99 (1879).

78 Ibid., paragraph 3.

79 Ibid., paragraph 9.

80 Ibid.

81 Kawohl and Kretschmer, 'Johann Gottlieb Fichte, and the Trap of *Inhalt* (Content) and *Form*: An Information Perspective on Music Copyright', 214.

self-evident'[82] presupposition that 'we are the rightful owners of a thing the appropriation of which by another is physically impossible'.[83] This inalienable thing, as Fichte would clarify, was the 'mind'[84] or 'spirit' [*Geist*] of the person. For Fichte, it was the mind that gave ideas their perceptible form, without which ideas would be incapable of being thought, much less of being presented to another. The perceptibility of form was stressed in his recognition that there were no 'pure ideas without sensible images [*reine Ideen ohne sinnliche Bilder*]',[85] the latter of which had to be supplied by the individual mind. In the case of books, it was the mind of the writer that gave perceptible form to the ideas presented in the books. It was impossible for this form to be appropriated. To read the book was to 'assimilate [*aufnehmen*]'[86] its ideas to the reader's own 'system of thought [*Gedankensystem*]',[87] which meant giving a new form to those ideas that necessarily diverged from the preceding form given by the author. To publish the book with permission was to exercise the usufruct the author had granted to the publisher, which involved the passing of a property right but not the property itself. To reprint the book without permission was to appropriate not the form of its ideas but only the usufruct that the author alone was capable of granting. In all three instances the literary form remained the inalienable property of the author by virtue of its origination in the latter's mind. Insofar as copyright expression, too, is understood as causally deriving from its author-creator, the doctrine could be said to grant a similar sort of priority to the author's mental labour. However, copyright law does not go so far as to articulate any equivalent concept of inalienable property in the book that is generated by mental processes of formation and assimilation unique to the minds of authors and readers.

The theory of mind that defines Fichte's concept of form leads us closer to the place of materiality in his essay. Notions of materiality have already surfaced in our reprisal of Fichte's twofold distinction between the physical and the ideal and between content and form, structuring it from within. In the initial fold, the matter of the book was valuable to Fichte as that which served to be negated to identify the ideal object in which authors and readers were truly interested. It was against the 'printed paper'[88] of the book that its ideal dimension was defined, the latter of which was prioritised as being the ultimate object of the book transaction. Nonetheless, as if defying conceptual repression, the negated term would return in the second fold, this time informing both sides of the binary forming the book's ideal aspect. The content and ideas presented in the book were understood to be its 'material

82 'Fichte: Proof of the Unlawfulness of Reprinting, Berlin (1793)', 446.
83 Ibid.
84 Ibid., 450.
85 Ibid., 451.
86 Ibid.
87 Ibid.
88 Ibid., 447.

aspect',[89] suggesting that those ideas shared a material basis with the printed paper. The materiality of ideas would be reaffirmed in Fichte's recognition of the impossibility of 'pure ideas without sensible images'[90] and of the concomitant necessity of ideas to bear perceptible form. Thus, despite being the prioritised term in the second fold, the form of ideas, too, was understood in terms of the visible letters appearing on the page: 'the phrasing and wording in which [ideas] are presented'.[91] Literary property was, at once, material property. Rather than being external to the proof advanced by the philosopher of German Idealism, materiality was the integral structural motif that defined its basic distinction.

Yet, as Fichte's underlying theory of mind would suggest, the literary form in which the author held perpetual property bore an ultimately subjective aspect that exceeded its ostensibly objective presentation in the material book. This meant that Fichte's understanding of literary form was not reducible to the combination of letters printed in the book. Rather, it continually extended from the mind that had produced it, enduring as something beyond the book's surface. A clue to the subjectivity of form was given in Fichte's recognition of form as being no less inalienable, no less 'physically impossible'[92] to appropriate, than the mind that had generated it. Form could not be the object of theft because, against the appearance of the book, it remained bound to its originating mind. In their own ways, Kretschmer-Kawohl and Mario Biagioli have similarly observed the non-exhaustion of literary form by the arrangement of letters in the book. Kretschmer-Kawohl have twice noted a 'tension'[93] and 'contradiction'[94] in Fichte's concept of form, which at once referred to 'the process of formation'[95] of the literary work and its 'result'.[96] The former sense was dependent on the individual who had given the form, be they the author who had articulated the book's ideas or the reader who had appropriated them, whereas the latter seemed to pertain to the book itself or at least some aspect of it.[97] Biagioli has emphasised that, unlike intellectual property law, Fichte did not reify or 'fetishize'[98] the book as that in which the author held property, but instead simply suggested that it bore 'material traces'[99] of something else he called 'form'. What has been commonly noted is that Fichte understood

89 Ibid.
90 Ibid., 451.
91 Ibid., 447.
92 Ibid., 446.
93 Martin Kretschmer and Friedemann Kawohl, 'The History and Philosophy of Copyright', in *Music and Copyright*, ed. Simon Frith and Lee Marshall (London: Routledge, 2004), 21–52.
94 Kawohl and Kretschmer, 'Johann Gottlieb Fichte, and the Trap of *Inhalt* (Content) and *Form*: An Information Perspective on Music Copyright', 213.
95 Kretschmer and Kawohl, 'The History and Philosophy of Copyright', 32.
96 Ibid.
97 Kawohl and Kretschmer, 'Johann Gottlieb Fichte, and the Trap of *Inhalt* (Content) and *Form*', 213.
98 Biagioli, 'Genius against Copyright', 1867.
99 Ibid., 1865.

form to be something necessarily exceeding the material combination of letters in the book precisely because it remained attached to the mind in which it had originated. Hence, the apparent reassertion of materiality in Fichte's concept of form is complicated by its underpinning theory of mind, whose relationship with the material remains ambiguous. It is unclear if Fichte understood the mind itself to bear any material basis, notwithstanding its predominant association with the ideal. What we can say, though, is that Fichte conceived of literary form as extending beyond the printed words of the book. Further, this object of literary property is recognised to be created by the author alone and, by virtue of the singularity of its creation, to be immune from appropriation.

Unlike Fichte's account, Kant's proposed solution to the problem of reprinting in late eighteenth-century Germany did not rely on any concept of intellectual property. As discussed in Chapters 1 and 2, Kant advanced a non-proprietary perspective on author's rights that was grounded in a concept of the book as communicative medium and visual object in particular. For Kant, the book served to relay to the public a speech necessarily spoken in its author's name. 'In a book, as a writing, the author *speaks* to his reader; and the one who has printed the book *speaks*, by his copy, not for himself but simply and solely in the author's name. He presents the author as speaking publicly and only mediates delivery of his speech to the public.'[100] The right that the author held in relation to the book was conceived not as any proprietary right but as a personal right of self-expression that extended from the author's personhood. In Kant's view, the author had an 'inalienable right (*ius personalissimum*)'[101] for the speech to be communicated in his own name. Under this 'most personal right',[102] it was ultimately the author who spoke through the book printed by the publisher. Pursuant to the same fundamental right, the author granted the publisher the right to publish the book by means of a contract.[103] To reprint the book without such a right was to wrong both the legitimate publisher and the author: doing so not only subtracted the profits of the former[104] but further, in so relaying the speech without his permission, violated the latter's 'innate right in his own person',[105] that is, to speak only as he willed.

Notice that, even as Kant prioritised the author as the ultimate subject in whose name the book's speech was necessarily communicated, he credited the publisher's involvement in the production of the book. More so than in Fichte's essay, the publisher arose as a key figure without whom the book would not be presented to the reading public. Whereas Fichte had focused on the author's act of giving form to ideas as the central act that created literary property, it was the process of 'publishing'

[100] Kant, 'On the Wrongfulness of Unauthorized Publication of Books (1785)', 30.
[101] Ibid., 35.
[102] Ibid.
[103] Ibid., 33.
[104] Ibid., 29–30.
[105] Ibid., 35.

[*Verlag*] and its significance to the problematic that Kant sought to clarify from the outset:

> Some regard the publishing of a book [*den Verlag eines Buchs*] as a use of property in a copy (whether the copy has come to the possessor as a manuscript from the author or as a print of the manuscript from an already existing publisher) and then want, nevertheless, to restrict the use of this right by the reservation of certain rights, either of the author or of the publisher appointed by him, so that unauthorized publication of it would not be permitted; they can never succeed in this. For the author's property in his thought (even if one grants that there is such a thing in terms of external rights) is left to him regardless of the unauthorized publication; and, since there cannot reasonably be an express consent of one who buys a book to such a restriction of his property, how much less will a merely presumed consent suffice for his obligation?[106]

For Kant, it was simply misleading to see publishing as the exercise of a proprietary right in the written manuscript or printed book because the author's right in his thoughts was essentially inalienable and, thus, not of a proprietary nature. As the right was 'left to [the author] regardless of the unauthorized publication', it should be understood to be a personal right instead. As we have recalled, Kant's subsequent reconstrual of publishing as a process of relaying the author's speech was based on such a personal understanding of the author's communicative right, that is, a right to have the speech communicated in their own name that existed by virtue of their personhood. In so conceiving of the book as communicative medium, Kant did not lose sight of the publisher's role in literary production.

Further, Kant saw the very visuality of the printed book to be that which afforded its relay of the author's speech to the public. Whereas copyright scholars have tended to interpret Kant's essay as prescribing a speech act theory of the literary work,[107] the essay also sharply registered the medial-material conditions of possibility of literary communication. The optical medium of print, Kant observed, was the material basis on which eighteenth-century book publishing occurred: '[The publisher] indeed provides in his own name *the mute instrument for delivering the author's speech to the public*; [footnote inserted] but to *bring his speech to the public* by printing it, and so to show himself as the one through whom the author speaks to the public, is something he can do only in the name of another.'[108] As discussed in Chapter 1, Kant explained in the accompanying footnote that the printed book was 'mute' because it relayed the author's speech not by means of sound as in the instances of the 'megaphone' or 'mouth', but rather by means of the letter: 'This is what is essential here: that what is thereby delivered is not a *thing* but an *opera*,

[106] Ibid., 29.

[107] See Drassinower, *What's Wrong with Copying?*; Borghi, 'Copyright and Truth'; Barron, 'Kant, Copyright and Communicative Freedom'.

[108] Kant, 'On the Wrongfulness of Unauthorized Publication of Books (1785)', 30.

namely *speech*, and indeed by letters. By calling it a mute instrument I distinguish it from one that delivers speech by sounds, such as a megaphone or even the *mouth* of another.'[109] In this contrast between acoustic and optical media, the materiality of the letter, specifically the visibility of the printed letter, rears to prominence. Prior to the evolution of audiobooks, books could relay the speech of the author only by means of the visible letters printed on the page. The opticality of print would be re-emphasised by Kant in a passage on the nature and legal status of the book in *Die Metaphysik der Sitten* ['The Metaphysics of Morals'] (1797): 'A book is a writing (it does not matter here, whether it is written by hand or set in type, whether it has few or many pages) which represents a discourse that someone delivers to the public by visible signs.'[110] Though eventually elided in favour of their continuity as visual methods of communication, the taxonomic difference between handwriting and typesetting evidently surfaced in Kant's reflections on the book.

These interests in the publisher and publishing, and in the opticality of the book and its typesetting, would resurface in Kant's brief reflection on eighteenth-century German typefaces in *Der Streit der Fakultäten* ('The Conflict of the Faculties') (1798).[111] There we find an acuter recognition of the perceptual materiality of type than in the earlier text, which accentuates the distance between Fichte's and Kant's perspectives on the medium of literature. Whilst the *Berlinische Monatsschrift* had silently served as the enlightenment periodical that conveyed Kant's proposed regime of author's rights in 1785, its typeface and typesetting would become the very subject matter of discussion in the later text. Specifically, Kant announced his support for the periodical's use of the Breitkopf Fraktur typeface because its letters were, in his view, less straining on the reader's eyes than roman types were.[112] This position was advanced against the then-prevailing '*fashion* in printing'[113] to set letters in the supposedly more attractive roman types. Dismissing the preference for roman types as one of several 'wretched affectations'[114] of book printers in his day,[115] Kant asserted instead that letters 'have no intrinsic beauty at all'.[116] Consistent with his concept of the book as communicative medium and visual object, Kant prioritised the functionality of type, particularly the ease with which it permitted one's reading of the text. Johann Gottlob Immanuel Breitkopf, the Leipzig typefounder and publisher who had designed the Fraktur typeface deployed in the German periodical, was cited as an authority for the position that roman type 'tires the eyes more

[109] Ibid.
[110] Kant, 'The Metaphysics of Morals (1797)', 437.
[111] Immanuel Kant, *The Conflict of the Faculties*, trans. Mary J. Gregor (New York: Abaris Books, 1979), 209–13.
[112] Ibid., 211.
[113] Ibid.
[114] Ibid.
[115] Ibid., 209.
[116] Ibid., 211.

quickly than does Gothic type'.[117] Kant would conclude by directing printers to the printed pages of the *Berlinische Monatsschrift* as the exemplary publication: 'for no matter what page one opens it to, the sight of it will strengthen the eyes perceptibly when they have been strained by reading the kind of print described above [footnote inserted]'.[118] As suggested by the accompanying footnote, Kant's acute sensitivity to the opticality of the printed page was owed to his own perceptual experiences as a reader. Not only had he already gone blind in the left eye some years before writing the passage, but he also continued to suffer from a recurrent, intermittent condition of being temporarily overcome by 'a certain brightness [that] suddenly spreads over the page'.[119] This bodily affliction stressed the importance of visual perception to the activity of reading.

I am suggesting that, more so than Fichte, Kant understood the reading of print to be a corporeal experience, namely an interactive activity between the bodies of type and readers. For Fichte, it was the mind that gave form to ideas, thereby establishing the author's perpetual ownership of literary form. Though literary form was affirmed to bear a material basis, such materiality was seen to consist only in an imaginable combination of words that, ultimately, transcended the visible letters printed in the book. The printed book only mattered as the medium of exchange between the minds of authors and readers. For the author, the book bore partial record of the literary form s/he had created and forever owned. For the reader, the book was simply a repository of ideas to be appropriated through the no-less-writerly act of giving original form to those ideas. From within each of the perspectives, the book ceded visibility and priority to the pertinent form and its generative mind. Kant, on the contrary, kept in sight the book as an optical medium composed of letters printed on paper. Instead of proposing any concept of intellectual property that exceeded the material dimensions of the book, Kant saw the book as a material artefact to be interacted with first and foremost through the organ of the eyes. Before the book could be read for its interpretable meaning or 'speech', it had first to be seen as a material composition of type set on paper. Reading, or what Fichte understood to be the application of one's mind, could not take place without the sensory perception of printed matter, that is, the phenomenal encounter between eye and page. It is this corporeal dimension of reading, relatively muted in Fichte's account, that distinguishes Kant's from his student's.

In Kant's recognition of the visual materiality of the printed book, particularly that of its typeface and typesetting, we find both an anticipation and a potential problematisation of the doctrine of typographical copyright. On the one hand, Kant's acknowledgement of the publisher's contribution to the production of the printed text coheres with typographical copyright's recognition of the skill and labour

[117] Ibid.
[118] Ibid.
[119] Ibid.

invested in the publication of the book and its typographical arrangement in particular. This continuity insists notwithstanding the obvious difference that copyright law sees the publisher's contribution to be sufficient to grant the publisher a property right in the edition's typography, whereas Kant declined to see the publisher as an intellectual proprietor. On the other hand, in so identifying the opticality of print and the corporeal experience of reading, Kant provided an arguably richer perspective on the materiality of book than that of copyright law. For whilst the typographical arrangement of the book only matters to the copyright system as evidence of the publisher's skill and labour that warrants protection, the visual materiality of the book in Kant's account implies a dimension of historical interactions between bodies that far exceed the copyright perspective. For Kant, Breitkopf Fraktur was the exemplary typeface that best relayed the speech made in the name of the author in each of the essays published in the *Berlinische Monatsschrift*. The communicative affordance of the typeface made it significant to enlightenment practice.

PRODUCING BREITKOPF FRAKTUR

Typographical copyright takes the labour of the publisher in literary production to be the decisive criterion that grants them ownership of the typographical arrangement of the published edition. If an equivalent law were to have operated during the time of the publication of Kant's and Fichte's essays in the *Berlinische Monatsschrift*, the periodical editor-publishers, Friedrich Gedike and Johann Erich Biester, would have had a property right in the typography of the issues in which the essays appeared. Reprinting those issues without permission would have infringed the copyright held by Gedike and Biester, who would have been treated as if they were the author-creators of each typographical arrangement. Their typographical authorship would have co-subsisted with the literary authorship of Kant, Fichte and other writers who composed the individual pieces in each issue.

It is my argument that the historical processes of literary production detract from this neat bifurcation of the literary artefact into intellectual works created by publishers and authors. As discussed in Chapter 2, the signature marks, catchwords, front matter and other material paratexts of Kant's essay evidence the technologically mediated labour of not only the named publishers and authors but also others working within and outside the printing house, including compositors, printers, binders, advertisers, readers and so forth. Together with the postal system, text- and bookmaking processes participated in the gargantuan print apparatus that mediated the German Enlightenment. It was through the very medium of print that Kant, Gedike, Biester and others sought to advance public enlightenment and deal with print proliferation. Authorship in the German Enlightenment was intimately bound up with a broader medial-material assemblage, without which essays, periodicals and books would not have been possible. To claim sole proprietorship in some aspect of literary production, be it the typographical layout or literary work, is to deny that the other surrounding processes materially contributed to its emergence.

The making of typefaces such as Breitkopf Fraktur is one historical thread that unsettles copyright's proprietary approach to literature. For Lord Hoffmann, the typeface of a publication only mattered as a part of the 'typographical vocabulary' in which the publisher's labour of creating the overall design is expressed. Nonetheless, we may note that before any ascription of the utilised typeface to the publisher's mental labour, the typeface has first to be made available as a technical possibility in which the contents are to be set. The historicity of typefaces is, to an extent, recognised in modern copyright law's willingness to grant copyright in typefaces to their designers in certain jurisdictions.[120] For instance, sections 55(1)–(3) of the CDPA 1988 acknowledge the possibility of there being 'copyright in an artistic work consisting of the design of a typeface'[121] for a term of twenty-five years from its first appearance in the market. Apprehended as an 'artistic work'[122] in which copyright could subsist, the typeface and its protection are similarly brought under the rubric of authorship, in which a human designer is seen to be its creator.[123] Even where a computer has generated the typeface as artistic work, the law ascribes its authorship to some underlying creative personality: 'the person by whom the arrangements necessary for the creation of the work are undertaken'.[124] Despite collaborating to reproduce the myth of authorship, the doctrines of typographical copyright and copyright in typeface design bring to light some of the technical preconditions for the production of books that perturb the legal insistence on authorial creation.

Kant's endorsement of the '*Breitkopf* characters'[125] printed in the *Berlinische Monatsschrift* offers us an inroad into the history of the typeface. When citing that periodical as the model for print in 1798, Kant emphasised the readability of its typeface and typesetting, which aligned with the communicative aim of publication. The modern conception of the 'aesthetics' of type, construed as pertaining to questions of 'beauty'[126] and 'taste',[127] was de-prioritised in favour of its ancient sense of relating to 'sense perception',[128] particularly the sense of sight: 'for no matter what page one opens [the *Berlinische Monatsschrift*] to, the sight of it will strengthen the eyes perceptibly when they have been strained by reading the kind of print described

[120] The United States is one of the few jurisdictions that do not recognise copyright in typefaces: see Gloria C. Phares, 'An Approach to Why Typography Should Be Copyrightable', *The Columbia Journal of Law & the Arts* 39, no. 3 (2016): 417–20.

[121] Copyright, Designs and Patents Act 1988, section 55(1).

[122] Ibid., section 4(1).

[123] Ibid., sections 9(1) and 9(3).

[124] Ibid., section 9(3).

[125] Kant, *The Conflict of the Faculties*, 211.

[126] *Oxford English Dictionary*, 2nd ed. (Oxford: Oxford University Press, 2004), s.v. 'Aesthetics', definitions 4 and 5.

[127] Ibid.

[128] As recorded in the *Oxford English Dictionary* entry, 'aesthetics' derives from the ancient Greek *αἰσθητικός*, meaning 'of or relating to sense perception, sensitive, perceptive'.

above'.[129] Despite his 1785 comments on literary materiality, Kant enacted an 'ethic of typographical invisibility'[130] or transparency that would continue to predominate in modern Western publishing and bookmaking. Under that paradigm, the best typeface and typesetting effaced themselves to reveal the printed contents. In 1951, a similarly practical and communicative account of typography was articulated by Stanley Morison:

> Typography may be defined as the art of rightly disposing printing material in accordance with specific purpose; of so arranging the letters, distributing the space and controlling the type as to aid to the maximum the reader's comprehension of the text. Typography is the efficient means to an essentially utilitarian and only accidentally aesthetic end, for enjoyment of patterns is rarely the reader's chief aim.[131]

Echoing Kant's disapproval of the use of grey rather than black ink for its 'softer and more agreeable'[132] contrast on white paper, Morison argued that 'there [was] little room for "bright" typography'.[133] All decisions in typography, whether they relate to composition, imposition, impression or paper, were to be made in the service of readability and communication within societal traditions and publishing contexts. Though recognising its historical decline in use, Morison noted some merits of black letter, affirming that it was 'in design more homogenous, more lively and more economic a type than the grey round roman we use'.[134] Kant's defence of the Breitkopf Fraktur typeface based on its perceptual advantage over roman types was, thus, not peculiar to the philosopher, but instead reflected the predominant modern understanding of type as a practical means of literary dissemination.

Though named in support of Kant's case for the superior readability of German scripts,[135] the Leipzig typefounder Breitkopf did not share the philosopher's contempt for roman types, nor did he necessarily privilege the functionality of type over its aesthetic beauty. The beauty of roman types arose as a topic for reflection in a 1777 essay where Breitkopf praised the letters cut by the Parisian typefounder Pierre Simon Fournier le jeune. In *Nachricht von der Stempelschneiderey und Schriftgießerey. Zur Erlaüterung der Enschedischen Schriftprobe* ('Breitkopf on

[129] Kant, *The Conflict of the Faculties*, 211.

[130] Paul C. Gutjahr and Megan L. Benton, 'Introduction: Reading the Invisible', in *Illuminating Letters: Typography and Literary Interpretation*, ed. Paul C. Gutjahr and Megan L. Benton (Amherst: University of Massachusetts Press, 2001), 4.

[131] Stanley Morison, *First Principles of Typography* (Cambridge: Cambridge University Press, 1951), 5.

[132] Kant, *The Conflict of the Faculties*, 211.

[133] Morison, *First Principles of Typography*, 5.

[134] Ibid., 7.

[135] Kant did not cite the specific reference in which Breitkopf purportedly noted that Roman letters were more straining on the eyes than German ones were.

Punchcutting and Typefounding'[136]), Breitkopf criticised a claim made by a Dutch typefounder, Joh. Enschedé, that the latter's typefoundry in Holland was 'the best and most beautiful'[137] in all of Europe.[138] The typefoundry's most recent typefaces were partially cut by the German punchcutter, Joan Michaël Fleischmann, whom Enschedé recognised to be 'the greatest or the most accomplished type-cutter since the invention of printing'.[139] Against the use of these superlatives to describe Enschedé's own typefoundry and punchcutter, Breitkopf sought to show that Fournier's typefoundry in Paris was in fact superior, a key reason being that the latter's types were cut by the artist Fournier himself. In Breitkopf's view, 'the best and most beautiful'[140] typefaces were those whose full range of sizes exhibited the greatest regularity, consistency and harmony in appearance. He compared the pleasure of viewing these typefaces to that of seeing a beautiful work of art: 'it is a pleasant, appealing sight, where the eye is just as much delighted when types of different sizes appear on a page as by a beautiful painting'.[141] Because of this demand for consistency, Breitkopf stressed that the types had to be 'cut from one and the same hand by a single artist'.[142] The advantage of Fournier's foundry over Enschedé's consisted precisely in the fact that Fournier had personally cut all of the typefaces according to a common design, whereas Enschedé had employed multiple typecutters. Juxtaposing Enschedé type specimens against Fournier's, Breitkopf observed that the former not only omitted certain type sizes but also were only partly cut by Fleischmann, such that the type specimens lacked the uniform beauty of the Fournier's. 'How pleasantly one is moved by the consistency of [Fournier's] round *Romain* or roman types, cut according to a common design, which one reads with pleasure; none of the type specimen from the other, previously distinguished Parisian typefoundries come close; not the typefaces of the Sanlecques or those of Granjon.'[143] In Breitkopf's praise of Fournier's letters we see the Leipzig typefounder's clear admiration for the beauty of roman types. In the course of elaborating on the aesthetic principles of typefaces, Breitkopf went further to suggest that 'a full round letter [was] always more pleasant to the eye than

[136] See the English translation by Dan Reynolds: J. G. I. Breitkopf, *Breitkopf on Punchcutting and Typefounding: A Critique of Enschedé's 1768 Type Specimen*, trans. Dan Reynolds (Berlin-Neukölln, 2019).

[137] Ibid., 1.

[138] Enschedé's claim was made in his preliminary note to the 1768 type specimen catalogue published by his printing house in Haarlem, whose review by Christoph Gottlieb von Murr in the *Journal zür Kunstgeschichte und zur allgemeinen Litteratur* (Journal of Art History and Literature') in 1776 served as the occasion for Breitkopf's criticism of Enschedé in the 1777 essay: see the translator Dan Reynold's introduction, especially pages ii and v.

[139] Breitkopf, *Breitkopf on Punchcutting and Typefounding*, 3.

[140] Ibid., 1.

[141] Ibid.

[142] Ibid.

[143] Ibid., 6.

a long and condensed one',[144] which lends itself to be read as an implicit comparison between roman and black letter types. The rest of the essay was punctuated with exclamations about the beauty of the former. Considerations of the readability of letters arose only in occasional discussions of letters that were so tiny as to be nothing but 'pure torture'[145] for typecutters, printers and readers, or whose strokes and lines were 'too fine'[146] to be read and 'burdensome to the reader's eyes'.[147] German types and typefoundries were mentioned only in the concluding paragraphs, where Breitkopf reflected on the limits of typefounding in German as compared to that in France, Holland and the Netherlands. Christian Zinck, a punchcutter and typefounder in Wittenberg, was cited as possibly matching Fournier in vocational excellence 'if only [Zinck] had possessed a good eye for beauty and correctness, in addition to his industriousness'.[148] Further, Breitkopf recognised that the existence of two German types, namely Schwabacher and Fraktur, alongside that of roman and italic styles, made it difficult for German typefoundries to produce artists like Fournier capable of cutting every type.[149] Much had to be done for leading German typefoundries like Breitkopf's to produce type specimens as beautiful and as complete as Fournier's roman letters.[150]

Breitkopf's 1777 essay suggests that the visual materiality of type is by no means definitively or exhaustively explained by Kant's communicative and functionalist account. Unlike Fichte's movement beyond the surface of the text to the so-called ideal form belonging to the author, Kant's account retained its focus on the visible letters of the publication as the material means that relayed a speech necessarily spoken in the author's name. However, the optical medium need not be subordinated to the prescribed role of delivering any message defined in reference to the authorial figure. Rather, as suggested by Breitkopf, both the printed letters and the printing types that were cut for their production could be regarded as works of art that were, in themselves, pleasing to the eyes. Whereas Kant thought that the 'letters, considered as pictures, have no intrinsic beauty at all',[151] Breitkopf recognised their potential for 'beautiful regularity'[152] and the aesthetic pleasure that 'geometrically-correct'[153] typefaces gave. 'The beauty of every typeface consists in the correct relation of the strokes with the space between the lines, which cannot be neglected even in the intervals between one letter and the next; in the correct height and depth of the ascender'd and descender'd letters; and in the proper length

[144] Ibid., 3.
[145] Ibid., 7.
[146] Ibid., 9.
[147] Ibid.
[148] Ibid., 11.
[149] Ibid.
[150] Ibid.
[151] Kant, *The Conflict of the Faculties*, 209–11.
[152] Breitkopf, *Breitkopf on Punchcutting and Typefounding*, 3.
[153] Ibid., 2.

of the lines'.[154] The proportions of type could be determined with precision, not unlike those of sculptures. Roman types were not to be categorically dismissed for allegedly interfering with the reading of books, but instead admired as crafted objects whose aesthetic appeal was not necessarily in tension with their functionality.

Other than exhibiting an emphasis of the aesthetic beauty of type, Breitkopf's text also prompts the questioning of his putative creation of the typeface bearing his last name. Recall that when the Wittenberg typefounder Zinck was mentioned, it was to call attention to the gap between Zinck's craftsmanship and Fournier's. Breitkopf had not only been familiar with Zinck's work but in fact enlisted his help for the making of the Breitkopf Fraktur typeface more than two decades prior. As recorded in Christina Killius's account of the 'origins' of the typeface, the letters of Breitkopf Fraktur were first cut by Zinck and two other punchcutters, Johann Michael Schmidt and Johann Peter Artopacus, in the Leipzig typefoundry around 1750.[155] Not unlike Enschedé, Breitkopf had relied on the labour of others to produce the typeface that would later bear his sole name. The 'authorship' of the typeface was thus separated from its very originary moment. Indeed, the visible irregularities of the script evidenced this co-production, and could well have informed Breitkopf's later comments about the aesthetic requirement for typefaces to be cut by the same hand.[156] As Killius put it, 'Breitkopf Fraktur appeared somewhat inconsistent [*uneinheitlich*] because of the multiple typecutters. That is why the publisher advocated as early as 1776 that a good type foundry should have all its typefaces designed by an artist in order to achieve the greatest possible consummation and harmony.'[157]

This recorded collaboration in the initial cutting of Breitkopf Fraktur coheres with Harry Carter's history of the manufacture of types.[158] Before the appearance of letters as two-dimensional ink marks on paper, first the three-dimensional metal types had to be made. 'Type is something that you can pick up and hold in your hand.'[159] Though printers financed the operations by purchasing the types at book fairs and foundries, their making was undertaken by other skilled artists, namely punchcutters, matrix and mould makers and casters.[160] The technical skills required for the completion of these tasks derived from trades that historically predated letterpress printing, including coin and seal engraving (for punchcutting), goldsmithery (for matrix- and mould-making) and pewtery (for typecasting).[161]

[154] Ibid.

[155] Christina Killius, *Die Antiqua-Fraktur Debatte um 1800 und ihre historische Herleitung* (Wiesbaden: Harrassowitz Verlag, 1999), 327.

[156] For an image of the Breitkopf Fraktur script taken from Albert Kapr, *Fraktur: Form und Geschichte der gebrochenen Schriften* (Mainz: H. Schmidt, 1993), see Killius, 328.

[157] Killius, *Die Antiqua-Fraktur Debatte um 1800 und ihre historische Herleitung*, 327; my translation.

[158] Harry Carter, *A View of Early Typography: Up to About 1600* (London: Hyphen Press, 2002).

[159] Ibid., 5.

[160] Ibid., 10.

[161] Ibid., 13.

Punchcutters worked to cut by hand relief patterns of the letters on the end of long pieces of steel.[162] These completed 'punches'[163] were then struck into blocks of copper, creating impressions of each letter and thereby forming 'matrices'.[164] After each matrix had been carefully trimmed or 'justified'[165] to give the preferred alignment, it was fixed in a two-part contraption called a 'mould'[166] so that molten metal (typically an alloy of lead, tin, antimony and copper)[167] could be poured into the matrix while the matrix was held in place. Printing types were thus cast, the requisite number of which in a particular size constituted a 'fount'.[168] Printers could contract with specialist casters for the making of types using the matrices and moulds that they had purchased, though by the early seventeenth century most were already purchasing ready-made founts.[169] The co-cutting of those punches for the initial casting of Breitkopf Fraktur was but one moment in the longer production lines that manufactured the types utilised in printing houses of the period.

The technical derivation of typefounding from older trades suggests that the material history of typefounding predates the founding of any specific type. From Killius's account of the 'origins' of Breitkopf Fraktur we can further identify at least two sets of techno-cultural inheritances on which the design of Breitkopf Fraktur had probably drawn. First, Albrecht Dürer's writings on applied geometry, including his discussion on the production of roman types, had been closely studied by Breitkopf and shaped his own perspective on typefounding, particularly his demand for geometrical correctness.[170] Other than Dürer's texts, Breitkopf owned an extensive collection of books on the art of printing that contributed to his understanding of it.[171] Second, the design of Breitkopf Fraktur was based on a classical model of Fraktur, the Neudörffer-Andreä Fraktur, which dates back to the early sixteenth century.[172] Thus, printing types are iterations of prior historical forms. In the 1777 essay, Breitkopf suggested that even the letters cut by the 'peerless' Fournier had identifiable precedents: 'Fournier is not entirely the inventor of these cursive types; P. Moreau, a Parisian writing master who was granted a privilege to build a foundry and printing establishment in 1640, had the idea first.'[173] Indeed, he noted that the technology of printing types historically derived from handwritten scripts:

[162] Ibid., 6. For a schematic representation of a punch, a matrix, and a type, see Philip Gaskell, *A New Introduction to Bibliography* (New Castle, DE: Oak Knoll Press, 1995), 11.

[163] Carter, *A View of Early Typography: Up to About 1600*, 6.

[164] Ibid.

[165] Ibid., 11.

[166] Ibid.

[167] Ibid., 21.

[168] Ibid., 7.

[169] Gaskell, *A New Introduction to Bibliography*, 12.

[170] Killius, *Die Antiqua-Fraktur Debatte um 1800 und ihre historische Herleitung*, 327.

[171] Ibid.

[172] Ibid.

[173] Breitkopf, *Breitkopf on Punchcutting and Typefounding*, 9.

> It is the imitation of handwriting that led to the invention of printing. The first examples of the art were nothing else than copies of the common handwriting then used in Germany, just as the Manutius italic was a copy of the roman chancellory hand. Subsequent type-cutters only improved these features, and have endeavoured to give them a definite and steady form, and this is the reason why they have actually been confirmed as types for use in printing.[174]

The history of Breitkopf Fraktur incessantly points backwards to an earlier point in time, moving from an apparently self-contained form invented in Leipzig around 1750 to its precursors in the sixteenth century and, even further, to the material form of writing that it supposedly superseded.

I have been suggesting that the making of Breitkopf Fraktur was not only owed to the multiple hands that cut it but also indebted to prior knowledges and practices that animated its production. Theories and practices of punchcutting and type-founding, only crudely indexed in the proper names of Breitkopf, Zinck, Schmidt, Artopacus, Dürer, Neudörffer and Andreä, were part of the historical processes that produced it. Emergent from a dense history of collaboration, influence, imitation, adaptation and renewal, the material typeface undercuts the idea of sole proprietorship attached to its name and enshrined in copyright doctrine.

(NOT) PERCEIVING BREITKOPF FRAKTUR

Before specifying some ways in which Breitkopf Fraktur was seen and ignored in the late eighteenth century, let us note that there would have occurred a series of processes in literary production between the printing type's initial manufacture and the reader's later perception of its inked impressions on paper. Evidencing the socio-technological basis of the printed book, these intermediary stages may be sketched in reference to bibliographical studies of the hand-press period of print (1500–1800) that gave rise to the German periodical.[175] After having procured the Breitkopf Fraktur types, the Berlin publishing house Haude and Spener (with whom Gedike and Biester had contracted to print the periodical issues) would task their workers with various modes of interacting with those printing types and their impressions. The metal types would be stored in 'cases', namely large wooden trays split into compartments assigned to each of the different symbols (and blanks) that made up the fount of type.[176] From these cases the compositor retrieved particular types that would be assembled into words, lines and pages, the arrangement of which were based on the handwritten manuscripts supplied by Gedike and Biester.[177] Specifically, each line of type was gathered on a hand-held tray called a

[174] Ibid., 10.

[175] See Gaskell, *A New Introduction to Bibliography*, 5–159.

[176] For an image of what an arrangement of compartments for a case of German types might look like, see Gaskell, *A New Introduction to Bibliography*, 35.

[177] Ibid., 40.

'composing stick', before being tied with a string and transferred to trays large enough hold an entire page of type called 'galleys'.[178] Pages of type set on a whole sheet of paper were locked into position by a pair of iron frames called 'chases', thereby becoming 'formes' prepared for printing.[179] Known as 'imposition', this process of setting pages into formes was shaped by the spatial dimensions of the paper on which the text was to be printed.[180]

The presswork of this period typically involved a wooden hand-press operated by two pressmen.[181] After placing a forme on a small table mounted behind one of the side-frames of the hand-press ('ink block'), the first pressman would use a pair of stuffed leather pads ('ink balls') to rub black ink (a mix of varnish and lampblack) onto the surface of the type.[182] After the forme was transferred onto a block of marble or limestone called the 'press stone', the other pressman would work to lower paper (probably wetted the night before so as to aid its absorption of the ink) onto it.[183] Once each forme had been printed off, it was usually passed back to the compositor for the stripping and cleaning of its type (by scrubbing it with an alkaline solution and rinsing it with water)[184] and the return of the type to the cases.[185] After both sides of the sheets of paper had been printed, the warehouse-keeper would hang them up on racks to dry.[186] Once that was done, the sheets would be sorted and folded into the gatherings that constituted each copy of the periodical issue.[187] Once stitched, each issue would be ready for sale and delivery at various sites and in various modes, whether sold at retail bookshops and book fairs or sent via the postal system to the regular subscribers of the periodical. As the publishers of the *Berlinische Monatsschrift*, Gedike and Biester would have financed and asserted some degree of control over each of these processes of print production, including their selection of the printing house.[188] Nonetheless, it was still only by virtue of this assemblage of industry actors interacting with the technologies available to them that the printed publication finally appeared before the reader.

Fichte, Kant and Breitkopf have provided us with three ways in which Breitkopf Fraktur was (not) perceived by late eighteenth-century readers. Each of their essays directs us to the corporeal basis on which the typeface interacted with readers of the *Berlinische Monatsschrift*. For Fichte, the combination of letters and words in the

[178] Ibid., 43.
[179] Ibid., 42.
[180] Ibid., 56.
[181] For an image of a modern replica of a late eighteenth-century English common press, see Gaskell, *A New Introduction to Bibliography*, 119.
[182] Ibid., 125
[183] Ibid., 129.
[184] Ibid., 109.
[185] Ibid., 53.
[186] Ibid., 143
[187] Ibid., 144.
[188] See Gaskell, *A New Introduction to Bibliography*, 179.

printed book only acted as a material index of the inalienable proprietary 'form' generated by the author's mind. Notwithstanding his intimations about the materiality of ideas and the ideal aspects of the book, the particular typeface in which the book was set was invisible to Fichte, who prioritised instead the minds of authors and readers. Kant, on the other hand, kept in view the surface of the printed book, noting its operation as an optical medium that relied on the encounter between eyes and the printed letters of the book for the relay of a speech necessarily spoken in the author's name. Differences in typeface readability, particularly the contrast between the '*Breitkopf* characters' and the '*Didot* characters' (an Antiqua or roman variant),[189] were directly remarked upon, with Kant preferring the former for being less tiring to read. Still, Kant's functionalist account of the book, in so prescribing to the typeface the definitive function of communicating a speech bound to the personhood of the author, disclosed a hidden allegiance to the modern ethics of typographical transparency. The visual and corporeal materiality of type, which Kant's account already suggests, is brought into sharper focus in Breitkopf's account of the aesthetic beauty of types. Rather than being optical instruments that simply facilitate the expression of the author's personhood, types and their impressions on paper could also be seen as artistic objects capable of generating pleasure in readers by virtue of their geometrical proportions and consistency in appearance. Whereas the minds of authors and readers were prioritised in Fichte's account, the eyes and bodies of the persons interacting with print in historical time rose to prominence in Kant's and Breitkopf's accounts. From the latter two perspectives, typefaces needed to be assessed for their perpetual effects on corporeal subjects.

To supplement Breitkopf's perspective, let us note that perceptions of the comparative beauty of types tend to be entwined with those of the cultures that produced them. As a blackletter script, Breitkopf Fraktur would have evoked both the visceral and cultural associations of the script. In the preface to his redesign and republication of the Breitkopf Fraktur typeface in 1793, Breitkopf observed that German typefaces tended to be reproached for looking 'gothic',[190] that is, for their association with datedness, ugliness and barbarism.[191] This 'negative image'[192] of blackletter was offered by Killius as an explanation for the general reluctance of typographers to reform Fraktur until well into the eighteenth century. Breitkopf's work with Fraktur resisted contemporary efforts to abolish blackletter typefaces and pressures to make them closer in appearance to roman typefaces. Despite admiring the rounded characters of roman typefaces, Breitkopf sought to preserve the defining

[189] Kant, *The Conflict of the Faculties*, 211.

[190] See Killius, *Die Antiqua-Fraktur Debatte um 1800 und ihre historische Herleitung*, 329.

[191] See also Gerald Newton, '*Deutsche Schrift*: The Demise and Rise of German Black Letter', *German Life and Letters* 56, no. 2 (2003): 185; *Oxford English Dictionary*, 2nd ed. (Oxford: Oxford University Press, 2004), s.v. 'Gothic'.

[192] Killius, *Die Antiqua-Fraktur Debatte um 1800 und ihre historische Herleitung*, 326; my translation.

characteristics of Fraktur, namely its 'long, narrow and broken'[193] letters, while demanding for 'geometrical correctness'[194] in its redesign.

In some twentieth-century Anglophone accounts of blackletter types we can find reiterations of the earlier aesthetic dismissal of Fraktur with added tinges of xenophobia and a certain disdain for Germanic culture.[195] Consider, for instance, Daniel Berkeley Updike's history of German types, 1500–1800.[196] While accounting for the historical differentiation between two categories of blackletter types, Fraktur and Schwabacher, Updike utilised a slew of derogatory adjectives and phrases to describe examples of each in selected publications. The early Fraktur in which Hans Schösperger's *Diurnale* (1514) was set was said to consist of descenders that were 'all too restless'[197] and of capital letters with 'eccentric curves'[198] that were 'particularly disagreeable and vulgar'.[199] Similarly, the cursive Schwabacher type deployed in Chrystoph Froschauer's *Kunstrich Buch* (1567) was described as having 'imitated the German handwriting of that period–a fussy, restless kind of character, which is distracting to the rye and has somewhat the appearance of ravelled carpet-threads'.[200] Compare these denunciations of blackletter types with Updike's approval of the sixteenth-century roman types used in *Canones Apostolorum* (1525): the latter edition was noted to be set in a 'larger and better roman character, accompanied by a charming type',[201] and overall 'an elegant piece of work'.[202] The occasional applaudable use of roman types was said to have declined across the sixteenth and seventeenth centuries and, finally, 'succumbed'[203] to the popular taste for Fraktur in the eighteenth century.[204] Other instances of the simultaneous criticism of blackletter typefaces and the people who produced them would recur across Updike's account. 'These types are characteristically German–which is, artistically, seldom a compliment!'[205] Perhaps the clearest sign of contempt for German culture would appear in his depiction of the printed editions of *Historia von D. Johann Fausten*, printed in Frankfurt in 1586, as being 'very ugly and very

[193] Ibid., 329.
[194] Ibid., 327.
[195] Other than Updike's account (discussed later in the chapter), see S. H. Steinberg, *Five Hundred Years of Printing* (Mineola, NY: Dover Publications, Inc., 1955). See also Peter Bain and Paul Shaw, 'Introduction: Blackletter vs Roman: Type as Ideological Surrogate', in *Blackletter: Type and National Identity*, ed. Peter Bain and Paul Shaw (New York: Princeton Architectural Press, 1998), 13: 'Steinberg called blackletter the "main obstacle to Germany's full share in the life of the civilized world."'
[196] Updike, *Printing Types*, 139–58.
[197] Ibid., 140.
[198] Ibid.
[199] Ibid.
[200] Ibid., 142.
[201] Ibid.
[202] Ibid.
[203] Ibid., 145.
[204] Ibid.
[205] Ibid., 140.

obviously Teutonic'.[206] Updike's extreme account suggests that, against any pretensions to universality and objectivity, questions of beauty were bound up with those of cultural differences, with aesthetic judgements being shaped by the wider sociopolitical context in which they were made.

I would add that the cultural-political significance of Breitkopf Fraktur in late eighteenth-century Germany may well contest Kant's communicative-functionalist account of type. Being an 'improved' Fraktur typeface that nonetheless stayed to the broken character of the script, Breitkopf Fraktur would have metonymically invoked the symbolic associations of Fraktur and blackletter types more generally. As historical studies of blackletter have suggested, Fraktur was not simply a neutral medium assessed based on its aesthetic or communicative merits, but instead bore the face of German national identity.[207] As previously discussed in reference to Woodmansee, the Holy Roman Empire of the late eighteenth century was a highly fragmented political entity composed of more than three hundred states with separate governments and laws. Nonetheless, the German language was understood to be the cultural glue that held together the disparate states. In Johann Gottfried Herder's definition of nation, for instance, a common language used by the constitutive members of a group was identified to be the most important medium that held them together as a community. For Herder, a nation was 'a community that was made of kinship and history and social solidarity and cultural affinity and was shaped over time by climate and geography, by education, by relations with its neighbours and by other factors, and was held together most of all by language, which expressed the collective experience of the group'.[208] As one of the four blackletter types that emerged in German-speaking localities during the Middle Ages and retained its popularity well beyond the late eighteenth century,[209] Fraktur came to be perceived to be the visual-material form of the language that united the Germanic peoples. Despite their formal differences, Textura, Rotunda, Schwabacher and Fraktur were grouped as scripts of the Middle Ages whose 'darkness of the characters overpowers the whiteness of the page',[210] hence the name 'blackletter'. The emergence of the rounder, more broadly spaced roman types in the late fifteenth century, and its competition with blackletter types since then, further enforced the division between

[206] Ibid., 146.

[207] See Peter Bain and Paul Shaw, eds., *Blackletter: Type and National Identity* (New York: Princeton Architectural Press, 1998); Newton, '*Deutsche Schrift*: The Demise and Rise of German Black Letter'.

[208] Johann Gottfried Herder, *Ideen zur Philosophie der Geschichte der Menschheit* ['Outlines of a Philosophy of the History of Man'] (1800), translated and cited in Bain and Shaw, 'Introduction: Blackletter vs Roman: Type as Ideological Surrogate', 13.

[209] The other three categories of blackletter type are Textura, Rotunda and Schwabacher: see Bain and Shaw, 10. For a timeline of milestone events in the development of blackletter type between 1455 and 1995, see Paul Shaw, 'Timeline of Typography and Events 812–1995', in *Blackletter: Type and National Identity* (New York: Princeton Architectural Press, 1998), 22–66.

[210] Bain and Shaw, 'Introduction: Blackletter vs Roman: Type as Ideological Surrogate', 10.

German national identity and that of the wider European community.[211] As Peter Bain and Paul Shaw put it, Fraktur and other blackletter types had been 'the visual embodiment of German national identity since the days of Luther'.[212] Martin Luther's 1522 German translation of the New Testament had been fully set in blackletter, the body text taking the form of Schwabacher, and the title text, Fraktur.[213] The historical emancipation of the German peoples from the Roman Catholic Church was thus associated with these blackletter types.[214] The subsequent redesign, reproduction and reuse of Fraktur by Breitkopf and others would carry forward the cultural-political history of the German type and its symbolic resonances.

The aesthetic and cultural-political dimensions of type are even more discernibly suppressed in Fichte's idealism. Fichte insisted on looking beyond the typography of the book to the mind that supposedly produced and owned the form evidenced in it, thereby eliding the materialities and meanings of blackletter type. This prioritisation of the authorial mind underlying the book was not missed by Friedrich Kittler in the latter's discussion of the techno-institutional conditions or *Aufschreibesystem* ('discourse network') that generated the myth of authorship circa 1800.[215] Though Fichte's 1793 essay was only mentioned in passing as 'one of the essays that led to the codification of authors' copyrights',[216] Kittler commented extensively on Fichte's reflections on reading and his pedagogical method as a university lecturer at Jena, suggesting the latter to be one of the exemplary representatives of the traditions of German Idealism and Romanticism that similarly prioritised the imagination (synonymous with 'mind' or 'spirit') over the letter. These passages from Fichte, I suggest, reflect his insistent prioritisation of authorial minds over the bodies of books, which screened the latter's operation as subjectivising techniques that generated authorial subjects like himself.

In Fichte's guidance to the reader on how his treatise *Grundlage der gesammten Wissenschaftslehre* ('Foundations of the Science of Knowledge') (1794) should be read, he wrote that it 'cannot be communicated in any way by the mere letter, but must be imparted by the spirit',[217] thereby reasserting the priority of the latter. 'It could not be otherwise in a science that returns to the very foundations of human knowledge, in that the very enterprise of the human spirit proceeds from the

[211] Phillipp Th. Bertheau, 'The German Language and the Two Faces of Its Script: A Genuine Expression of European Culture?', in *Blackletter: Type and National Identity* (New York: Princeton Architectural Press, 1998), 22.

[212] Bain and Shaw, 'Introduction: Blackletter vs Roman', 14.

[213] Bertheau, 'The German Language and the Two Faces of Its Script', 26.

[214] Yvonne Schwemer-Scheddin, 'Broken Images: Blackletter between Faith and Mysticism', in *Blackletter: Type and National Identity* (New York: Princeton Architectural Press, 1998), 52.

[215] Kittler, *Discourse Networks 1800/1900*.

[216] Ibid., 160.

[217] Johann Gottlieb Fichte, *Grundlage der gesammten Wissenschaftslehre* (1794), cited in Kittler, *Discourse Networks 1800/1900*, 154.

imagination, and in that the imagination cannot be grasped except through the imagination.'[218] Notice that the imagination was set up as the transcendental ground for the very production of knowledge, including that of itself, relegating the letter to a secondary and derivative status. Whilst the book consisted of letters, it was dependent on the reader's use of their own imagination to generate knowledge of the imagination itself. In other words, to 'understand' the subject matter of the book, the reader had to become an author like himself: that is, not just a body that writes, but more fundamentally a mind that 'imagines' or gives form to ideas.

A similar call to authorship was sounded earlier in Fichte's *Plan anzustellender Rede-Übungen* ('Plan for Speech Exercises') (1787), which advocated for the subordination, even disappearance, of the letter by prescribing authorship as a remedy for the reader's spiritual 'stagnation'.[219] Two modes of reading were juxtaposed against each other: whilst 'to follow another's train of thought'[220] – that is, to trace the letters printed in the book – 'slackens the soul and lulls it with a certain indolence',[221] to 'develop one's own thoughts'[222] instead and 'put oneself confidently and subtly in the spirit of the author'[223] would help to 'interrupt the stagnation thus induced in the human spirit'.[224] Fichte further claimed that it was by becoming an author that the fullest understanding of the author could be gained by the reader: 'Certainly no one can completely understand a writer and feel himself his equal who is not already in some sense a writer himself.'[225] We may note that, in Fichte's emphasis on understanding the author by becoming one, the book all but recedes from view. The materiality of the book gives way to authorial formation. Lost in the reverie of authorship, Fichte went so far as to suggest that authorship could take place in the absence of prior books: 'There is certainly no greater spiritual pleasure for those capable of it than that which one experiences through, or during, writing itself, and which . . . would remain so even in a world where no one read or heard of anything read.'[226] The practice of writing itself was imagined to be an immensely pleasurable activity that could take place without the practice of reading. Fichte's valorisation of the imagination extended to the extinction of letters. As Kittler put it, 'The clear implication is that, in the writing of the *Science of Knowledge* as well the imagination had surpassed all letters.'[227]

[218] Ibid.
[219] Johann Gottlieb Fichte, *Plan anzustellender Rede-Übungen* (1787), cited in Kittler, *Discourse Networks 1800/1900*, 155.
[220] Ibid.
[221] Ibid.
[222] Ibid.
[223] Ibid.
[224] Ibid.
[225] Ibid.
[226] Ibid.
[227] Ibid.

Fichte's fantasy of the disappearance of books was re-staged in the first university lectures that he gave in Jena. Departing from the practice of assigning and paraphrasing textbooks of older thinkers, which Kittler observed to be a convention extending from the earlier discourse network of *res publica litteraria* (the 'Republic of Scholars'), Fichte read aloud from his own newly written work, that is, instalments of what would later be published as *Grundlage der gesammten Wissenschaftslehre*.[228] In so doing, Fichte not only performed his pedagogical duties as an author who exerted his imagination as if in the absence of prior books but also urged his students to enact authorship by giving form to the ideas that arose in the lectures. It was as if eighteenth-century authors were independent of books, publishers and the wider print machinery. 'Where previously the printing press and professors simply republished the whole world of books, the author-ego (to use his favorite term) Fichte published himself.'[229] Instead of books, authors themselves were reproduced. For Kittler, Fichte was enacting precisely what the discourse network of 1800 demanded: the identification of the imaginative author-poet as the foundation of the European system of knowledge.

As a philosophical proponent of German Idealism, Fichte cooperated with the poets of German Romanticism to imagine the transcendence of the spirit and imagination over the material letter. An emblematic scene in Romantic literature that depicted the tradition's 'invisibilisation' of the letter, as previously discussed in Chapter 1, was Anselmus's enthrallment by Serpentina's voice over against the manuscript that as copying.[230] Fichte was one of the late eighteenth-century authors who joined Anselmus in doubly ignoring the letters he was transcribing and the wider techno-institutional network to which he and the work were coupled. Unlike Kant and Breitkopf, Fichte did not attend to the Fraktur letters in which his 1793 periodical essay was set, nor those of his other publications. The typeface and what it might index about the historical context in which it was produced and used remained invisible to the philosopher.

Had Fichte attended to the materiality of the Fraktur letters in which his texts were set, he might have realised that the so-called transcendental and transcendent mind of the author was likely the effect of broader subjectivating processes that relied on the optical medium (see Figure 3.2). To cite one of these techniques: as Kittler has noted, the discourse network of 1800 was characterised by the mass printing, distribution and use of state-sanctioned ABC books or primers that enlisted mothers as the primary instructors in their children's education:

> The list of such books is long: Friedrich Wilhelm Wedag, *Handbook of Early Moral Education, Intended Primarily for Use by Mothers, in Epistolary Form* (1795); Samuel Hahnemann, *Handbook for Mothers, or Rules for the Early Education of*

228 Ibid., 156. See also Kittler, 'Towards an Ontology of Media', 28.
229 Kittler, *Discourse Networks 1800/1900*, 156.
230 Hoffmann, 'The Golden Flower Pot', 34; Kittler, *Discourse Networks 1800/1900*, 100.

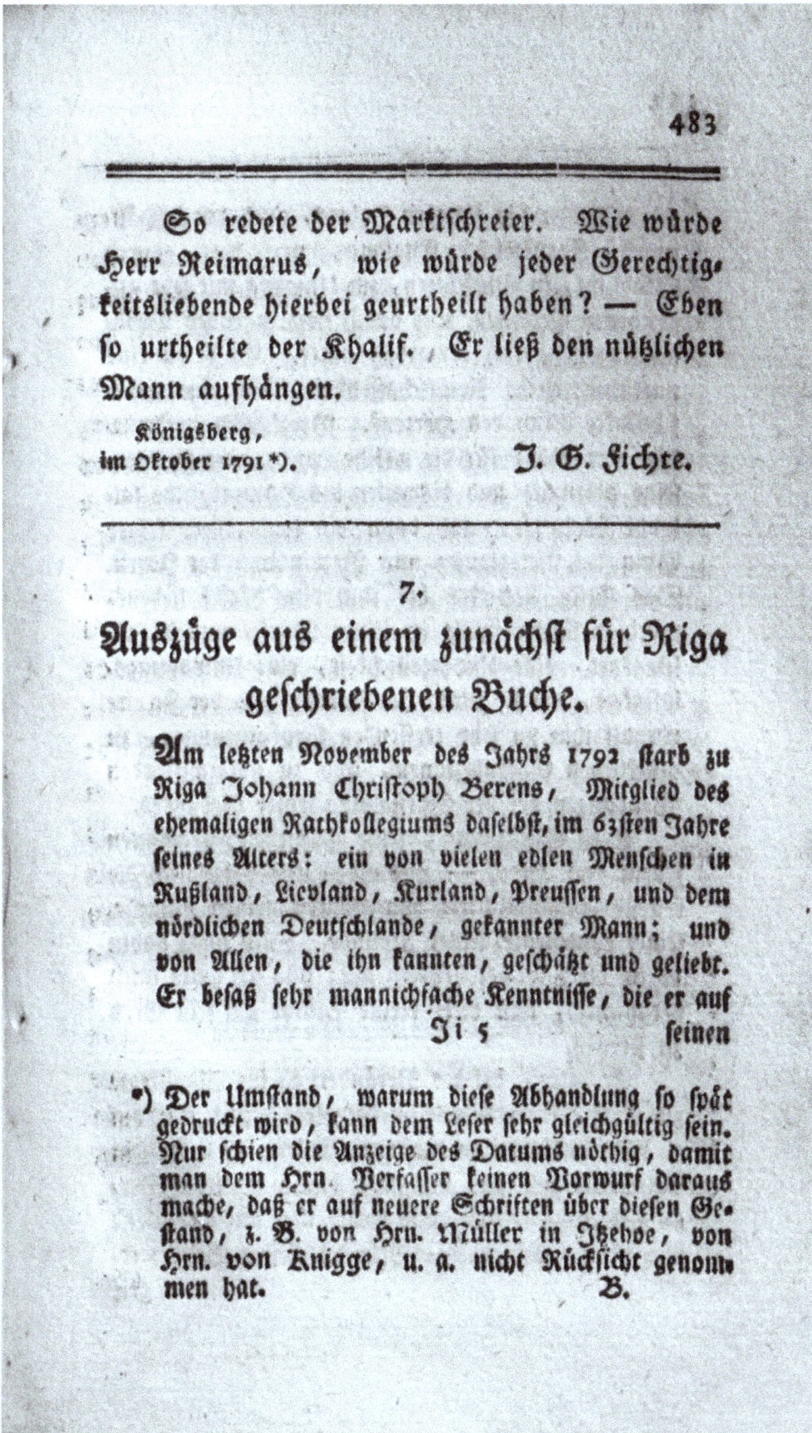

483

So redete der Marktschreier. Wie würde Herr Reimarus, wie würde jeder Gerechtigkeitsliebende hierbei geurtheilt haben? — Eben so urtheilte der Khalif. Er ließ den nützlichen Mann aufhängen.

Königsberg,
im Oktober 1791 *). J. G. Fichte.

7.

Auszüge aus einem zunächst für Riga geschriebenen Buche.

Am letzten November des Jahrs 1792 starb zu Riga Johann Christoph Berens, Mitglied des ehemaligen Rathkollegiums daselbst, im 63sten Jahre seines Alters: ein von vielen edlen Menschen in Rußland, Lievland, Kurland, Preussen, und dem nördlichen Deutschlande, gekannter Mann; und von Allen, die ihn kannten, geschätzt und geliebt. Er besaß sehr mannichfache Kenntnisse, die er auf

Ii 5 seinen

*) Der Umstand, warum diese Abhandlung so spät gedruckt wird, kann dem Leser sehr gleichgültig sein. Nur schien die Anzeige des Datums nöthig, damit man dem Hrn. Verfasser keinen Vorwurf daraus mache, daß er auf neuere Schriften über diesen Gegenstand, z. B. von Hrn. Müller in Itzehoe, von Hrn. von Knigge, u. a. nicht Rücksicht genommen hat. B.

FIGURE 3.2 Last page of Fichte's 1793 essay.

> *Children (after the Principles of J. J. Rousseau)* (1796); Christoph Wilhelm Hufeland, *Good Advice for Mothers on the Most Important Points of Physical Education in the First Years* (1799); Johann Heinrich Pestalozzi, How Gertrude Teaches Her Children, an Attempt to Provide Guidance for Mothers in the Self-Instruction of Their Children (1801); *The Mother's Book, or Guidelines for Mothers in Teaching Children to Observe and Speak* (1803); Christian Friedrich Wolke, *Instructions for Mothers and Child Instructors on the Teaching of the Rudiments of Language and Knowledge from Birth to the Age of Learning to Read* (1805); Heinrich Stephani, *Primer for Children of Noble Education, Including a Description of My Method for Mothers Who Wish to Grant Themselves the Pleasure of Speedily Teaching Their Children to Read* (1807).[231]

Though set in Fraktur, these primers were created to be read not by children, but rather by mothers who thereby learnt how to use their own mouths to teach their children to vocalise the sounds of the alphabet.

> Did you know, ladies, that you can close the oral cavity without any help from the lips, simply by firmly pressing the forward part of the tongue tightly against the gums and thereby forcing the same original voice sound to travel also through the nasal passage? If you try this, you will find that you have made a voice sound different from the previous ones, which is designated *n* in our speech notation.[232]

Instead of Fraktur letters, then, the mother's mouth and the sounds it produced were the chief sensory phenomena that first made the child a literate subject. Psychically, this meant that the child's future acts of reading the book would entail the unseeing of the letters and the hallucination of a voice that recalled the mother's. 'And when later in life children picked up a book, they would not see letters but hear, with irrepressible longing, a voice between the lines.'[233] In so prescribing the maternal instruction that substituted the voice for the letter, the ABC books of 1800 inaugurated the birth of poet-authors such as Anselmus, Fichte and the German Romantics. Despite contributing to the alphabetisation of the author, those Fraktur letters effaced themselves, enduring only as traces in Breitkopf's updated script. By virtue of their Breitkopf characters, Fichte's and Kant's essays subsist as palimpsests of the historico-material means by which authorial subjects were produced in their time.

In as early as 1982, Walter Ong had suggested the figure of the proprietary author to be a perceptual effect of the print medium and its typography.[234] The image of an

[231] Ibid., 27–28.

[232] Heinrich Stephani, *Fibel für Kinder von edler Erziehung, nebst einer genauen Beschreibung meiner Methode für Mütter, welche sich die Freude verschaffen wollen, ihre Kinder selbst in kurzer Zeit lesen zu lehren* ['Primer for Children of Noble Education, Including a Description of My Method for Mothers Who Wish to Grant Themselves the Pleasure of Speedily Teaching Their Children to Read'] (1807), cited in Kittler, *Discourse Networks 1800/1900*, 34.

[233] Ibid.

[234] Walter J. Ong, *Orality and Literacy: The Technologizing of the Word*, 30th Anniversary Edition (London: Routledge, 2012), 128–29.

authorial mind that stood over against an object it had created, versions of which were theorised in Fichte's essay and redoubled in the various author-centric doctrines of copyright, was traced to the visual space of the printed page and its ostensible promise of intellectual proprietorship:

> Print created a new sense of the ownership of words ... Typography had made the word into a commodity ... By removing words from the world of sound where they had first had their origin in active human interchange and relegating them definitively to visual surface, and by otherwise exploiting visual space for the management of knowledge, print encouraged human beings to think of their own interior conscious and unconscious resources as more and more thing-like, impersonal and religiously neutral. Print encouraged the mind to sense that its possessions were held in some sort of inert mental space.[235]

As a visible embodiment of the abstract literary work, the printed page seemed to reflect a mind of no less objectively ascertainable dimensions. Ong pointed us to what resembled a modern iteration of Jacques Lacan's mirror stage.[236] Just as the function of the 'I' had formed pursuant to the infant's *méconnaissance* ['misrecognition'][237] of its ideal specular image as its present and future self, so too did the proprietary author emerge from a misidentification of the ostensibly self-contained printed page as external analogue of the author's inner mind. In both instances, the complex historical processes that produced the image of the author-ego were submerged beneath it.

This chapter's review of the production and perception of the Breitkopf Fraktur typeface has disclosed a similar elision of the literary artefact in contemporary copyright doctrine and Fichte's account of the book. Whereas the law acts as if the literary artefact could be bifurcated into its constitutive literary (and other cultural) works and its overall typographical arrangement, the historical itinerary of the typeface disavows such a simple division, illustrating instead an array of criss-crossing interactions between human bodies and print technologies. Though registered in Kant's account of the book as communicative medium, this corporeal dimension of literature ultimately exceeds it by bringing to light those aesthetic and cultural-political dimensions of type that defy any prevailing emphasis on communication and authorship. The materialities of type suggest the printed book itself to be doubly involved in the propagation and negation of the myth of proprietary authorship.

235 Ibid.

236 Jacques Lacan, 'The Mirror Stage as Formative of the I Function: As Revealed in Psychoanalytic Experience', in *Écrits: The First Complete Edition in English* (New York: W. W. Norton & Company, 2006), 75–81.

237 Ibid., 80.

4

A Biography of I. Kant

LEGALITIES OF THE AUTHORIAL NAME

Perhaps attesting to the global dominance of the myth of proprietary authorship, it is rare to find contemporary print publications that do not bear the name of their authors. Writers have tended to assert their moral right to be identified as authors of their works.[1] Often foregrounded on the front cover and title page of the book, the authorial name affixed to the text is of evidentiary significance to contemporary copyright systems.[2] Not only may the authorial name be relied upon as probative proof of literary ownership; it further places the burden of proof on any party seeking to dispute ownership in jurisdictions such as the United Kingdom, Australia and many civil law and European nations.[3] For instance, section 104(2)(a) of the Copyright, Designs, and Patents Act 1988 ('CDPA 1988)' provides that the person whose name appears on the publication 'shall be presumed, until the contrary is proved—to be the author of the work'.[4] Similarly, article 15(1) of the Berne Convention for the Protection of Literary and Artistic Works 1886 states that the appearance of the author's name on the literary work 'in the usual manner' is sufficient for the author to enforce the protected rights 'in the absence of proof to the contrary'.[5] Though no equivalent presumption of authorship operates in the United States and Canada, the authorial name printed in the certificate of

[1] In the United Kingdom, this moral right is asserted under section 78 of the Copyright, Designs and Patents Act 1988.

[2] For an overview of the norms organised around the author in UK copyright law, see Lionel Bently et al., *Intellectual Property Law* (Oxford: Oxford University Press, 2022), 125–40.

[3] For a list of some pertinent statutory provisions, see Jane Ginsburg, 'The Concept of Authorship in Comparative Copyright Law', *Depaul Law Review* 52 (2003): 1069, fn. 18.

[4] Copyright, Designs and Patents Act 1988, section 104(2)(a). The presumption is inapplicable in certain exceptional instances such as works produced in the course of employment: see section 104(2)(b) of the same Act.

[5] Berne Convention for the Protection of Literary and Artistic Works (1886), article 15(1).

registration of copyright issued by their respective copyright and intellectual property offices is similarly presumed to be a valid index of authorship.[6]

Whilst of evidentiary value, the authorial name affixed to the text is neither determinative of the work's authorship nor a requirement for copyright to subsist in the work. The doctrine of joint authorship, for instance, may be invoked to contest a claim to exclusive authorship.[7] In the United Kingdom, an unnamed participant in the creation of the literary work may argue that the work is a product of 'collaboration'[8] with the named author, in which the former's contribution 'is not distinct from that of the other author',[9] to qualify for joint authorship under section 10(1) of the CDPA 1988. *Kogan v Martin*[10] was a recent case before the Court of Appeal that addressed the question of joint authorship in a screenplay, a text that straddled the literary and dramatic categories of the copyright work. Beyond its doctrinal significance,[11] *Kogan v Martin* registers the law's treatment of the authorial name as a potential screen that obscures the truth of the work's creation. The claimant, whose name had appeared as the sole screenwriter in all typed versions of the screenplay, had sought a declaration that he was, indeed, the sole author of the work.[12] Conversely, the defendant, who had been romantically involved with the claimant during the writing of the first three drafts and allegedly made pertinent contributions to their writing that accrued to the final version, made a counterclaim for copyright infringement on the basis of her alleged ownership of a share of the copyright in the screenplay as its joint author. Though the court of first instance ruled in favour of the claimant, the Court of Appeal ordered a retrial of the case on several grounds of error, including the trial judge's failure to see that the dramatic genre of the work called for a recognition of the defendant's 'non-textual input',[13]

6 See Title 17 of the United States Code, section 410(c); Copyright Act (R.S.C., 1985, c. C-42), section 53(2).

7 For a recent account of the doctrine of joint authorship in UK copyright law, see Daniela Simone, '*Kogan v Martin*: A New Framework for Joint Authorship in Copyright Law', *Modern Law Review* 83, no. 4 (2020): 877–92.

8 Copyright, Designs and Patents Act 1988, section 10(1).

9 Ibid.

10 [2019] EWCA Civ 1645; [2020] E.C.D.R. 3.

11 Daniela Simone has argued that *Kogan v Martin* paid heed to 'the reality of collaborative creativity' (892), both in the Court of Appeal's positing of a four-part test for joint authorship that was attentive to the context of the creative process and the nature of the subject matter, and in its own demonstration of a 'more comprehensive and nuanced approach' (881) to the evidence that far exceeded the narrow vision of the Court of first instance: see Simone, '*Kogan v Martin*'.

12 These include the certificates of the first three drafts registered with the Writers Guild of America, the emails sent to various finance companies, and the film's credits. On the appearance of the claimant's name in these various 'private' and 'public' forms, see *Martin v Kogan* [2018] F.S.R. 9 (2017), paragraphs 56, 81, 97; *Kogan v Martin* [2020] E.C.D.R. 3 (2019) paragraphs 71, 99; *Martin v Kogan* [2021] E.C.D.R. 26 (2021), paragraphs 40, 186, 193, 204, 205, 260, 291, 377.

13 On these non-textual contributions, see *Kogan v Martin* [2020] E.C.D.R. 3 (2019), paragraphs 121–138.

ranging from the inclusion of a song performance to ideas relating to character and plot development, as possibly yielding joint authorship. Subsequently, in the second trial, the Intellectual Property Enterprise Court held that the defendant's devising of those musical, character and plot elements of the screenplay indeed entailed the 'creation, selection, and gathering together of concepts and emotions which the words have fixed in writing'[14] so as to constitute original authorial contributions amounting to one-fifth of the screenplay's creation. Against the statutory presumption of authorship provided under section 104(2) of the CDPA 1988, *Kogan v Martin* suggests that copyright law may not trust claims to sole intellectual proprietorship performed by authorial names, but rather seeks to look behind the material façade and assess the actual authorial contributions to the creative process. Notwithstanding the appearance of the claimant's name in every version of the screenplay and in its various institutional and public forms, both the Intellectual Property Enterprise Court and the Court of Appeal were willing to recognise the possibility of there being an uncredited joint author to whom the work was originally indebted.

Let us add that the absence of specification of the authorial name on the material form of the work does not preclude the subsistence of copyright. Under the doctrine of unknown authorship,[15] which applies where the authorial identity is not known, the duration of copyright in a literary work takes as its reference point not the year in which the author dies but that in which the work was made or first made available to the public.[16] As presently provided, the copyright term ends seventy years thereafter.[17] Where only the publisher's name appears on the work when it was first published somewhere that qualifies it for copyright protection, the law presumes the publisher to be the copyright owner.[18] Despite the importance of authors to copyright law as one of the pillars on which its doctrinal edifice stands, the law recognises and provides for situations of authorial anonymity. First an index, then a screen, the authorial name is now shown to be entirely dispensable to contemporary regimes of copyright.

The practice of affixing authorial names to publications, I suggest, has mostly been treated by copyright law and discourse in ways that presuppose, rather than detract from, the myth of proprietary authorship. Where collaboration in the making of works is affirmed (as under the doctrine of joint authorship), it is done only to determine which individuals have been assigned ownership rights on their grounds of their creation of such works. The extent to which the printed authorial name might have materially constituted, even undermined, the proprietary paradigm of

[14] *Martin v Kogan* [2021] E.C.D.R. 26 (2021), paragraph 319, citing *Kogan v Martin* [2020] E.C.D.R. 3 (2019), paragraph 41.

[15] For the definition of 'unknown authorship', see Copyright, Designs and Patents Act 1988, section 9(4).

[16] Ibid., sections 12(2) and 12(3).

[17] Ibid.

[18] Ibid., section 104.

literature is left unnoticed and undiscussed. It is as if the authorial name were but one of its inert objects of regulation.

The potential agency of the authorial name, likewise, goes unheeded in literary studies of anonymous and pseudonymous publishing. Authorial anonymity has persisted as a legal possibility in England since at least the latter half of the seventeenth century.[19] This has led some literary scholars, such as Robert Griffin, to question the apparent priority that Foucault granted to the authorial name.[20] Foucault's theorisation of the 'author-function' – that is, the role of the authorial figure in discourse – opens by differentiating the author's name from the proper name, the distinction of which invites a close association of the *figure* of the author with the author's *name*. Whereas the proper name 'Pierre Dupont' more simply designates and describes a particular person, the author's last name 'Shakespeare' further classifies a number of texts as being written by that author and him alone, establishing between these texts relationships of 'homogeneity, filiation, reciprocal explanation, authentification, or of common utilization'.[21] Against the tendency to equate the authorial name with the authorial figure, Griffin argues that the author-function could just as well operate in anonymous and pseudonymous texts, where the legal name of the author is not printed on the title page.[22] By the mid-eighteenth century, for instance, it had become commonplace to use the phrase 'by the author of' in publications following earlier unattributed works, which just as effectively

[19] It is rather the printer's name that has had to be printed in publications. Presently, pursuant to the Second Schedule of the Newspapers, Printers, and Reading Rooms Repeal Act of 1869 and the amending Printer's Imprint Act of 1961, each printer is required to print 'his or her name and usual place of abode or business' (section 2) and the same details of the publisher 'upon the first or last leaf of every paper or book' (section 2) that falls under these Acts. For historical accounts of the legal regulation of printers' and authors' names, see Eric Barendt, *Anonymous Speech: Literature, Law and Politics* (Oxford: Bloomsbury Publishing, 2016), 82–93; Fredrick Seaton Siebert, *Freedom of the Press in England 1476-1776: The Rise and Decline of Government Controls* (Urbana: University of Illinois Press, 1952); Colin Manchester, 'The Newspapers, Printers and Reading Rooms Repeal Act 1869: A Case for Repeal?', *Legal Studies* 2, no. 2 (1982): 180–88; Robert J. Griffin, 'Anonymity and Authorship', *New Literary History* 30, no. 4 (1999): 877–95.

[20] Michel Foucault, 'What Is an Author?', in *Language, Counter-Memory, Practice: Selected Essays and Interviews: Selected Essays and Interviews by Michel Foucault*, ed. Donald F. Bouchard (Ithaca, NY: Cornell University Press, 1977), 113–38; Griffin, 'Anonymity and Authorship'. Other than Griffin's work, see Mark Vareschi, *Everywhere and Nowhere: Anonymity and Mediation in Eighteenth-Century Britain* (Minneapolis: University of Minnesota Press, 2018); Janet Wright Starner and Barbara Howard Traister, eds., *Anonymity in Early Modern England: 'What's in a Name'* (Surrey: Ashgate, 2011); Robert J. Griffin, ed., *The Faces of Anonymity: Anonymous and Pseudonymous Publication, 1600-2000* (New York: Palgrave Macmillan, 2003). To be clear, most of these studies are not dismissive of Foucault, but rather keen on extending his insights into the historicity of the author-function to contexts where the authorial name is in some way absent.

[21] Foucault, 'What Is an Author?', 1977, 123.

[22] Griffin's broad definition of anonymity includes pseudonymity, the practice of using a name other than the author's legal name: see Griffin, 'Anonymity and Authorship', 882.

grouped those texts as a set to be read as written by the same author.[23] Relatedly, the phrase 'by a lady', which was mostly used in Jane Austen's novels in the early nineteenth century, brought the pertinent texts under the authorship of a particular gender and class, regardless of the actual identities of the authors.[24] De-linking the author's name and the author-function allows Griffin to observe the thriving of anonymous publishing during the eighteenth and nineteenth centuries (despite the commodification of the author's name),[25] and certain advantages the practice granted to writers, including those of social and political protection.[26] He further notes that copyright could subsist in both onymous and anonymous literary publications, which might or might not be held by the authors.[27]

Griffin's commentary on the history of anonymous publishing in England demonstrates a distrustful and diminishing take on the printed authorial name that eventually coincides with that of copyright law.

> The conclusion is inescapable. Naming and copyright protection operate on separate levels of discourse and involve separate decisions on the part of the writer (if indeed the writer is consulted). When copyright historians discuss the author as owner, the author is an abstract legal identity which does not need to have a specific name for it to function in legal discourse.[28]

Whilst at times helpfully indicating the identities of authors as potential first owners of copyright, the printed authorial name is ultimately seen to be an expendable product of commercial publishing that distracts us from the deeper questions of authorship that warrant attention. For the Court of Appeal in *Kogan v Martin*, it is the potential reality of a second feminine author suppressed beneath the established screenwriter's name that the copyright doctrine of joint authorship must evolve to uncover. As for Griffin, it is the existence of publishing practices conducted in the absence of the author's name – or, better yet, in the play of 'masks'[29] or 'faces of anonymity',[30] phenomena no less concrete than those surrounding the author's name – that must now be accounted for in histories of professional authorship.[31]

[23] Ibid., 880.
[24] Ibid.
[25] Griffin argues that anonymous publishing was 'at least as much a norm as signed authorship' during the eighteenth and nineteenth centuries: see Griffin, 'Anonymity and Authorship', 882.
[26] On some of the more specific motivations for publishing anonymously and their supporting historical examples, see Griffin, 'Anonymity and Authorship', 885–86.
[27] Griffin, 'Anonymity and Authorship', 889. Jane Austen, for example, often retained copyright in her anonymously published novels, the cost of printing being borne by her and their distribution being achieved by way of booksellers who partook of the profits: see Jan Fergus and J. Luke Wood, *Jane Austen: A Literary Life* (New York: Palgrave Macmillan, 1991).
[28] Griffin, 'Anonymity and Authorship', 889–90.
[29] See Griffin, *Faces of Anonymity*, 10.
[30] Ibid.
[31] See also Robert J. Griffin, 'The Profession of Authorship', in *A Companion to the History of the Book*, ed. Simon Eliot and Jonathan Rose, 2nd Edition (London: John Wiley & Sons, 2020).

The author-function may operate without the authorial name, the fact of which potentially contests studies that assume synonymity between them.

Against the tendency to diminish the authorial name as a material practice involved in the historical (de)constitution of the proprietary author, this chapter seeks to reconstitute the materiality of the authorial name and its implications on authorship in reference to Kant's 1785 essay in the *Berlinische Monatsschrift*. My argument is that Kant's authorial name, 'I. Kant', implemented an ethical author-function, one responsive to the demands of enlightenment practice, that well exceeds the perspectives under copyright law and literary studies of anonymous publishing. I begin by revisiting Foucault's 1969 essay on authorship, attending to both its textual ambiguities and four-part theorisation of the author-function for guidance on approaching Kant's treatment of the authorial name. Then, I examine Kant's 1785 essay for what it indicates about the author-function in late eighteenth-century Germany, considering not only the deployment of the authorial name at the rhetorical level of the text but also the textual and typographical (dis)placements of Kant's name, both within and outside the May 1785 issue of the periodical, and during and beyond the author's lifetime. In so following the anthumous and posthumous movements of 'I. Kant', I chart a biography of Kant's authorial name that clarifies his interventions as a media theorist and practitioner.

MATERIALITIES OF THE AUTHOR-FUNCTION

The textual ambiguities surrounding Foucault's 'What Is an Author?' (1969), a work divided into two or more versions, presuppose a literary apparatus not unlike the print machinery that had produced Kant's 1785 essay.[32] Despite the apparent ease with which we cite the title and its accompanying date, it is as yet unclear to which text we are, and should be, referring. One of the basic functions of the title is to identify a text.[33] By naming the text the title works to 'designate it as precisely as possible and without too much risk of confusion'.[34] In print publishing, the title usually appears at the time of the publication of the first edition of the text.[35] With respect to Foucault's text, it was in 1969 when the original French essay entitled

[32] See Stuart Elden, 'The Textual Issues around Foucault's "What Is an Author?"', *Progressive Geographies* (blog), 11 April 2017, https://progressivegeographies.com/2017/04/11/the-textual-issues-around-foucaults-what-is-an-author/ (accessed 9 September 2024); Stuart Elden, 'What Is Author? From Paris to Buffalo', *Progressive Geographies* (blog), November 2021, https://progressivegeographies.com/resources/foucault-resources/foucault-minor-resources/what-is-an-author-from-paris-to-buffalo/ (accessed 9 September 2024).

[33] For Genette's account of the title as paratext, see Gérard Genette, *Paratexts*, 55–103. For a helpful overview of modern titology, see Victoria Louise Gibbons, 'Toward a Poetics of Titles: The Prehistory', PhD thesis, Cardiff University, 2010, 23–53.

[34] Genette, *Paratexts*, 79.

[35] Ibid., 66. See also Colin Manchester, 'The Newspapers, Printers and Reading Rooms Repeal Act 1869: A Case for Repeal?', *Legal Studies* 2, no. 2 (1982): 180–88.

Qu'est-ce qu'un auteur was published in the year's third issue of the *Bulletin de la Société française de Philosophie*.[36] Earlier that year, on 22 February 1969, Foucault had delivered a version of the text as a lecture before the French Society of Philosophy in Paris. The original published essay was later edited, translated into English under the title, 'What Is an Author?', and published in a collection of Foucault's essays, *Language, Counter-Memory, Practice: Selected Essays and Interviews* (1977).[37] By citing the English title and the year of appearance of the original French essay, I purport to refer to the translated text while recognising the original date of its appearance and reserving the possibility of returning to the original text, lecture and their constitutive paratexts as might be helpful.[38]

The situation is complicated by the presence – and, indeed, absence – of other texts against which the identity of our chosen text is defined. Another version of 'What Is an Author?', or another translated text that bears the same title, authorial name and other close resemblances to the first, has been published and reprinted in other anthologies. The first known printed collection in which the other text appeared was *Textual Strategies: Perspectives in Post-Structuralist Criticism* (1979).[39] Some key differences between the two texts include the second text's omission of the first's contextual introduction,[40] and the inclusion of a new part towards the end of the second text that specified the author's ideological operation as a 'principle of thrift in the proliferation of meaning'.[41] One of the explanations given for this difference in the second text is premised on another talk on the author-function given by Foucault at SUNY Buffalo in March 1970. According to the editor's preface to *Textual Strategies*, the second text was his own translation of Foucault's second talk, the latter of which was identified as a 'version'[42] of the first given at the French Society of Philosophy and later published in its bulletin. The

36 Michel Foucault, 'Qu'est-ce qu'un auteur', *Bulletin de la Société française de Philosophie* 63, no. 3 (1969): 73–104. The following publication history is partially recorded in the introductory editorial comments of Michel Foucault, *Dits et écrits: 1954-1988*, ed. Daniel Defert, François Ewald, and Jacques Lagrange, vol. 1 (Paris: Gallimard, 1994), #69. See also the opening editorial footnote of Foucault, 'What Is an Author?', 1977, 113.

37 Foucault, 'What Is an Author?', 1977.

38 For Foucault's contemporaneous discussions of the author-function, see Michel Foucault, 'The Enunciative Function', in *The Archaeology of Knowledge and the Discourse on Language*, trans. A. M. Sheridan Smith (New York: Pantheon Books, 1972), 88–105; Michel Foucault, 'The Discourse on Language', in *The Archaeology of Knowledge and the Discourse on Language*, trans. A. M. Sheridan Smith (New York: Pantheon Books, 1972), 215–37.

39 Foucault, 'What Is an Author?', in *Textual Strategies: Perspectives in Post-Structuralist Criticism*, ed. and trans. Josué V. Harari (Ithaca, NY: Cornell University Press, 1979), 141–60.

40 See Foucault, 'What Is an Author?', 1977, 113–15.

41 Foucault, 'What Is an Author?', 1979, 159. On other terminological and editorial changes, see Stuart Elden, 'The Textual Issues around Foucault's "What Is an Author?"'; Stuart Elden, 'What Is Author? From Paris to Buffalo'.

42 Josué V. Harari, ed., *Textual Strategies: Perspectives in Post-Structuralist Criticism* (Ithaca, NY: Cornell University Press, 1979), 13.

translation was not only published with the 'permission'[43] of both the author Foucault and the French Society of Philosophy but also edited with an 'American readership in mind'[44]; the author having given the editor a 'free hand'[45] to do so. That the second version of Foucault's text ends on an apparently more 'political note'[46] than the first version is understood by the editor-translator to be indicative of a broader shift in Foucault's research interests from questions of language to those of history and politics.

Whereas the existence of two published texts does not necessarily impede analysis but could, on the contrary, enable it, the discovery of a third unpublished text still in manuscript form, one that might unsettle prior assumptions and findings, would complicate the matter further. The front matter of *Textual Strategies* presents the second Foucault text as an edited and translated version of the second talk. This textual identity is co-legitimated by *Dits et écrits*, probably the leading edition of Foucault's *oeuvre*, whose copy of Foucault's *Qu'est-ce qu'un auteur* gives an editorial introductory nod to the translated version of 'What Is an Author?' in *Textual Strategies* and its reprint in *The Foucault Reader*.[47] Specifically, it is claimed there that Foucault 'equally authorises' (*autorisa indifféremment*)[48] the first French text and the English translation of what purports to be the Buffalo lecture. Stuart Elden notes that what appears as #69 in *Dits et écrits* is a composite edition of Foucault's essay, one consisting of the first French text and some passages purportedly from the original Buffalo lecture.[49] However, Elden suggests that the second Foucault text in *Textual Strategies* might in fact have been based on the first lecture delivered in Paris, more so than on the lecture delivered at SUNY Buffalo.[50] In Elden's words, 'what claims to be the Buffalo text was actually something else – essentially a version of the Paris lecture, in a different translation, with some edits and a little of the actual Buffalo lecture appended'.[51] The insertions in #69 of *Dits et écrits* are, rather, French translations of the English translated text in *Textual Strategies*. The 'actual Buffalo lecture' or 'full Buffalo lecture', as Elden has more recently brought to our attention in November 2021, 'exists in the archive, and has not been published'.[52] At least until the original Buffalo lecture has been made publicly available, it would

43 Ibid.

44 Ibid.

45 Ibid.

46 Ibid., 43. This claim is, of course, contestable. Questions of language may be thoroughly historical and political.

47 Michel Foucault, 'What Is an Author?', in *The Foucault Reader*, ed. Paul Rabinow (New York: Pantheon Books, 1984). See Foucault, *Dits et écrits*, #69.

48 Foucault, *Dits et écrits*, #69.

49 Elden, 'The Textual Issues around Foucault's "What Is an Author?"'

50 Elden, 'What Is Author? From Paris to Buffalo'.

51 Ibid.

52 Ibid.; see the opening parenthesis, 'Update November 2021'.

remain unclear whether – and if so, how far – the first and second texts depart from the Buffalo manuscript, and what could be made of these differences.

My interest is not in identifying any 'true' nor 'definitive' textual expression of Foucault's ideas on authorship, but in foregrounding the literary machinery behind these textual ambiguities surrounding Foucault's work. Despite the prevailing juridical emphasis on the author as creator and owner of the original literary work, the literary artefact arises only pursuant to the interactions between multiple actors, including editors, translators, publishers and scholars. In Chapters 2 and 3, we considered the assemblage of print actors, technologies, and practices that produced Kant's 1785 essay in the *Berlinische Monatsschrift* periodical.[53] Kant's authorial 'speech', which presented the printed text as a speech articulated in the author's name, depended on this very machinery for its presentation before the late eighteenth-century German public. In the instance of Foucault's 1969 essay, we see in operation a similar literary apparatus on which the making, distribution and reading of the text is materially dependent. The two published versions of 'What Is an Author?', not to mention the third unpublished manuscript in the archive and the other 'original' French texts, all depend on a plurality of actors, objects and practices for their public appearance. This non-exhaustive series of (con)textual elements, which Genette federated under the abyssal category of the paratext, well exceed the proprietary paradigm of authorship.

Yet, the discourse involving 'What Is an Author?' – including my earlier analysis – has continuously sought recourse to the author Foucault as the figure authorising each text that bears the original or translated title, in each instance authenticating the text as written by, or in some other way associated with, the author. My citation of each version of the text doubly depends on its title and the name of the author affixed to it. The relevant editors and translators of Foucault's essay, particularly those of *Textual Strategies* and *Dits et écrits*, cite Foucault as the personal authorial figure who consented to the making of the text at hand, legitimating it as reflecting, or at least originating from, the lectures he had given in Paris and New York. Elden's careful mapping of the different versions of the text, the appended editorial comments and the inconsistencies between them has proceeded on the basis that there is an original manuscript, the 'full Buffalo lecture'[54] in the Foucault archive, against which any claim to textual veracity and accuracy is to be measured. Both the authorial name and the individual person it purportedly designates are summoned, expressly or implicitly, to identify, describe, classify and evaluate the text in each instance.

At play in this discourse is the basic classificatory operation of the authorial figure that Foucault has conceptualised as the author-function. As previously discussed, Foucault's initial discussion of the author-function proceeded by distinguishing the

[53] See Chapters 2 and 3.

[54] Elden, 'What Is Author? From Paris to Buffalo'.

modern understanding of the authorial name from the proper name. Whereas the proper name conventionally serves to identify and describe some individual, the author's name goes further to 'group together a number of texts and thus differentiate them from others'.[55] This classification also entails the establishing of various relationships between the included texts: in the instance of those different versions of Foucault's 'What Is an Author?', the author is deployed as a figure of 'authentification',[56] inviting them to be accepted as legitimate specimens of the author's oeuvre, and to be read alongside one another as kindred texts affording 'reciprocal explanation'.[57] The third and perhaps most crucial point is that the recognition of there being a particular author to a text, most obviously through the authorial name affixed to it, defines the being (or 'manner of existence'[58]) of the text and the discourse in which it participates. An essay bearing an authorial name, and Foucault's canonised name in particular, tends to spare it the fate of cultural oblivion. 'Discourse that possesses an author's name is not to be immediately consumed and forgotten; neither is it accorded the momentary attention given to ordinary, fleeting words. Rather, its status and its manner of reception are regulated by the culture in which it circulates.'[59] Elden's careful reading of those works bearing Foucault's name attests to the present endurance of the author-function in the given sense.

Whilst recognising there could be multiple author-functions, or differences in the author-function as it operates in various discourses at any given time, Foucault outlines what he considers to be four of 'the most obvious and important'[60] features of the author-function in 'books or texts with authors'.[61] In what follows, I review these four features of the author-function, which collectively present an alternative way of approaching the authorial name to copyright doctrine. My suggestion is that Foucault's second and third suggestions, when considered alongside Chartier's critical commentary, direct us to the materialities of the author-function, which would guide my subsequent analysis of Kant's authorial name.

The first aspect of the author-function discussed by Foucault is its historical legalities, specifically its evolved proprietary and penal characteristics. He relates the author-function in modern discourse to the legal-institutional order of Western civilisation, suggesting that the law both reflects and entrenches our modern understanding of authors as owners of property in books. Alluding to the first copyright laws of the eighteenth and early nineteenth centuries, Foucault notes that the present status of books as objects of property owned by authors is a result of

55 Foucault, 'What Is an Author?', 1977, 123.
56 Ibid.
57 Ibid.
58 Ibid.
59 Ibid.
60 Ibid., 130.
61 Ibid., 124.

'legal codification . . . accomplished some years ago'.[62] Prior to ratifying the myth of the proprietary author, Foucault adds, the law had first inducted the author as a penal subject – one who was 'subject to punishment . . . to the extent that his discourse was considered transgressive'.[63] Though Foucault does not specify a date for this initial penal subjectivation of the author, the English laws providing for the (non-)printing of authorial names suggests that it dates back to at least the mid-sixteenth century.[64] Foucault's identification of two historically successive senses of the author reflects his acute recognition of the historicity of the author-function and its co-evolution with law. In copyright history, there have been many incisive responses to Foucault's call to study the juridical correlate of the author, including key classics of the early 1990s focusing on localities in eighteenth-century Europe, which have in turn attracted their share of critical replies.[65]

The second aspect of the author-function concerns its discursive and historical specificity: 'it does not operate in a uniform manner in all discourses, at all times, and in any given culture'.[66] This proposition is, to some extent, continuous with Foucault's opening suggestion about the historical transformation of the author from a penal subject into an owner of literary property. Whereas the emphasis in

62 Ibid. Foucault also notes that the proprietary function of the author in modern discourse was preceded by the author becoming 'subject to punishment', which coheres with our earlier review of anti-sedition laws demanding the disclosure of authorial identities on title pages in early modern England.

63 Ibid.

64 See Barendt, 82–89. See also Roger Chartier's discussion of a 1544 catalogue, the Sorbonne's Index, that used the category of the author as its principle for designating books censored by the Faculty of Theology of Paris, which supports Foucault's proposed connection between judicial responsibility and the author-function: Roger Chartier, 'Figures of the Author', in *The Order of Books: Readers, Authors, and Libraries in Europe between the Fourteenth and Eighteenth Centuries*, trans. Lydia G. Cochrane (Stanford, CA: Stanford University Press, 1994), 49.

65 See Introduction. Three of the early landmark monographs focusing on Germany, Britain, and France, respectively, are Martha Woodmansee, *The Author, Art, and the Market: Rereading the History of Aesthetics* (New York: Columbia University Press, 1994); Mark Rose, *Authors and Owners: The Invention of Copyright* (Cambridge, MA: Harvard University Press, 1993); Carla Alison Hesse, *Publishing and Cultural Politics in Revolutionary Paris*, 1789-1810 (Berkeley: University of California Press, 1991). For two helpful reviews of Woodmansee's and Rose's works, see Rosemary J. Coombe, 'Challenging Paternity: Histories of Copyright', *Yale Journal of Law & the Humanities* 6, no. 2 (1994): 397–422; Kathy Bowrey, 'Law, Aesthetics and Copyright Historiography: A Critical Reading of the Genealogies of Martha Woodmansee and Mark Rose', in *Research Handbook on the History of Copyright Law*, ed. Isabella Alexander and H. Tomás Gómez-Arostegui (Cheltenham: Edward Elgar Publishing, 2016), 27–52. See also Roger Chartier's book-historical studies of the author-function, which have implicitly critiqued genealogies of authorship that narrowly focused on statutory articulations: Roger Chartier, 'Figures of the Author'; Roger Chartier, 'Foucault's Chiasmus: Authorship between Science and Literature in the Seventeenth and Eighteenth Centuries', in *Scientific Authorship: Credit and Intellectual Property in Science*, ed. Mario Biagioli and Peter Galison (London: Routledge, 2003), 13–31; Roger Chartier, *The Author's Hand and the Printer's Mind*, trans. Lydia G. Cochrane (Cambridge: Polity Press, 2014).

66 Foucault, 'What Is an Author?', 1977, 130.

the first is on coincidences between the cultural and juridical expressions of authorship, that in the second is on potential divergences in the significance of authors in specific discourses. By way of illustration, Foucault posits a reversal or chiasmus concerning the organisation of so-called scientific texts ('dealing with cosmology and the heavens, medicine or illness, the natural sciences or geography'[67]) and literary texts ('stories, folk tales, epics and tragedies'[68]) around the practice of (not) naming the author, which supposedly occurred during the early modern period. According to Foucault, in the Middle Ages, literary texts were disseminated without interest in their authors' identities, whilst scientific texts required the validation of their authors, whose names had to be therein indicated. However, by early modernity, the two positions had reversed: scientific texts relied instead on impersonal conceptual systems for the validation of their truth-claims, whilst the demand for disclosing the identities of literary authors arose, with each anonymous literary publication becoming 'a puzzle to be solved'.[69]

Chartier casts doubt on Foucault's chiasmus of literary and scientific authorship by citing countervailing examples from book history. Contrary to Foucault's claim of medieval indifference to authorial identities in literary texts, Chartier notes particular strategies adopted by the Parisian *rhétoriqueurs* (including Jean Molinet, André La Vigne and Pierre Gringore) between 1450 and 1530 to establish their presence as individual owners and controllers of their literary texts.[70] On top of relying on the limited system of privileges to control the publication and distribution of their books, the Parisian authors had their identities indicated in title pages, colophons and frontispieces, including in the form of a portrait of the author writing the work.[71] These material methods of authorial self-promotion evidence the operation of the author-function well before early modernity. Foucault's claim about the impersonality of early modern scientific texts is similarly undermined in Chartier's reference to the widespread textual practice of dedications to patrons whose superior socio-economic status to some extent assured the credibility of scientific truth-claims.[72] Consider, for instance, Galileo Galilei's *Sidereus nuncius*, whose account of astronomical discoveries, including the Medicean Stars, was dedicated to the Grand Duke of Tuscany, Cosimo II de' Medici, celebrating the latter as 'the primordial inspiration and the first author of the work presented to him'.[73] Rather than

67 Ibid., 125.

68 Ibid.

69 Ibid., 126.

70 Chartier, 'Foucault's Chiasmus', 24. Chartier cited the work of Cynthia J. Brown in support: see Cynthia J. Brown, *Poets, Patrons, and Printers: Crisis of Authority in Late Medieval France* (Ithaca, NY: Cornell University Press, 1995), 7.

71 Chartier, 'Foucault's Chiasmus', 24.

72 Ibid., 22.

73 Ibid. Chartier cited the work of Mario Biagioli in support: see Mario Biagioli, 'Galileo the Emblem Maker', *Isis* 81, no. 2 (1990): 230–58; Mario Biagioli, *Galileo, Courtier: The Practice of Science in the Culture of Absolutism* (Chicago: University of Chicago Press, 1993).

indicating any absence or diminution of the author-function, the dedication reflected its enduring operation by way of transfer to the sovereign as 'the discoverer and owner of the natural reality'.[74] The insistence of the author-function across the medieval and early modern periods, with respect to both literary and scientific texts, and as mediated and evidenced by their material forms, would seem to refute Foucault's historical claim, or at least necessitate further qualification.[75]

Chartier's attention to the material form of the book and its deep involvement in the author-function attests to both an acceptance and sharpening of Foucault's third observation about the author-function's reliance on particular methods and procedures. Foucault understood that the attribution of books to authors did not happen 'spontaneously'[76] (that is, without identifiable cause), but instead depended on 'a series of precise and complex procedures'.[77] Specifically, Foucault noted that the modern recognition of authors as individuals whose '"profundity' and "creative" power'[78] gave rise to the literary work is, in fact, an aspect or extension of a contingent textual practice. This individualisation of the author is but one of the 'projections, in terms always more or less psychological, of our way of handling texts ... [which] vary according to the period and the form of discourse concerned'.[79] In so connecting our understanding of authorship with our textual dealings, Foucault already recognised the essential involvement of books in the author-function. Through his book-historical contributions to the discourse on authorship Chartier goes further to foreground the material form of the book as an index of those textual practices and understandings of authorship. In other words, the author-function is evidenced in the materiality of books – title pages, colophons, front pages, dedications and so forth – by which it operates. Whereas copyright historians tend to focus on the juridical conditions for authorship, Chartier calls attention to the evolving material conditions on which our correlative understandings of the author have been, and continue to be, based.

Despite the historical importance of title pages and other preliminary materials in defining the reception of texts and their connection with authors, these original paratextual matter tend not to be reproduced in contemporary translations and editions of texts. In Chapters 2 and 3, I noted the exclusion of catchwords, signature marks and the various front matter of Kant's 1785 essay in the *Berlinische Monatsschrift* from the *Cambridge Edition*, and on its typographical shift from the Breitkopf Fraktur typeface to the Times New Roman font. Chartier has observed a

[74] Chartier, 'Foucault's Chiasmus', 22.

[75] See Mario Biagioli and Peter Galison's edited collection of studies on scientific authorship: Mario Biagioli and Peter Galison, eds., *Scientific Authorship: Credit and Intellectual Property in Science* (London: Routledge, 2003).

[76] Foucault, 'What Is an Author?', 1977, 127.

[77] Ibid., 130.

[78] Ibid., 127.

[79] Ibid.

similar publishing practice in respect of medieval and early modern texts, including the two parts of Cervantes's *Don Quixote*, originally entitled *El Ingenioso Hidalgo Don Quixote de La Mancha*.[80] Contemporary French translations of these texts have tended not to reprint their original title pages and other preliminary materials (first published in 1605 and 1615), as if these front matter were inconsequential to our understanding of the work.[81] Consequent to such exclusions, contemporary readers are separated from some of the key paratextual indices of the author-function as it had operated in the early seventeenth century, including the typographical placement of the authorial name on the original title pages, thereby contributing to the work's de-historicisation and our limited engagement with the history of authorship.

The fourth and last feature of the author-function noted by Foucault entails a methodological differentiation of the actual person of the author from the author as a product of discourse. On the one hand, there is the writer-in-the-flesh whose actions at a particular place and time contributed to the production of the text. But on the other, there is the discursive author, the meaningful figure of discourse whose conditions of possibility Foucault calls attention to with the term 'author-function'. Maintaining this distinction allows us to see a 'variety of egos',[82] or plurality of authors, that may arise in a single text. Foucault offers the example of a generic mathematical treatise, where it is possible to find at least three authorial egos attached to its different parts. In the preface, there is the 'I' who factually outlines 'the circumstances of composition'[83]; in the body, we find an 'I' performing the pertinent 'demonstration'[84]; and, perhaps towards the end of the book, there might be a reflective self looking back on 'the goals of his investigation, the obstacles encountered, its results, and the problems yet to be solved'.[85] Similarly, Chartier cites the literary example of *Don Quixote*, in which a reader may find at least four authors.

> The 'authors' of the novel multiply: there is the 'I' of the prologue who announces that the work is his; then there is the author of the first eight chapters who upsets the 'I-reader' inscribes in the text when he suddenly interrupts his narration ("This caused me great annoyance'); there is also the author of the Arabic manuscript; finally, there is the Morisco author of the translation that is the text read by the 'I-reader' and by the reader of this novel.[86]

80 See Introduction for my prior discussion of Chartier's analysis of the title page of part I of *Don* Quixote. On Chartier's account of the preliminary materials of part II and their comparison with those of an earlier apocryphal version, see Chartier, *The Author's Hand and the Printer's Mind*, 140–49.

81 Ibid., 139.

82 Foucault, 'What Is an Author?', 1977, 131.

83 Ibid., 130.

84 Ibid.

85 Ibid.

86 Chartier, 'Figures of the Author', 46.

In each of these instances, the 'author' is cited as a unifying figure that ensures the integrity of the discourse, even though the dispersion of authors points to the instability of the authorial identity named on the title page – the person of whom copyright law now recognises to be the owner and creator of the literary work.

I have been suggesting alongside Chartier that the history of authorship co-evolves with the history of the book. 'Such a perspective allows us to understand that the author-function is not only a discursive function, but also a function of the materiality of the text.'[87] The materialities of the book, including that of the placement of the authorial name on the title page and its other parts, are some of the key conditions through which the author-function operates. As the original 1605 title page of part I of *Don Quixote* indicates,[88] the printed authorial name may anticipate the juridical recognition of the author as proprietary creator of the literary work under copyright law. But it may also subvert the myth by directing us to the adjoining historical conditions that are processually constitutive of the book, including the contributions of other print actors and practices relating to the book's financial support, publication and dissemination. The book itself, and the visual space it presents, is shown to be involved in the configuration and transmission of authorship, mediating its ascription to the author as creator. What the book affords, also, as a material index of the historical conditions and processes of literary production is a de-constitution of the myth of proprietary authorship. In so recording some potential tensions between the juridical and historical accounts of literary production, the authorial name and its analysis paves the way for an alternative mode of dealing with texts that de-prioritises authors, which is a possibility that Foucault suggests to have long been posed in literary modernism and intimated in Beckett's question, 'What matter who's speaking?'[89]

Whilst useful in pointing to the discursive specificity and historical contingency of authorship, Foucault's differentiation of the discursive author from the authorial person inadvertently screens the transactions between them. The person of the author – that is, the writer who wrote the manuscript to be fed into the print machinery – could well be part of the process that shaped the book and its articulation of authorship. Vice versa, the discursively and materially constituted sense of authorship might likely be involved in the formation of the author's self-understanding. If the book depends on the person of the author and other agents of literary production for its emergence, then this relationship remains relevant to our understanding of authorship. As a book historian aware of the sociality of texts, Chartier does not exclude the person of the author and other human bodies from his

[87] Chartier, 'Foucault's Chiasmus: Authorship between Science and Literature in the Seventeenth and Eighteenth Centuries', 28.

[88] Roger Chartier, *The Author's Hand and the Printer's Mind*, trans. Lydia G. Cochrane (Cambridge: Polity Press, 2014), 139. See Introduction.

[89] Samuel Beckett, *Texts for Nothing* (London: Calder & Boyars, 1974), 16; cited in Foucault, 'What Is an Author?', 1977, 115.

analysis of the materialities of the author-function. For instance, in the chapter after Chartier's analysis of the prefatory materials of *Don Quixote*, Cervantes returns as a body engaged in a series of interactions with and within the print machinery of the Spanish Golden Age, including his writing of the autograph manuscript for the printing of the first part of *Don Quixote* in the print shop of Jean de la Cuesta in 1604, his probable revisions of the fair copy and his introduction of certain modifications into the subsequent textual editions of 1605 and 1608.[90] Chartier's point is that early seventeenth-century books such as *Don Quixote* were not identical to the so-called original autograph manuscripts, but instead were products of a complex publishing apparatus – hence the title 'Publishing Cervantes'. Not always respected, the writer's wishes were constantly threatened by the fragility and complexity of the publishing process, including but not limited to editorial interventions. Consistent with Kittler's observation about the alphabetisation of eighteenth-century German and European authors,[91] I would suggest that Cervantes probably had to be trained to act like a seventeenth-century Spanish author. This training would have included not only his own alphabetisation but also his induction into the socio-technological systems of print and patronage. It might be that any adequate analysis of the materialities of the author-function would have to take account of the interaction between textual and human bodies. The person of the author, I contend, is far from irrelevant to the author-function.[92]

IN THE NAME OF DIGNITY

Examined at the rhetorical level of Kant's 1785 essay, the author's name and related idiom of acting in one's or another's name disclose the importance of the personal author to Kant's argument for the wrongfulness of reprinting. These nominal figures, which drew upon Kant's secular humanist philosophy and concept of personal dignity, were the basis on which Kant defined and advanced a non-proprietary understanding of enlightenment authorship. Not so much the author-creator of contemporary copyright law bearing exploitable economic rights in their work, it was the dignified human being with an inalienable right in their own person and speech that defined the possessive determiner 'my' in Kant's account of literature.

Kant eschewed the proprietary idiom in his 1785 essay. As discussed in Chapter 3, Kant's proof opened with a scathing dismissal of the perspective on publishing as

[90] Roger Chartier, 'Publishing Cervantes', in *The Author's Hand and the Printer's Mind*, trans. Lydia G. Cochrane (Cambridge: Polity Press, 2014), 150–57.

[91] See Introduction and Chapters 1 and 3 for my prior discussions of Kittler.

[92] On a similar observation about the difficulty in separating the personal author from the discursive author in literary analysis, see Adrian Wilson, 'Foucault on the "Question of the Author": A Critical Exegesis', *The Modern Language Review* 99, no. 2 (2004): 339–63; which draws on Seán Burke, *The Death and Return of the Author: Criticism and Subjectivity in Barthes, Foucault and Derrida* (Edinburgh: Edinburgh University Press, 1992).

involving the exercise of some property right in a text, be it a handwritten manuscript or a print copy.[93] Not unlike Fichte, Kant did not consider it to be possible for the author to so alienate his thoughts as to give rise to any owned commodity.[94] Whereas Fichte still deployed the language of property and ownership (in the sense of literary property forever owned by the author whose mind had given form to it) to justify the wrongfulness of reprinting, Kant relied instead on a communicative account of publishing that utilised the rhetoric of names. 'But I believe there are grounds for regarding publication not as dealing with a commodity *in one's own name* [*in seinem eigenen Namen*], but as *carrying on an affair in the name of another* [*die Führung eines Geschäftes im Namen eines andern*], namely the author, and that in this way I can easily and clearly show the wrongfulness of unauthorized publication.'[95] Kant's construal of the book as a visual record of speech necessarily spoken in the author's name was the conceptual basis on which the rights of the legitimate publisher against unauthorised reprinting were vindicated.

The phrases 'in one's own name' and 'in the name of another' lent support to Kant's case for author's and publisher's rights through their semantic associations with theological and secular law. As recorded in the *Oxford English Dictionary*, the expression 'in — 's name (in the name of —)' has been a means of 'invoking or expressing reliance on or devotion to a divine being'[96] since at least the early medieval period. The earliest quotation consists of the Trinitarian formula of baptism from the Lindisfarne Gospels, which dates back to the early seventh century: '*Baptizantes eos in nomine patris et fili et spiritu sancti*: fulwuande hia in noma fadores & sunu & halges gastes.'[97] Relatedly, the phrase has been used as part of 'solemn adjurations',[98] where Christian figures ('God, Christ, the saints, the Devil or hell'[99]) or else personifications of more secular phenomena ('mercy',[100] 'goodness',[101] 'Wisdom'[102]) have been called to witness the situation at hand, attesting to its seriousness and importance. Whereas these definitions have relied on divine or abstract figures to authorise the pertinent context or action, the third sense of the phrase that most closely resembles its use in Kant's essay invokes the authority of human individuals, whether that for whom one is 'acting as deputy'[103] or oneself. To act 'in one's own name' is to act 'on one's own behalf, independently, without

93 Kant, 'On the Wrongfulness of Unauthorized Publication of Books (1785)', 29.

94 'Fichte: Proof of the Unlawfulness of Reprinting, Berlin (1793)', Primary Sources on Copyright (1450-1900), eds L. Bently & M. Kretschmer, accessed 9 September 2024, www.copyrighthistory.org/cam/tools/request/showRecord.php?id=record_d_1793. See Chapter 3.

95 Kant, 'On the Wrongfulness of Unauthorized Publication of Books (1785)', 29.

96 *Oxford English Dictionary*, 2nd ed. (Oxford: Oxford University Press, 2004), s.v. 'Name', P2a.

97 Ibid.

98 Ibid., P2b.

99 Ibid.

100 Ibid.

101 Ibid.

102 Ibid.

103 Ibid., P2d.

the authority of another'.[104] Previously dependent on theological figures of authority, the individual is now capable of authorising themselves to act in some manner, and of authorising another to act on their behalf. Notwithstanding such a definitional claim to self-sufficiency and independence, the textual examples given have tended to suppose the existence of some underpinning socio-juridical order that legitimates the said individuals as proper name bearers: 'To sue an Action of dette in his own name' (1444)[105]; 'You who in the name of the rest were Solliciters in this business' (1631).[106] Similarly, Kant grounded his agential account of the publisher in what Kant considered to be the properly juridical understanding of the author as a rights-bearing individual 'with an innate right in his own person'.[107] From the personhood of the author extended the author's 'inalienable right . . . always *himself* to speak through anyone else, the right, that is, that no one may deliver the same speech to the public other than in his (the author's) name'.[108] Kant noted that with the author's right in relation to the book came at least three obligations: the author '[was] bound as if he were doing it [i.e., publishing the book] himself'[109]; the publisher who had been contractually empowered to relay this speech to the public must fulfil this obligation, even after the author's death; and the unauthorised printer was barred from reprinting the book, the doing of which wronged both the publisher and author. Thus, a system of rights and obligations surrounding the person of the author purportedly underpinned, structured and ratified Kant's definition of publishing. By the essay's conclusion, Kant would align his case against wrongful reprinting with the Roman legal tradition, suggesting that it extended from the latter: 'If the idea of publication of a book as such, on which this is based, were firmly grasped and (as I flatter myself it could be) elaborated with the requisite eloquence of Roman legal scholarship, complaints against unauthorised publishers could indeed be taken to court without it being necessary first to wait for a new law.'[110] First semantically authorising Kant's account, the theological inheritance of naming soon ushered in and subsisted alongside the latter's secular perspective on print publishing and its involved persons.

Kant's proposed system of rights and obligations with respect to publishing, which affirmed the personhood and authority of the author, cohered with his preceding account of enlightenment as involving the public use of reason: that is, the exercise of 'an unrestricted freedom to make use of his own reason and to speak in his own

[104] Ibid.

[105] Ibid. The quotation is from *Rolls of Parliament* (*Rotuli parliamentorum*), 1278–1503 (1761–77).

[106] Ibid. The quotation is from William Gouge, *Gods Three Arrowes: Plague, Famine, Sword, in Three Treatises* (London: George Miller, 1631).

[107] Kant, 'On the Wrongfulness of Unauthorized Publication of Books (1785)', 35.

[108] Ibid.

[109] Ibid., 32.

[110] Ibid. For an account of Kant's discussion of the mandate and how far it could be said to derive from Roman law, see Alain Pottage, 'Literary Materiality', in *Routledge Handbook of Law and Theory*, ed. Andreas Philippopoulos-Mihalopoulos (London: Routledge, 2019), 409–29.

person'[111] before 'the entire public of the *world of readers*'.[112] As noted in Chapter 1's review of Kantian copyright scholarship, it is possible to see Kant's account of author's and publisher's rights as the legal arrangement to protect the 'communicative freedom'[113] of persons (in late eighteenth-century Germany, and perhaps even today), including both the right to speak publicly and to do so in one's capacity as a rational being unencumbered by civil or religious duties. The two main examples Kant gave of speakers divided in their capacities as (passive) institutional subjects and (active) rational discussants were those of the clergyman and the citizen.[114] As employee of the church, the clergyman was bound to instruct his congregation according to the church's teachings. Similarly, as legal (and, in eighteenth-century Germany, monarchical) subject, the citizen was obligated to obey the prevailing laws. But neither position should prevent the individual from critiquing the doctrines and practices in their capacity as scholar addressing the public by one's writings. The authority to reason publicly derived from no higher source than the very dignity of the person: the '*government* ... finds it profitable to itself to treat the human being, *who is now more than a machine*, in keeping with his dignity'.[115] Personal dignity, which in Kant's moral philosophy was inseparable from the rationality of persons,[116] acted as the common basis that founded both enlightenment practice and the legal arrangement that secured it. As Barron has suggested, Kant's proposed regime of rights for publishers and authors promoted the public use of reason by ensuring the continuing willingness of publishers to purchase authorial manuscripts for profitable printing.[117] Presenting the author as an authoritative figure capable of authorising the public communication of the author's speech – that is, the printing of a book by which a speech to the public was made 'simply and solely in the author's name'[118] – could be situated within and alongside Kant's critical humanist philosophy, supporting and deriving support from it. Naming authors as bearers of dignity at the heart of enlightenment practice was the rhetorical strategy by which Kant advanced his account of enlightenment authorship.

KANT QUA MEDIA THEORIST AND PRACTITIONER

Beyond the rhetorical significance of names in enlightenment authorship, Kant understood the printing of authorial names in publications to be the material basis on which authors could be made responsible for their public speech. It is this idiom of authorial responsibility, I suggest, that distinguishes Kant's account of authorship

[111] Kant, 'An Answer to the Question: What Is Enlightenment? (1784)', 19.
[112] Ibid., 18.
[113] Barron, 'Kant, Copyright and Communicative Freedom', 39.
[114] Kant, 'An Answer to the Question: What Is Enlightenment? (1784)', 18–22.
[115] Ibid., 22.
[116] See Kant, 'Groundwork for the Metaphysics of Morals (1785)', 73.
[117] Barron, 'Kant, Copyright and Communicative Freedom', 34.
[118] Kant, 'On the Wrongfulness of Unauthorized Publication of Books (1785)', 30.

from that of copyright law. Kant advocated for onymous publishing: the actual affixing of authorial names to works. In his March 1795 letter to Friedrich Schiller, Kant advised Schiller to disclose the names of the authors who contributed to *Die Horen*, a newly launched monthly literary magazine edited by the latter.[119] In an earlier letter enclosed with two issues of the periodical, Schiller had asked Kant to contribute to it.[120] Instead of printing the authorial name on each piece constitutive of each issue of *Die Horen*, Schiller released a list of contributors to the periodical in his opening editorial foreword (see Figure 4.1).[121] Included in the name list was Fichte, who had not only contributed a piece to the first issue of *Die Horen* but also written to Kant supporting Schiller's request.[122] Schiller's decision to publish individually authored writings as the undifferentiated output of a 'society' [*Gesellschaft*] involved in the making of the periodical cohered with his aim of 'combining several of the most deserving writers in Germany into one continuous work'.[123] While politely declining to contribute to the periodical, Kant suggested that the periodical was better off disclosing the authorial identity of each piece on the grounds of promoting individual accountability and meeting the demands of the reading public: 'I feel that it may harm your magazine not to have the authors sign their names, to make themselves thus responsible for their considered opinions; the reading public is very eager to know who they are.'[124]

In Kant's 1785 description of the publishing apparatus, the author was identified as the speaker who, though dependent on the publisher and the print machinery, was ultimately responsible for the speech relayed in and by the book. Authorised to relay the speech in the author's name, the publisher was not responsible for the speech's content: 'if he can do something only in another's name, he carries on this affair in such a way that by it the other is bound as if he were doing it himself'.[125] Notice that

[119] Immanuel Kant, 'To Friedrich Schiller, March 30, 1795', in *Correspondence*, trans. Arnulf Zweig (New York: Cambridge University Press, 1999), 497–98. The first issue of the periodical was published on 10 December 1794: see 'Die Horen', Friedrich Schiller Archiv, accessed 9 September 2024, www.friedrich-schiller-archiv.de/schriften/horen/.

[120] See Kant, 'To Friedrich Schiller, March 30, 1795', 498, editorial endnote 1.

[121] For a digitised version of the first volume of *Die Horen*, see Wikimedia Commons contributors, "File:Schiller Die Horen 1-1795.pdf," *Wikimedia Commons*, https://commons.wikimedia.org/w/index.php?title = File:Schiller_Die_Horen_1-1795.pdf&oldid = 499068440 (accessed 9 September 2024).
https://upload.wikimedia.org/wikipedia/commons/6/65/Schiller_Die_Horen_1-1795.pdf

[122] See Johann Gottlieb Fichte, 'Über Belebung und Erhöhung des reinen Interesse für Wahrheit.', Friedrich Schiller Archiv, 17 September 2013, www.friedrich-schiller-archiv.de/die-horen/die-horen-1795-stueck-1/iv-ueber-belebung-und-erhoehung-reinen-interesse-fuer-wahrheit/ (accessed 9 September 2024). On Fichte's letter to Kant, see Kant, 'To Friedrich Schiller, March 30, 1795', 498, editorial endnote 1.

[123] Friedrich Schiller, 'Vorwort', Friedrich Schiller Archiv, 17 September 2013, www.friedrich-schiller-archiv.de/die-horen/die-horen-1795-stueck-1/vorwort/ (accessed 9 September 2024); my translation.

[124] Kant, 'To Friedrich Schiller, March 30, 1795', 498.

[125] Kant, 'On the Wrongfulness of Unauthorized Publication of Books (1785)', 32.

VIII [12]

Zeiten zu erscheinen bestimmt ist, Vortreflichkeit im Einzelnen mit Abwechslung im Ganzen zu verbinden.

Folgende Schriftsteller werden an dieser Monatschrift Antheil nehmen:

Herr Hauptmann von Archenholz in Hamburg.
Seine Erzbischöffl. Gnaden Herr Coadjutor von Mainz
Freyherr von Dalberg in Erfurt.
Hr. Professor Engel aus Berlin.
— D. Erhardt in Nürnberg.
— Professor Fichte in Jena.
— von Funk in Dresden.
— Professor Garve in Breslau.
— Kriegsrath Genz in Berlin.
— Canonicus Gleim in Halberstadt.
— Geheimer Rath von Göthe in Weimar.
— D. Gros in Göttingen.
— Vice-Consistorial-Präsident Herder in Weimar.
— Hirt in Rom.
— Professor Hufeland in Jena.
— Legations-Rath von Humbold aus Berlin.
— Oberbergmeister von Humbold in Bayreuth.
— Geheimer Rath Jacobi in Düsseldorf.
— Hofrath Matthison in der Schweiz.
— Professor Meyer in Weimar.

FIGURE 4.1 List of contributors in Schiller's foreword to the first issue of *Die Horen*.

[13] IX

Hr. Hofrath Pfeffel in Colmar.
— Hofrath Schiller in Jena.
— Schlegel in Amsterdam.
— Hofrath Schütz in Jena.
— Hofrath Schulz in Mietau.
— Professor Woltmann in Jena.

Da sich übrigens die hier erwähnte Societät keineswegs als geschlossen betrachtet, so wird jedem deutschen Schriftsteller, der sich den nothwendig gefundenen Bedingungen des Instituts zu unterwerfen geneigt ist, zu jeder Zeit die Theilnahme daran offen stehen. Auch soll jedem, der es verlangt, verstattet seyn, anonym zu bleiben, weil man bey Aufnahme der Beyträge nur auf den Gehalt und nicht auf den Stempel sehen wird. Aus diesem Grunde, und um die Freyheit der Critik zu befördern, wird man sich erlauben, von einer allgemeinen Gewohnheit abzugehen, und bey den einzelnen Aufsätzen die Nahmen ihrer Verfasser, bis zum Ablauf eines jeden Jahrgangs verschweigen, welches der Leser sich um so eher gefallen lassen kann, da ihn diese Anzeige schon im Ganzen mit denselben bekannt macht.

Jena, den 10. Dec. 1794.

Schiller.

FIGURE 4.1 *(cont.)*

in Kant's later advice to Schiller, the author was similarly seen to be the personal speaker accountable for the opinions expressed in the periodical. Crucially, Kant identified the practice of having authors affix their names to their respective textual contributions, 'to have the authors sign their names',[126] to be the means by which authors were held responsible for their texts. Indicating the authorial name within the individual text was seen to be the technique by which accountability for the text was ensured. Kant accepted the practice to be a way of enforcing the borders of each text and individualising each contribution as a distinct speech traceable to some authorising person. Well before Foucault and Chartier, Kant understood the authorial name to be the material means of implementing the author-function.

Other than evincing the author's recognition of the materiality of the author-function, Kant's letter to Schiller recorded the autographic signing of Kant's authorial name. To be sure, Foucault did not consider private letters to be material forms organised around the figure of the author: unlike an essay or a book, 'a private letter may have a signatory, but it does not have an author'.[127] Yet, it has been a practice for the private correspondence of writers and other intellectuals to be later made public in the form of the printed book, which attests to the fluidity of texts as they migrate between genres, media and forms across time, potentially attracting and executing the author-function. In the case of Kant, it was after the author's death that his epistolary communications with other participants in the German print machinery and book trade came to be compiled and published as printed books.[128] The presentation of Kant's private letters to the public had not been authorised by Kant.[129] A print translation of Kant's letter to Schiller may be found in *Immanuel Kant: Correspondence* (1999), a selection of letters pertinent to philosophy, similarly published in *The Cambridge Edition of The Works of Immanuel Kant*.[130] At the bottom of the letter, typographically centred and split into two lines, is the author's sign-off: 'Your most devoted, loyal servant / I. Kant'.[131] In the original letter, Kant's signature served to identify the letter's sender through the abbreviated proper name and its handwritten form, whilst also forming part of the sender's best wishes to the recipient and affirming their friendship.[132] But Kant's name also acted as one of the mechanically – and, later, digitally – reproducible forms by which particular texts were included in the author's oeuvre.

126 Kant, 'To Friedrich Schiller, March 30, 1795', 498.
127 Foucault, 'What Is an Author?', 1977, 124.
128 On the posthumous publication of Kant's letters, see the editor's introduction to Immanuel Kant, *Correspondence*, ed. and trans. Arnulf Zweig (New York: Cambridge University Press, 1999), 2–3.
129 Ibid.
130 Kant, 'To Friedrich Schiller, March 30, 1795'.
131 Ibid., 498.
132 Ibid. The preceding part of the paragraph reads: 'And so, dearest sir, I wish your talents and your worthy objectives the strength, health, and long life they deserve, and also the friendship, with which you wish to honor one who is ever—.'

If we return to Kant's essay as it was originally published in the May 1785 issue of the *Berlinische Monatsschrift* (and subsequently bound in the fifth volume of the periodical), we shall find that the text concludes with a similar imprint of the author's name (see Figure 4.2). At the last line of the essay, near the bottom-right of the leaf bearing the page number '417', we find 'I. Kant' printed in the same Breitkopf Fraktur typeface in which the essay was set. Notice that both the alphabetical form of the author's name and its placement at the end of the text are all but identical to those of the letter. Despite the printed format, it is as if Kant had signed the essay. In both instances the author's name acts to identify the body of text that came before as a distinct record of a speech for which the named author is held accountable. Having received and read the letter signed by Kant, Schiller could write back to Kant and resume the 'literary discussions'[133] with which Kant had been 'delighted'[134] to engage. Readers of Kant's essay in the *Berlinische Monatsschrift* could comment on the argument in some format, whether in a private letter or in some publication like the periodical. For instance, Fichte could claim in a footnote to his own essay to have written it before reading Kant's and, having read it, to find it 'very encouraging to find [himself] on the same road as [Kant]'[135] (even though their arguments substantially differed).[136] Set in Breitkopf Fraktur, Kant's signature in the essay underwent depersonalisation in that it was no longer handwritten by the signatory but rather a product of the printing press operated by other workmen. Nonetheless, its newly acquired mechanical reproducibility within and alongside the essay facilitated the essay's dissemination to the public as a text with a known author.

In its categorisation of works under a single author, the authorial name 'I. Kant' might well have been involved in the propagation of proprietary authorship, both in and beyond Kant's time. The absence of copyright legislation in Germany until 1837 would not have precluded the existence of the perspective on authors as owners and creators of their works before then.[137] Though it was in eighteenth-century Britain where the earliest copyright statute arose and the ensuing literary property debate involving London and Scottish booksellers took place,[138] the

[133] Kant, 'To Friedrich Schiller, March 30, 1795', 497.

[134] Ibid.

[135] 'Fichte: Proof of the Unlawfulness of Reprinting, Berlin (1793)', 472.

[136] See Chapter 3's discussion of Fichte.

[137] See 'Prussian Copyright Act of 1837', Primary Sources on Copyright (1450-1900), eds L. Bently & M. Kretschmer, accessed 9 September 2024, www.copyrighthistory.org/cam/tools/request/showRecord.php?id = record_d_1837a.

[138] 'Statute of Anne' ('An Act for the Encouragement of Learning, by Vesting the Copies of Printed Books in the Authors or Purchasers of such Copies, during the Times therein mentioned)', Primary Sources on Copyright (1450-1900), eds L. Bently & M. Kretschmer, accessed 9 September 2024, www.copyrighthistory.org/cam/tools/request/showRecord.php?id = record_uk_1710. See also Rose, *Authors and Owners*. Chartier has suggested that the proprietary understanding of authorship preceded the Statute of Anne, appearing in Ben Johnson's and John Milton's contracts: see Chartier, 'Foucault's Chiasmus: Authorship between Science and Literature in the Seventeenth and Eighteenth Centuries', 18–20.

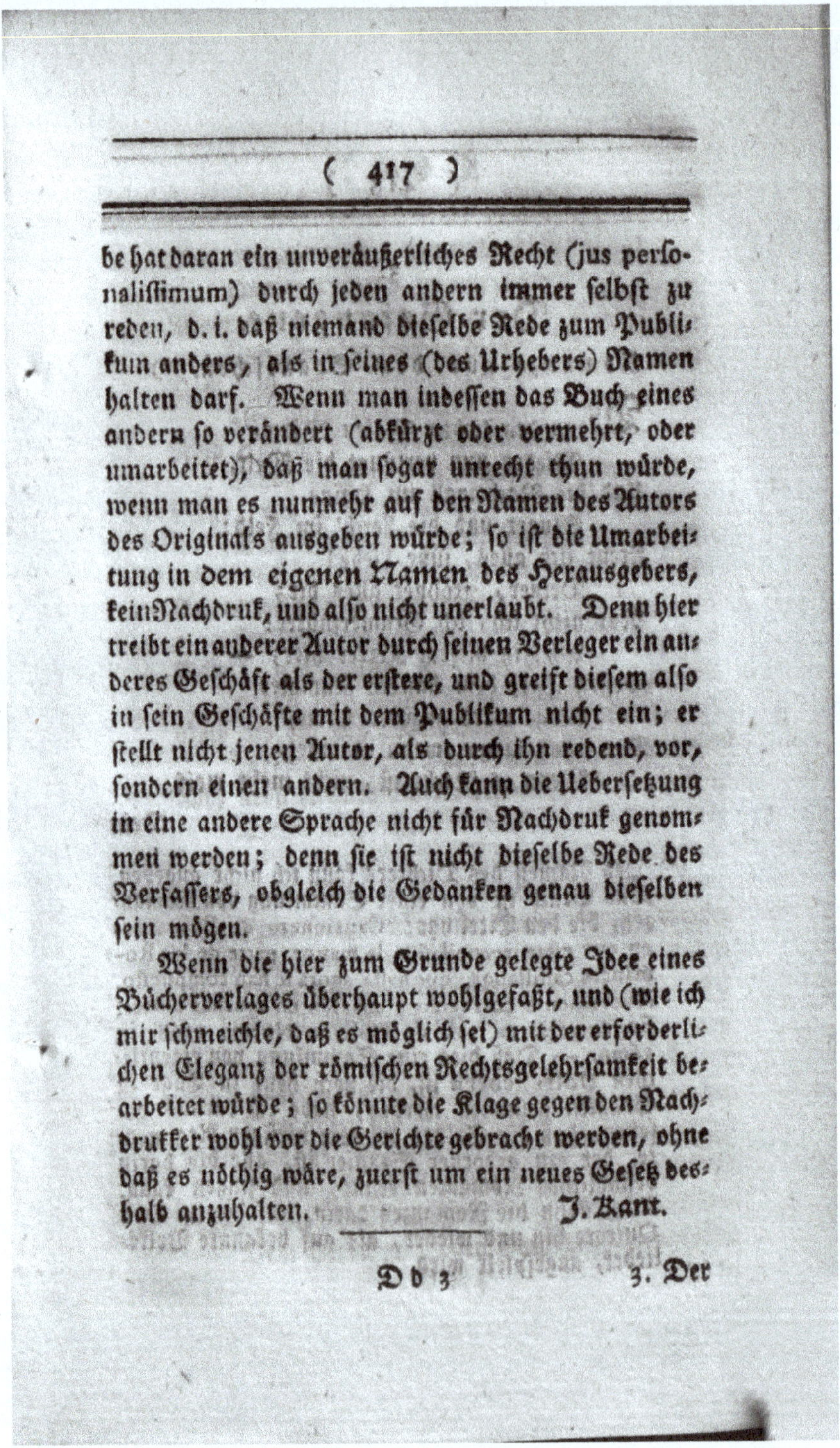

(417)

de hat daran ein unveräußerliches Recht (jus personalissimum) durch jeden andern immer selbst zu reden, d. i. daß niemand dieselbe Rede zum Publikum anders, als in seines (des Urhebers) Namen halten darf. Wenn man indessen das Buch eines andern so verändert (abkürzt oder vermehrt, oder umarbeitet), daß man sogar unrecht thun würde, wenn man es nunmehr auf den Namen des Autors des Originals ausgeben würde; so ist die Umarbeitung in dem eigenen Namen des Herausgebers, kein Nachdruk, und also nicht unerlaubt. Denn hier treibt ein anderer Autor durch seinen Verleger ein anderes Geschäft als der erstere, und greift diesem also in sein Geschäfte mit dem Publikum nicht ein; er stellt nicht jenen Autor, als durch ihn redend, vor, sondern einen andern. Auch kann die Uebersetzung in eine andere Sprache nicht für Nachdruk genommen werden; denn sie ist nicht dieselbe Rede des Verfassers, obgleich die Gedanken genau dieselben sein mögen.

Wenn die hier zum Grunde gelegte Idee eines Bücherverlages überhaupt wohlgefaßt, und (wie ich mir schmeichle, daß es möglich sei) mit der erforderlichen Eleganz der römischen Rechtsgelehrsamkeit bearbeitet würde; so könnte die Klage gegen den Nachdrukker wohl vor die Gerichte gebracht werden, ohne daß es nöthig wäre, zuerst um ein neues Gesetz deshalb anzuhalten. I. Kant.

Dd 3 3. Der

FIGURE 4.2 Last page of Kant's 1785 essay.

contemporaneous circulation in Germany of certain cultural texts that legitimated and rhetorically echoed the British literary property debate suggests that there probably was a 'transnational flow of ideas in this period'.[139] Edward Young's *Conjectures on Original Composition in a Letter to the Author of Sir Charles Grandison* (1759), whose account of the author as creator, genius and owner of property in their original work has been observed to underpin and anticipate copyright law's account of the proprietary author.[140] For Young, authorship was indissociable from genius and ownership: the original work 'rises spontaneously from the vital root of Genius',[141] organically extending from the writer himself; against the backdrop of merely imitative writings, the writer's original works 'will stand distinguished; his the sole Property of them; which Property alone can confer the noble title of an *Author*'.[142] Young's work did not receive much attention in England when it was first published in 1759, and so was of little direct influence on the contemporaneous literary property debate.[143] Nonetheless, Young's 'mystification of the author ... served the purposes of the ultimate proprietors of copyrights, the booksellers'.[144] Recognising the nobility of authors as owners of literary property legitimated transfers of title to the booksellers for exploitation in the book trade. Other than supporting the debate's commodification of literature, Young's work acceded to the terms of the debate by deploying the property idiom relied upon by both the proponents and opponents of perpetual copyright at common law in the British debate.[145] As Woodmansee has noted, in contrast to its mild English reception, two translations of Young's book appeared in Germany within two years of its original publication, which had a 'profound impact'[146] on the German debate on the book between 1773 and 1794. Young's theory of the author as original genius might have shaped Fichte's view on the author's mind as that which granted singular form to ideas in the book, such form being inalienable property forever owned by

[139] Coombe, 'Challenging Paternity: Histories of Copyright', 421.

[140] Edward Young, *Conjectures on Original Composition: In a Letter to the Author of Sir Charles Grandison* (London: A. Millar and R. and J. Dodsley, 1759). See Woodmansee, 'The Genius and the Copyright', 430–31; Rose, *Authors and Owners*, 117–22. As discussed in Chapter 3, however, Mario Biagioli has sharply reinterpreted Fichtean genius as copyright's *pharmakon*: see Biagioli, Mario Biagioli, 'Genius against Copyright: Revisiting Fichte's Proof of the Illegality of Reprinting', *Notre Dame Law Review* 86, no. 5 (2011): 1847–68.

[141] Young, *Conjectures on Original Composition*, 12.

[142] Ibid., 54.

[143] See Woodmansee, 'The Genius and the Copyright', 430.

[144] Rose, *Authors and Owners*, 120.

[145] For a review of the arguments in the literary property debate other than Rose's, see Brad Sherman and Lionel Bently, *The Making of Modern Intellectual Property Law* (Cambridge: Cambridge University Press, 2003), 9–42.

[146] Woodmansee, 'The Genius and the Copyright: Economic and Legal Conditions of the Emergence of the "Author"', 430. For Woodmansee's overview of the debate, see Ibid., 440–48.

the author.[147] The criterion of inalienability, or the impossibility of appropriation, distinguishes Fichte's account of literary property from English accounts that drew on Locke's possessive individualism. Thus, the understanding of books as original creations of proprietary authors was likely to have been present in some form in late eighteenth-century Germany. The practice of affixing an authorial name to a text, which perceptually groups the text with the named author, may well have perpetuated the myth of proprietary authorship.

Despite its probable propagation of the proprietary paradigm, the material form and placement of 'I. Kant' in the *Berlinische Monatsschrift* also afforded and supported Kant's theorisation of the book in non-proprietary terms. Read alongside Kant's argument, the nominal peritexts in the periodical's front matter and its contributing texts supported Kant's ascription of responsibility for the latter to their authors. Included in the title pages of the fifth volume and the May 1785 issue were the names of the editor-publishers, 'F. Gedike und J. E. Biester' (see Figures 2.2 and 4.3). Their roles in editing and publishing the periodical was posited and foregrounded in both the title wording, 'Berlinische / Monatsschrift / herausgegeben / von / F. Gedike und J. E. Biester', and the preface to each issue. For instance, in the preface to the first issue, Gedike and Biester presented not only their 'plan'[148] for the periodical, including the types of contributions pertinent to 'pleasant instruction and useful enlightenment'[149] they would 'gratefully accept',[150] but also their projected publishing of six to seven pieces in each monthly issue. Not unlike Kant's, their names were printed at the end of the text as its speaker, though the line further specified their roles as editor-publishers, 'Die Herausgeber. G. u. B' (see Figure 4.4).[151] Read alongside these other nominal peritexts that assert and disclose the publishers' identities, 'I. Kant' affirmed Kant's characterisation of the printed book as a speech to the public made by the publisher 'in the author's name'.[152] In other words, the printed authorial name formed part of the material basis for Kant's communicative account of the book. The book could be imagined as consisting in a reflexive ventriloquy where the puppet-publisher disavowed his responsibility for the authorial speech he transmited precisely because the book bore the names of the two pertinent actors: 'Through me a writer will by means of letters have you informed of this or that, instruct you, and so forth. I am not responsible for anything, not even for the freedom which the author assumes to

[147] On the influence of Young on Fichte, see Ibid., 444–46. As discussed in Chapter 3, Fichte's account of literary property departs from the Anglo-American account in regarding it to be inalienable.

[148] For the preface of the first issue, see www.digitale-sammlungen.de/de/view/bsb10926840?q=%28Berlinische+Monatsschrift.+1.+1783%29&page=8,9 (accessed 9 September 2024); my translation.

[149] Ibid.

[150] Ibid.

[151] Ibid.

[152] Kant, 'On the Wrongfulness of Unauthorized Publication of Books (1785)', 30.

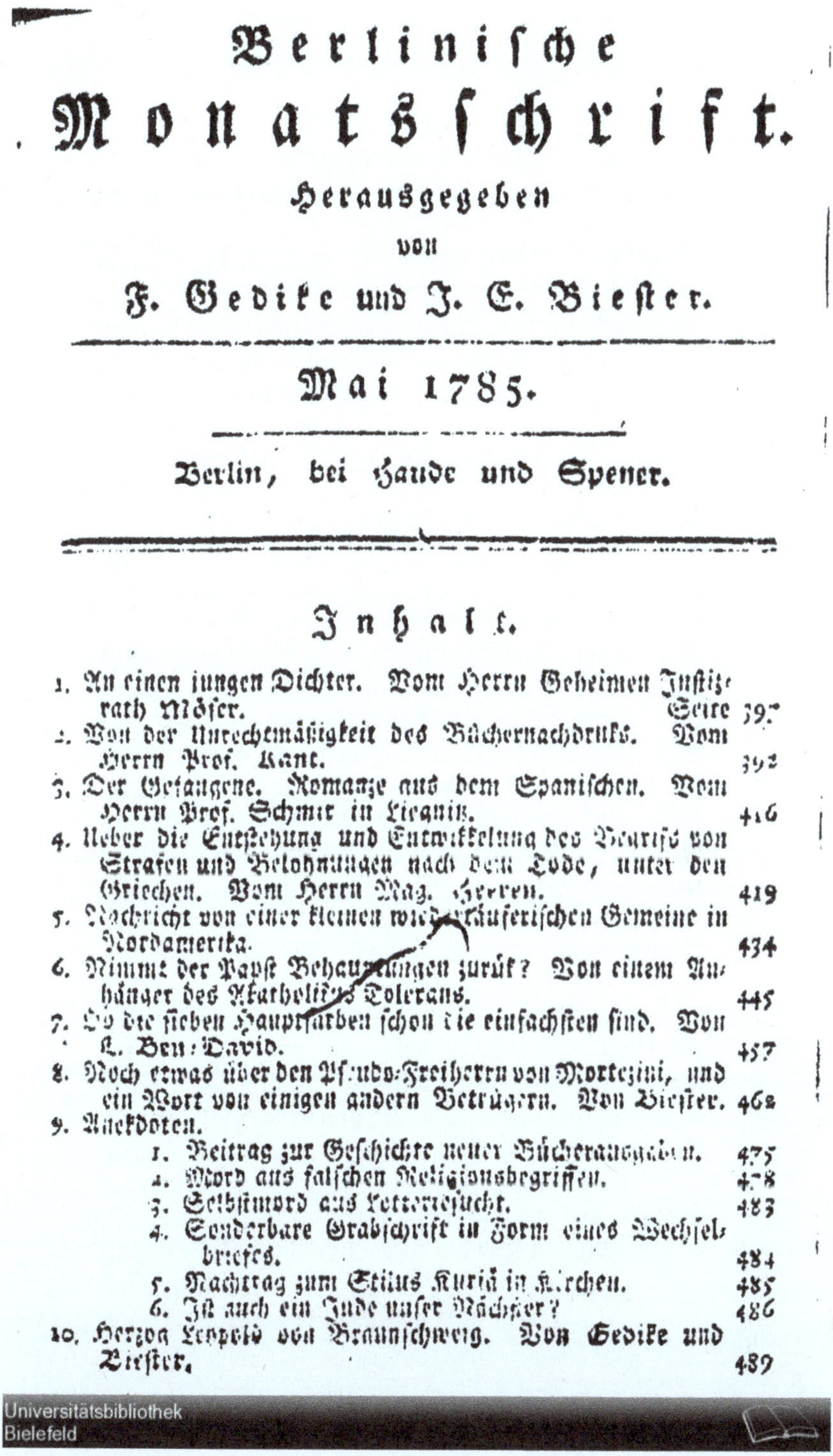

Berlinische
Monatsschrift.

Herausgegeben
von
F. Gedike und J. E. Biester.

Mai 1785.

Berlin, bei Haude und Spener.

Inhalt.

1. An einen jungen Dichter. Vom Herrn Geheimen Justizrath Möser. Seite 397
2. Von der Unrechtmäßigkeit des Büchernachdruks. Vom Herrn Prof. Kant. 392
3. Der Gefangene. Romanze aus dem Spanischen. Vom Herrn Prof. Schmit in Liegnitz. 416
4. Ueber die Entstehung und Entwickelung des Begrifs von Strafen und Belohnungen nach dem Tode, unter den Griechen. Vom Herrn Mag. Herren. 419
5. Nachricht von einer kleinen wiedertäuferischen Gemeine in Nordamerika. 434
6. Nimmt der Papst Behauptungen zurük? Von einem Anhänger des Katholischen Tolerans. 445
7. Ob die sieben Hauptfarben schon die einfachsten sind. Von L. Ben-David. 457
8. Noch etwas über den Pseudo-Freiherrn von Mortczini, und ein Wort von einigen andern Betrügern. Von Biester. 462
9. Anekdoten.
   1. Beitrag zur Geschichte neuer Bücherausgaben. 475
   2. Mord aus falschen Religionsbegriffen. 478
   3. Selbstmord aus Lotteriesucht. 483
   4. Sonderbare Grabschrift in Form eines Wechselbriefes. 484
   5. Nachtrag zum Stilus Curiä in Kirchen. 485
   6. Ist auch ein Jude unser Nächster? 486
10. Herzog Leopold von Braunschweig. Von Gedike und Biester. 489

FIGURE 4.3 Title page of the May 1785 issue of the *Berlinische Monatsschrift*.

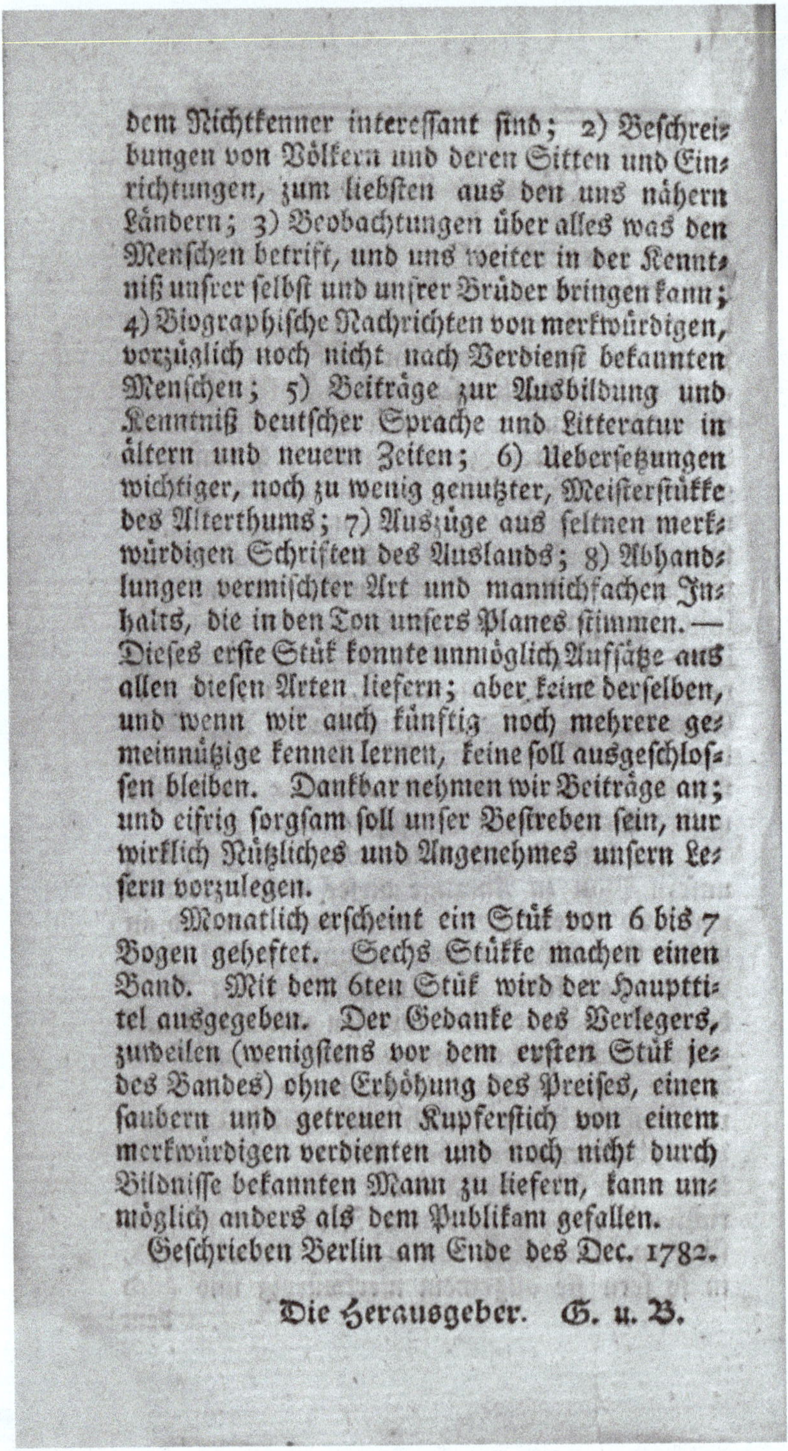

dem Nichtkenner interessant sind; 2) Beschreibungen von Völkern und deren Sitten und Einrichtungen, zum liebsten aus den uns nähern Ländern; 3) Beobachtungen über alles was den Menschen betrift, und uns weiter in der Kenntniß unsrer selbst und unsrer Brüder bringen kann; 4) Biographische Nachrichten von merkwürdigen, vorzüglich noch nicht nach Verdienst bekannten Menschen; 5) Beiträge zur Ausbildung und Kenntniß deutscher Sprache und Litteratur in ältern und neuern Zeiten; 6) Uebersetzungen wichtiger, noch zu wenig genutzter, Meisterstükke des Alterthums; 7) Auszüge aus seltnen merkwürdigen Schriften des Auslands; 8) Abhandlungen vermischter Art und mannichfachen Inhalts, die in den Ton unsers Planes stimmen.— Dieses erste Stük konnte unmöglich Aufsätze aus allen diesen Arten liefern; aber keine derselben, und wenn wir auch künftig noch mehrere gemeinnützige kennen lernen, keine soll ausgeschlossen bleiben. Dankbar nehmen wir Beiträge an; und eifrig sorgsam soll unser Bestreben sein, nur wirklich Nützliches und Angenehmes unsern Lesern vorzulegen.

Monatlich erscheint ein Stük von 6 bis 7 Bogen geheftet. Sechs Stükke machen einen Band. Mit dem 6ten Stük wird der Haupttitel ausgegeben. Der Gedanke des Verlegers, zuweilen (wenigstens vor dem ersten Stük jedes Bandes) ohne Erhöhung des Preises, einen saubern und getreuen Kupferstich von einem merkwürdigen verdienten und noch nicht durch Bildnisse bekannten Mann zu liefern, kann unmöglich anders als dem Publikum gefallen.

Geschrieben Berlin am Ende des Dec. 1782.

Die Herausgeber. G. u. B.

FIGURE 4.4 Last page of the editors' preface to the first issue of the *Berlinische Monatsschrift*.

speak publicly through me: I am only the medium by which it reaches you.'[153] With respect to Kant's 1785 essay, it was by means of the authorial name 'I. Kant' printed in the last line of the essay that responsibility for the essay qua speech was attributed to Kant.

It is my claim that Kant at once understood the medial-materiality of the printed book and insistently anchored it to the two involved persons of publisher and author. For Kant, the book was a visual-corporeal medium that depended on the manifold bodies of texts and humans for its making, distribution and use. Kant's description of the book as a 'mute instrument'[154] composed of 'letters',[155] along with his comments in *Der Streit der Fakultäten* ('The Conflict of Faculties') on typefaces such as Breitkopf Fraktur,[156] reflected his acute recognition of the book's opticality and artifice. At the same time, he declined to see it as some autonomous thing whose physical independence marked a space devoid of responsibility. Rather, aided by the convention of printing the names of the publisher and author on the book, Kant identified the publisher as a human 'medium' whose control of the publishing apparatus enabled the transmission of another's speech to the public, and the author as that human speaker accountable for the speech appearing in print. The objecthood of the book was, as it were, accompanied and ultimately circumscribed by the personal figures of the publisher and author and their perceived roles in producing it. Kant was a media theorist who recognised the dependence of authors on the print machinery, but also a humanist who affirmed human freedom and responsibility in his deployment of the authorial name.

Without delving into the personal and reputational reasons behind Kant's preference for onymous publishing,[157] let us note that Kant's attribution of responsibility for books (as printed matter and as speech) to publishers and authors in 1785 cohered with his epitextual observations about the burgeoning book trade and the ethics of authorship and publishing in the German Enlightenment. As discussed in Chapter 2, the phenomenon of print proliferation in eighteenth-century Germany, indexed in the catalogues of the Leipzig and Frankfurt book fairs and other quantitative records, gave rise to considerable anxiety amongst scholars and writers. In 1794 and 1795, the practices of indiscriminate reading and trifling chatter about books were condemned by critics as facets of a 'reading addiction'[158] and 'the plague

[153] Ibid.
[154] Ibid.
[155] Ibid.
[156] Kant, *The Conflict of the Faculties*, 209–13. See Chapter 3.
[157] Consider, for instance, his corroding relationship with Fichte indexed in his personal letters: see Kant, *Correspondence*. Kant only rarely published anonymously: see Steve Naragon, 'Chronology of Kant's Life', in *The Palgrave Kant Handbook*, ed. Matthew C. Altman (London: Palgrave Macmillan, 2017), xxxi–xliv.
[158] Johann Gottfried Hoche, *Vertraute Briefe über die jetzige Lesesucht und über den Einfluß derselben auf die Verminderung des häuslichen und öffentlichen Glücks* ('Intimate Letters: The Current Reading Addiction and Its Influence on the Reduction of Domestic and Public

of German literature'.[159] In the transcripts of Kant's *Vorlesungen über Philosophische Enzyklopädie* ('Lectures on the Philosophical Encyclopaedia) given sometime between 1767 and 1782,[160] Kant himself had described the reading public's excessive reading habits as a pathology, *Belesenheit*, a condition of overexposure to print without the requisite ability to separate the wheat from the chaff.[161] Accordingly, a book was first characterised as a threat to individual autonomy and the emancipatory practice of enlightenment in Kant's 1784 essay: 'If I have a book that understands for me, a spiritual advisor who has a conscience for, a spiritual advisor who has a conscience for me, a doctor who decides upon a regimen for me, and so forth, I need not trouble myself at all.'[162] For Kant, the surfeit of books, ceaselessly produced by the print machinery of the eighteenth century, was overwhelming the human being and preventing the use of one's own understanding to emerge from immaturity.

No less than authors who uncritically contributed to the clutter, publishers who financed and directed the assembly of books more for reasons of profit than for public enlightenment were censured by Kant. Unlike Kant's correspondence with Schiller, Kant's two letters addressed to Friedrich Nicolai entitled *Über die Buchmacherei* ('On Turning Out Books') (1798) were open letters made for the public's reading, first published as a pamphlet in Königsberg and then as part of a collection of Kant's shorter works in Leipzig and Jena in the same year.[163] As specified in the opening line identifying the addressee, each letter targeted one of two roles Nicolai played in the print machinery: the first reads, '*To Mr. Friedrich Nicolai, the author*'; the second, '*To Mr. Friedrich Nicolai, the publisher*'. With respect to the first, the very nomination of Nicolai as author might well have been derisive, for it was instead a text bearing Justus Möser's authorial name that

Happiness') (Hanover: Ritscher, 1794); translation from 'Proliferation', in *Interacting with Print: Elements of Reading in the Era of Print Saturation*, by The Multigraph Collective (Chicago: University of Chicago Press, 2018), 252.

159 Johann Georg Heinzmann, *Appel an Meine Nation: Über Die Pest Der Deutschen Literatur* ('A Plea to My Nation: On the Plague of German Literature') (Bern, 1795).

160 On some uncertainties surrounding when the lectures were delivered, see Manfred Kuehn, 'Dating Kant's "Vorlesungen über Philosophische Enzyklopädie"', *Kant -Studien* 74, no. 3 (1983): 302–13.

161 Immanuel Kant, 'Vorlesungen Über Philosophische Enzyklopädie', in *Gesammelte Schriften*, ed. Königlich Preussischen Akademie der Wissenschaften (Berlin: Walter de Gruyter, 1902), 29:30. See Chad Wellmon, 'Kant's Critical Technology', in *Organizing Enlightenment: Information Overload and the Invention of the Modern Research University* (Baltimore: Johns Hopkins University Press, 2015), 123–24.

162 Kant, 'An Answer to the Question: What Is Enlightenment? (1784)', 17. See Wellmon, 'Kant's Critical Technology', 124; Pasanek and Wellmon, 'Enlightenment, Some Assembly Required'.

163 Immanuel Kant, 'On Turning out Books: Two Letters to Mr. Friedrich Nicolai from Immanuel Kant', in *Practical Philosophy* (New York: Cambridge University Press, 1996), 617–27. For an account of the context surrounding these letters, see the editor's introduction: Ibid., 619–20. For a more extensive treatment of Nicolai's involvement in the eighteenth-century book trade, see Selwyn, *Everyday Life in the German Book Trade*.

occasioned Kant's reply. Möser was a German jurist and writer who contributed the letter to a young poet that immediately preceded Kant's 1785 essay in the same periodical issue (see Figure 2.1). In 1796, two years after Möser's death, the fragment *Über Theorie und Praxis* ('On Theory and Praxis') appeared in a posthumous collection of Möser's writings published by Nicholai.[164] Alluding in its title to another of Kant's essays first published in the *Berlinische Monatsschrift, Über den Gemeinspruch: Das mag in der Theorie richtig sein, taugt aber nicht für die Praxis* ('On the Common Saying: That May Be True in Theory, but It Is of No Use in Practice') (1793),[165] Möser's fragment opposed Kant's trenchant critique of hereditary nobility. Whereas Kant had argued in the essay that no people would freely agree to be ruled by higher fellow subjects with inherited prerogatives ('the hereditary privilege of ruling rank'[166]), Möser wrote a fictional counternarrative where persons consented to serfdom to meet their practical needs.[167] In the letter, Kant reasserted the primacy of reason as the faculty and principle that governed the question of which political arrangement people ought to agree to over and above any pragmatic or other empirical consideration.

> For this whole problem is to be judged (in the *Metaphysical First Principles of the Doctrine of Right*, p. 192), as a question belonging to the *doctrine of right*: whether the sovereign is *entitled* to found a middle estate between itself and the remaining citizens of the state; and hence the verdict is then that the people will not and cannot rationally resolve on such a subordinate authority, because otherwise it would be subject to the whims and crotchets of a subject that itself needs to be governed, which contradicts itself.[168]

After having '*parodied* into ridicule'[169] Möser's counternarrative, Kant concluded by returning to Nicolai as the individual most implicated by his critique. 'Mr Friedrich Nicolai, therefore, has come to misfortune with his interpretation and defense in the alleged concern of another (namely, Möser)'.[170] By using the adjective 'alleged' to describe Möser's fragment, Kant casted doubt on the authenticity of its authorship, suggesting that Nicolai himself might have written or substantially rewritten it while

[164] Justus Möser, *Vermischten Schriften*, ed. Friedrich Nicolai (Friedrich Nicolai, 1796). See the editor's introduction, Kant, 'On Turning out Books: Two Letters to Mr. Friedrich Nicolai from Immanuel Kant', 619.

[165] See Immanuel Kant, 'On the Common Saying: That May Be Correct in Theory, But It Is No Use in Practice (1793)', in *Practical Philosophy*, ed. Paul Guyer and Allen W. Wood, trans. Mary J. Gregor (Cambridge: Cambridge University Press, 1996), 279–309.

[166] Ibid., 297.

[167] For an account of the differences between Kant's and Möser's positions, see Jonathan B. Knudsen, *Justus Möser and the German Enlightenment* (Cambridge: Cambridge University Press, 1986), 176–86.

[168] Kant, 'On Turning out Books: Two Letters to Mr. Friedrich Nicolai from Immanuel Kant', 623–24.

[169] Ibid., 625.

[170] Ibid.

misattributing it to his late friend. Kant noted in the beginning of the letter the ambiguous origins of the fragment, it having been 'communicated to the latter [Mr. Nicolai] in manuscript, and as Mr. Nicolai assumed that Möser himself would have communicated it if he had brought it entirely to an end'.[171]

Read alongside these comments implicating Nicolai despite the letter's focus on the fragment bearing Möser's name, Kant's identification of Nicolai as author in the addressee line could be Kant's way of making the latter accountable for a speech made in Möser's name, but in fact was simply his own. For Kant, the printed authorial name had been misused by Nicolai to disavow himself of responsibility for the text, and was now redeployed by Kant to hold Nicolai to account before the reading public. The nomination may also be understood as Kant's negative appraisal of Nicolai's authorship to be merely derivative or imitative. Not only was Nicolai's 'completion' of Möser's work poor in the weakness of its argument, but Nicolai also proved incapable or afraid of exercising his own reason to produce any scholarly contribution to public enlightenment. His 'interpretation and defense'[172] of Möser was more a cowardly act of mimicry than a scholar's use of reason. In the terms of Kant's enlightenment essay, Nicolai remained mired in a '*self-incurred*'[173] state of immaturity, defined by a 'lack in resolution and courage to use [his own understanding] without direction from another'.[174] Under this latter reading, 'author' was deployed ironically to disclose and deride the insufficiency of Nicolai's contribution. In both instances, regardless of any personal feud Kant might have had with Nicolai,[175] the printed authorial name was understood by Kant to be materially connected to the assumption and attribution of scholarly responsibility in the practice of enlightenment.

Whereas the first letter dealt with the poverty of Nicolai's authorship, the second dwelt on the profitability of literary publishing that Nicolai had, on Kant's view, prioritised over other societal gains. A neat distinction on which Kant relied to criticise Nicolai's commercialism and at the same time clarify the ethics of publishing was that between '*prudence in publication*'[176] and '*soundness of publication*'.[177] A 'self-seeking'[178] publisher such as Nicolai pandered to and shaped the 'market'[179] and 'fashion'[180] of the book trade without regard for the 'inner worth and content of

[171] Ibid., 623.
[172] Ibid., 624.
[173] Kant, 'An Answer to the Question: What Is Enlightenment? (1784)', 17.
[174] Ibid.
[175] On Kant's displeasure with Nicolai's assessment of Kant's work, see the translator's introduction to Kant, 'On Turning out Books: Two Letters to Mr. Friedrich Nicolai from Immanuel Kant', 619–20. See also Selwyn, *Everyday Life in the German Book Trade*, 21–22.
[176] Kant, 'On Turning out Books: Two Letters to Mr. Friedrich Nicolai from Immanuel Kant', 626.
[177] Ibid.
[178] Ibid.
[179] Ibid.
[180] Ibid.

the commodities he publishes'.[181] As a result, the reading public was allowed to remain 'deceived'[182] and blind to the importance of theoretical works that sought to clarify and demonstrate 'judgements of reason'.[183] For Kant, it was instead the publication of 'labors in the sciences which [were] all the more serious and well-grounded'[184] than the farcical commodities turned out by Nicolai that truly mattered. By Kant's logic, it was Kant's Königsberg publisher, Friedrich Nicolovius, who instead materially advanced the German enlightenment by publishing the two open letters and Kant's other works such as *Die Metaphysik der Sitten* ('The Metaphysics of Morals').

Consistent with Kant's essays in the *Berlinische Monatsschrift*, the two open letters concluded with the printed authorial name 'I. Kant', at once identifying Kant as their responsible 'speaker' and affirming Kant's 1785 understanding of the ethics of authorship and its material basis. The proper names 'Justus Möser' and 'Friedrich Nicolai', printed on Möser's posthumous collection as the names of the author and publisher respectively, allowed Kant to identify and hold accountable the 'speaker (s)' whose speech and action, in his view, obstructed the advance of enlightenment. If their texts and activities were to contribute to the process of enlightenment, they had to be critically appropriated as materials with which to clarify the primacy of reason in questions of politics, authorship and publishing. Kant's own authorial name, 'I. Kant', rendered himself accountable for his 1798 intervention into the discourse while also inviting eighteenth-century German readers and us today to read those letters alongside his periodical essays and other writings. Those interventions reflected Kant's media-theoretical understanding of the authorial name as the material means by which responsibility was assumed and ascribed to individual participants in the German Enlightenment. The public use of reason materially depended on the printing of authorial names in textual publications. Rather than simply consolidating the myth of proprietary authorship (though that might well have been one of its effects), the authorial name was bound up in an ethics of authorship that Kant understood to be central to enlightenment practice.

KANT QUA PROPRIETARY AUTHOR?

Kant's argument for the wrongfulness of reprinting did not prevent his works from being reprinted and sold by illegitimate publishers and booksellers. In 1793, there appeared in Frankfurt and Leipzig an unauthorised edition of Kant's writings, *Zerstreute Aufsätze* ('Scattered Essays'), which included versions of both his 1784 and 1785 essays from the *Berlinische Monatsschrift* (see Figures 4.5 and

[181] Ibid.
[182] Ibid., 627.
[183] Ibid.
[184] Ibid.

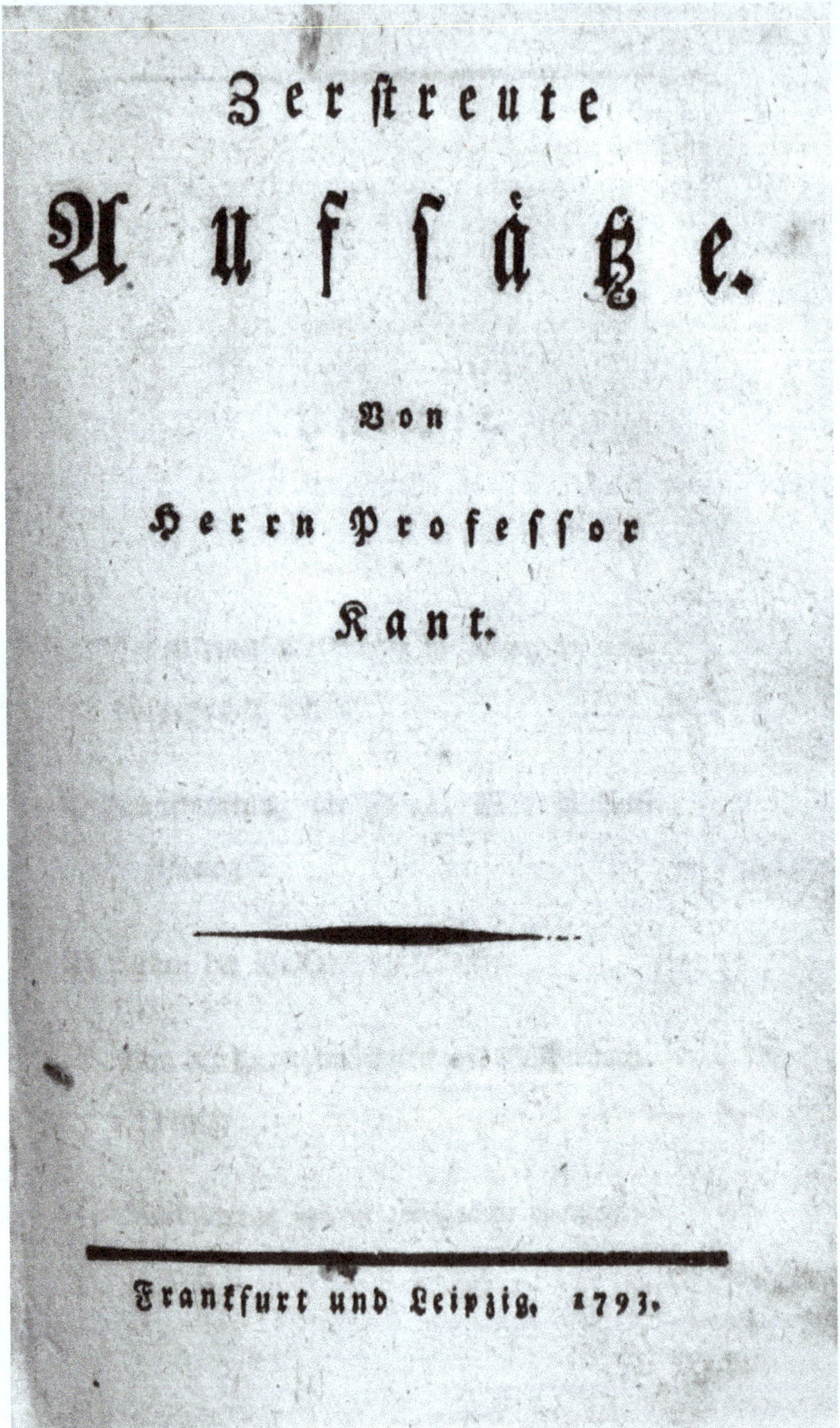

Zerstreute

Aufsätze.

Von

Herrn Professor

Kant.

Frankfurt und Leipzig, 1793.

FIGURE 4.5 Title page of Kant's *Zerstreute Aufsätze*.

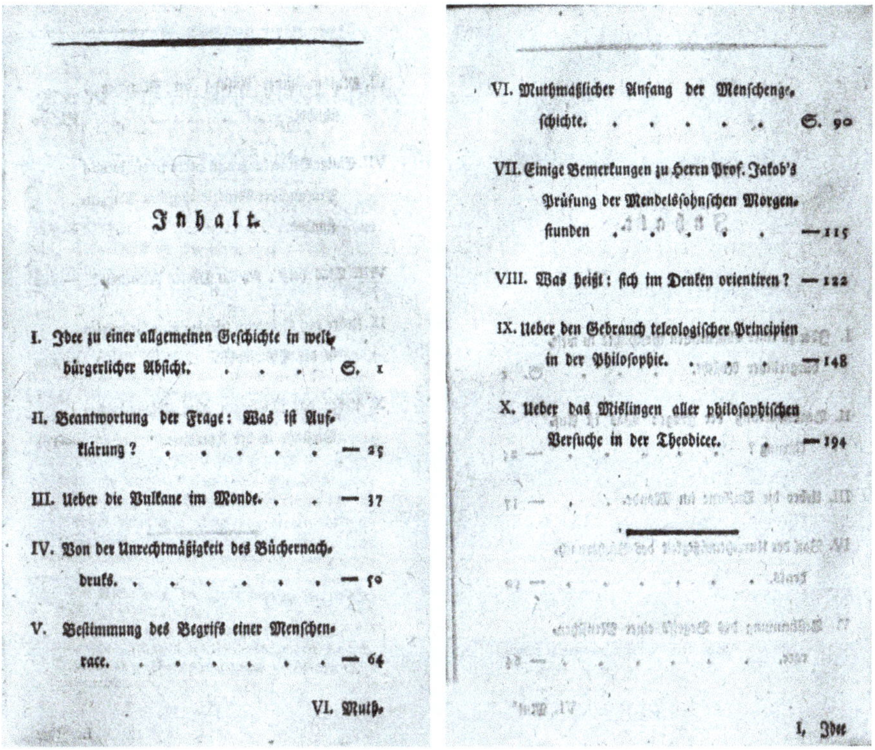

Inhalt.

I. Idee zu einer allgemeinen Geschichte in weltbürgerlicher Absicht. . . . . S. 1

II. Beantwortung der Frage: Was ist Aufklärung? . . . . . . — 25

III. Ueber die Vulkane im Monde. . . — 37

IV. Von der Unrechtmäßigkeit des Büchernachdruks. . . . . — 50

V. Bestimmung des Begrifs einer Menschenrace. . . . . — 64

VI. Muth-

VI. Muthmaßlicher Anfang der Menschengeschichte. . . . . . . S. 90

VII. Einige Bemerkungen zu Herrn Prof. Jakob's Prüfung der Mendelssohnschen Morgenstunden . . . . — 115

VIII. Was heißt: sich im Denken orientiren? — 122

IX. Ueber den Gebrauch teleologischer Principien in der Philosophie. . . — 148

X. Ueber das Mislingen aller philosophischen Versuche in der Theodicee. . — 194

I. Idee

FIGURE 4.6 Contents of Kant's *Zerstreute Aufsätze*.

4.6).[185] The illegitimacy of the text's reprinting is suggested by its title page that excluded the names of its editor, publisher and printing house. Such anonymity not only undermined the enforcement of the already limited system of print privileges in eighteenth-century Germany but also worked against the system of rights that Kant had conceived and attached to the printed book.

Though Kant's authorial name did appear in the 1793 edition, its form and placement so departed from that in the *Berlinische Monatsschrift* as to effect a subtle variation of the author-function as Kant had understood it. As previously noted, the authorial name in Kant's 1785 essay, 'I. Kant', was a print remake of Kant's autograph. In both the original contents of the May 1785 issue and the master contents of the fifth volume of the periodical, Kant's authorial name was printed after and alongside the essay title in a more formal fashion that included his gendered and academic titles while omitting his forename entirely: 'Vom herrn Prof. Kant'; 'Vom hrn. Prof. Kant' (see Figures 4.7 and 4.8). Whereas the title pages of the periodical

[185] For a digitised version of the text, see Immanuel Kant, 'Zerstreute Aufsätze (1793)', Münchener DigitalisierungsZentrum Digitale Bibliothek, accessed 9 September 2024, www.digitale-sammlungen.de/en/view/bsb10927121?page = ,1.

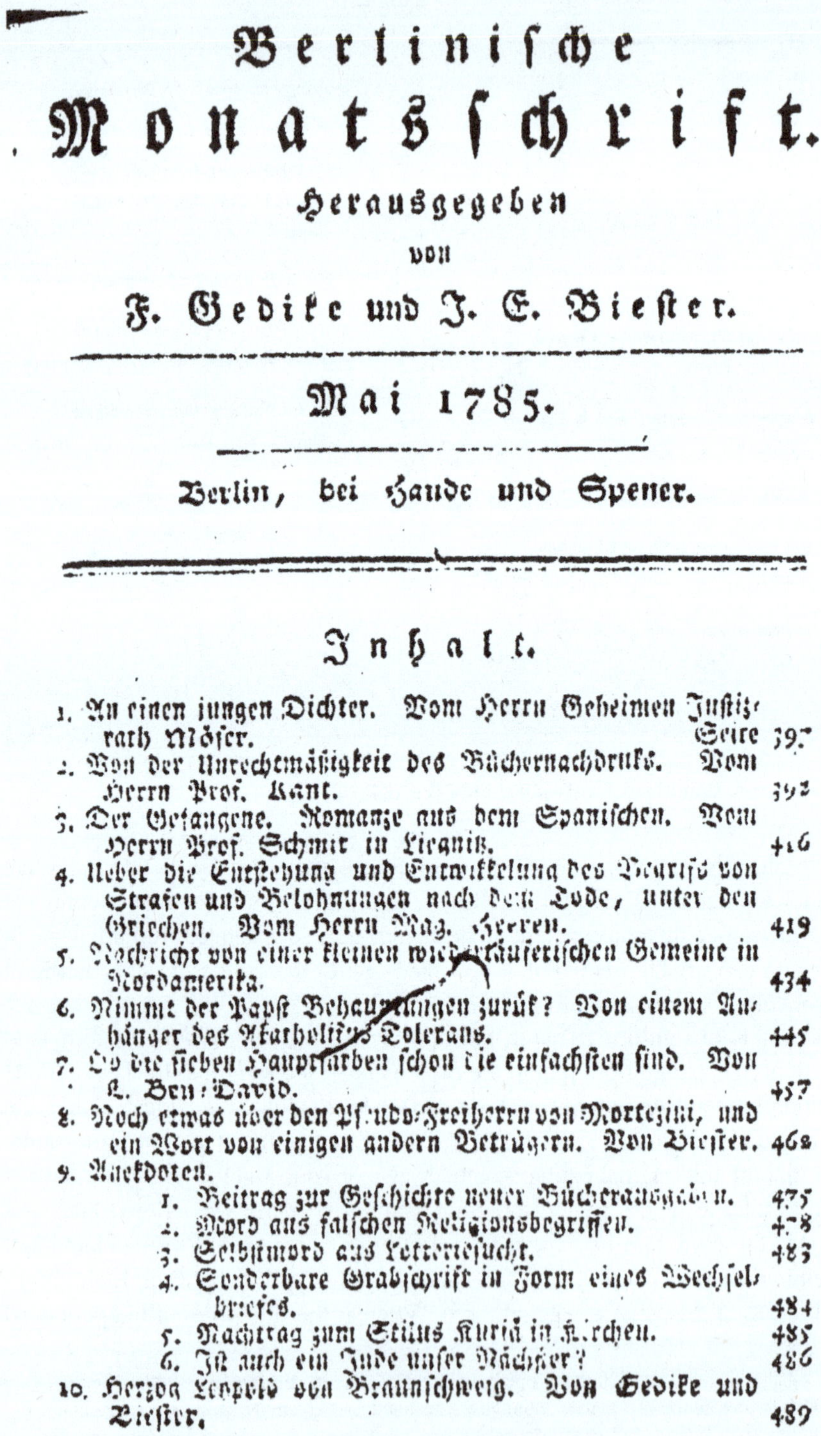

Berlinische Monatsschrift.

Herausgegeben
von
F. Gedike und J. E. Biester.

Mai 1785.

Berlin, bei Haude und Spener.

Inhalt.

1. An einen jungen Dichter. Vom Herrn Geheimen Justizrath Möser. Seite 385
2. Von der Unrechtmäßigkeit des Büchernachdruks. Vom Herrn Prof. Kant. 403
3. Der Gefangene. Romanze aus dem Spanischen. Vom Herrn Prof. Schmit in Lignitz. 416
4. Ueber die Entstehung und Entwikkelung des Begrifs von Strafen und Belohnungen nach dem Tode, unter den Griechen. Vom Herrn Mag. Heeren. 419
5. Nachricht von einer kleinen wiedertäuferischen Gemeine in Nordamerika. 434
6. Nimmt der Papst Behauptungen zurük? Von einem Anhänger des Akatholiken Tolerans. 445
7. Ob die sieben Hauptfarben schon die einfachsten sind. Von L. Ben-David. 457
8. Noch etwas über den Pseudo-Freiherrn von Mortezini, und ein Wort von einigen andern Betrügern. Von Biester. 462
9. Anekdoten.
   1. Beitrag zur Geschichte neuer Bücherausgaben. 475
   2. Mord aus falschen Religionsbegriffen. 478
   3. Selbstmord aus Lotteriesucht. 483
   4. Sonderbare Grabschrift in Form eines Wechselbriefes. 484
   5. Nachtrag zum Stilus Curiä in Kirchen. 485
   6. Ist auch ein Jude unser Nächster? 486
10. Herzog Leopold von Braunschweig. Von Gedike und Biester. 489

FIGURE 4.7 Original contents of the May 1785 issue of the *Berlinische Monatsschrift*.

Mai.

1. An einen jungen Dichter. Vom Herrn Geheimen Justizrath Möser. Seite 367
2. Von der Unrechtmäßigkeit des Büchernachdruks. Vom Hrn. Prof. Kant. 393
3. Der Gefangene. Romanze aus dem Spanischen. Vom Hrn. Prof. Schmit. 416
4. Ueber die Entstehung und Entwikkelung des Begrifs von Strafen und Belohnungen nach dem Tode, unter den Griechen. Vom Hrn. Mag. Heeren. 419
5. Nachricht von einer kleinen wiedertäuferischen Gemeine in Nordamerika. 434
6. Nimmt der Papst Behauptungen zurük? Von einem Anhänger des Akatholikus Tolerans. 445
7. Ob die sieben Hauptfarben schon die einfachsten sind. Von Herrn Ben David 457
8. Noch etwas über den Pseudo-Freiherrn von Mortezini, und ein Wort von einigen andern Betrügern. Von Biester. 462
9. Anekdoten.
   1. Beitrag zur Geschichte neuer Bücherausgaben 475
   2. Mord aus falschen Religionsbegriffen. 478
   3. Selbstmord aus Lotteriesucht. 482
   4. Sonderbare Grabschrift in Form eines Wechselbriefes. 484
   5. Nachtrag zum Stilus Kuriä in Kirchen. 485
   6. Ist auch ein Jude unser Nächster? 486
10. Herzog Leopold von Braunschweig. Von Gedike und Biester. 489

Junii.

FIGURE 4.8 Master contents of the May 1785 issue of the *Berlinische Monatsschrift*.

had foregrounded the names of the editor-publishers and printing house, the 1793 reprint instead designated the title 'scattered essays' as a single-authored collection re-grouped under the formal appellation adopted in those earlier content pages: 'Von / herrn Professor / Kant'.[186] The more 'personal' figure of 'I. Kant' (already to an extent depersonalised by the nominal abbreviation and the signature's remediation) gave way to the formal, revered figure of scholarly authority. Kant's interest in making authors responsible for their speech was subordinated to the more commercially relevant interest of securing the marketability of the literary commodity by attaching to it a brand name of an authoritative figure with institutional and gendered credentials. The eighteenth-century print machinery reworked the authorial name in accordance with the commercial imperative. Enclosed within a single-authored collection reprinted and sold for profit without the author's consent, Kant's essays on enlightenment and author's rights need not affirm the author's intended sign-off in the periodical whose typography he respected and recommended.[187]

Critical of the unauthorised reprinting of his own works, Kant relied on reputable daily periodicals to denounce and discredit pirated editions that came to his awareness, asserting his authorship in, and authority over, the original works through public notices that bore his authorial name. In the *Allgemeine Literatur-Zeitung*, a respected and prolific daily that rivalled Nicolai's *Allgemeine Deutsche Bibliothek*, there appeared at least two such notices in which the authority of 'I. Kant' was asserted to disavow the reprints.[188] On 12 June 1790, under the section *Literatur Zeigen* ('Literature Advertisements'), Kant posted an anti-advertisement of a reprint of his works indexed in a recent book catalogue (see Figure 4.9). The translation reads:

> In the Leipzig Catalogue of this year's Easter Fair, it is stated that amongst the books to be published is *I. Kant's Minor Writings, with Explanatory Notes* [*I. Kants kleine Schriften, mit erlaüternden Anmerkungen*] without the name of the editor or publisher. I hope that the person behind this idea would think of something else, and leave to the author the possibility of such arrangement along with the additional notes, which may concern the changes in such concepts that have since happened, but without prejudice to the notes that the editor might have made and which he could also make known without the text as he saw fit: otherwise, the authentic edition in collision with the illegitimate one would be detrimental to the latter in all respects.
>
> I. Kant.[189]

[186] Kant, 'Zerstreute Aufsätze (1793)'.

[187] Kant, *The Conflict of the Faculties*, 209–13. See Chapter 3.

[188] On the commercial success of the *Allgemeine Literatur-Zeitung* and the factors that contributed to it, see Thomas Broman, 'The Profits and Perils of Publicity: Allgemeine Literatur-Zeitung, the Thurn Und Taxis Post, and the Periodical Trade at the End of the Eighteenth Century', *Notes and Records: The Royal Society Journal of the History of Science* 69, no. 3 (2015): 267–71. Other than the first public notice discussed below, see the second from 1793: https://digipress.digitale-sammlungen.de/view/bsb10501996_00535_u001/1 (accessed 9 September 2024).

[189] See https://digipress.digitale-sammlungen.de/view/bsb10501984_00505_u001/1 (accessed 9 September 2024); my translation.

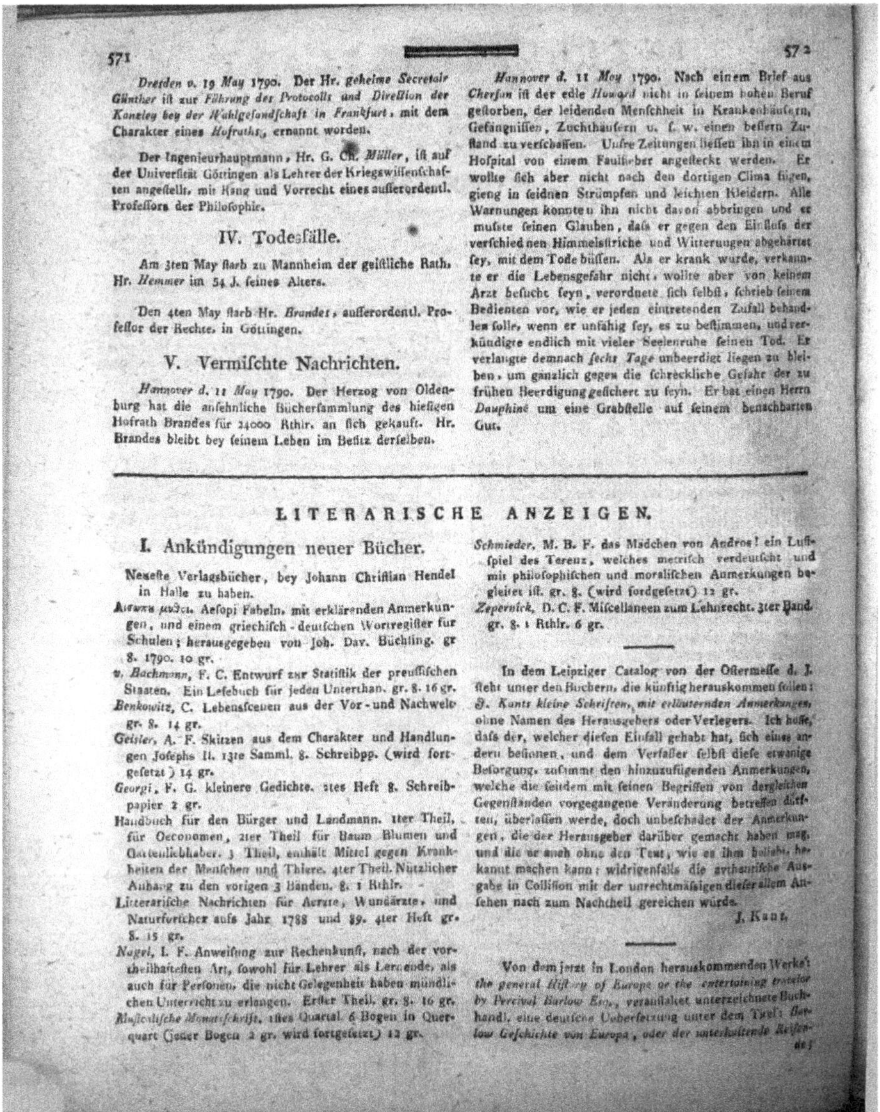

571

Dresden v. 19 May 1790. Der Hr. geheime *Secretair Günther* ist zur *Führung des Protocolls und Direction der Kanzley bey der Wahlgesandschaft in Frankfurt*, mit dem Charakter eines *Hofraths*, ernannt worden.

Der Ingenieurhauptmann, Hr. G. Ch. *Müller*, ist auf der Universität Göttingen als Lehrer der Kriegswissenschaften angestellt, mit Rang und Vorrecht eines ausserordentl. Professors der Philosophie.

IV. Todesfälle.

Am 3ten May starb zu Mannheim der geistliche Rath, Hr. *Hemmer* im 54 J. seines Alters.

Den 4ten May starb Hr. *Brandes*, ausserordentl. Professor der Rechte, in Göttingen.

V. Vermischte Nachrichten.

Hannover d. 11 May 1790. Der Herzog von Oldenburg hat die ansehnliche Büchersammlung des hiesigen Hofrath Brandes für 24000 Rthlr. an sich gekauft. Hr. Brandes bleibt bey seinem Leben im Besitz derselben.

572

Hannover d. 11 May 1790. Nach einem Brief aus *Cherson* ist der edle *Howard* nicht in seinem hohen Beruf gestorben, der leidenden Menschheit in Krankenhäusern, Gefängnissen, Zuchthäusern u. s. w. einen bessern Zustand zu verschaffen. Unsre Zeitungen liessen ihn in einem Hospital von einem Faulfieber angesteckt werden. Er wollte sich aber nicht nach den dortigen Clima fügen, gieng in seidnen Strümpfen und leichten Kleidern. Alle Warnungen konnten ihn nicht davon abbringen und er musste seinen Glauben, dass er gegen den Einfluss der verschiedenen Himmelsstriche und Witterungen abgehärtet sey, mit dem Tode büssen. Als er krank wurde, verkannte er die Lebensgefahr nicht, wollte aber von keinem Arzt besucht seyn, verordnete sich selbst, schrieb seinem Bedienten vor, wie er jeden eintretenden Zufall behandlen solle, wenn er unfähig sey, es zu bestimmen, und verkündigte endlich mit vieler Seelenruhe seinen Tod. Er verlangte demnach *sechs Tage* unbeerdigt liegen zu bleiben, um gänzlich gegen die schreckliche Gefahr der zu frühen Beerdigung gesichert zu seyn. Er bat einen Herrn *Dauphiné* um eine Grabstelle auf seinem benachbarten Gut.

LITERARISCHE ANZEIGEN.

I. Ankündigungen neuer Bücher.

Neueste Verlagsbücher, bey Johann Christian Hendel in Halle zu haben.

Αισωπου μυθοι. Aesopi Fabeln, mit erklärenden Anmerkungen, und einem griechisch-deutschen Wortregister für Schulen; herausgegeben von Joh. Dav. Büchling. gr 8. 1790. 10 gr.

v. Bachmann, F. C. Entwurf zur Statistik der preussischen Staaten. Ein Lesebuch für jeden Unterthan. gr. 8. 16 gr.

Benkowitz, C. Lebensscenen aus der Vor- und Nachwelt gr. 8. 14 gr.

Geisler, A. F. Skitzen aus dem Charakter und Handlungen Josephs II. 13te Samml. 8. Schreibpp. (wird fortgesetzt) 14 gr.

Georgi, F. G. kleinere Gedichte. 2tes Heft 8. Schreibpapier 2 gr.

Handbuch für den Bürger und Landmann. 1ter Theil, für Oeconomen, 2ter Theil für Baum Blumen und Gartenliebhaber. 3 Theil, enthält Mittel gegen Krankheiten der Menschen und Thiere. 4ter Theil. Nützlicher Anhang zu den vorigen 3 Bänden. 8. 1 Rthlr.

Litterarische Nachrichten für Aerzte, Wundärzte, und Naturforscher aufs Jahr 1788 und 89. 4ter Heft gr. 8. 15 gr.

Nagel, I. F. Anweisung zur Rechenkunst, nach der vortheilhaftesten Art, sowohl für Lehrer als Lernende, als auch für Personen, die nicht Gelegenheit haben mündlichen Unterricht zu erlangen. Erster Theil. gr. 8. 16 gr.

Musicalische Monatsschrift, 1tes Quartal 6 Bogen in Querquart (jeder Bogen 2 gr. wird fortgesetzt) 12 gr.

Schmieder, M. B. F. das Mädchen von Andros! ein Lustspiel des Terenz, welches metrisch verdeutscht und mit philosophischen und moralischen Anmerkungen begleitet ist. gr. 8. (wird fordgesetzt) 12 gr.

Zepernick, D. C. F. Miscellaneen zum Lehnrecht. 3ter Band. gr. 8. 1 Rthlr. 6 gr.

In dem Leipziger Catalog von der Ostermesse d. J. steht unter den Büchern, die künftig herauskommen sollen: *J. Kants kleine Schriften, mit erläuternden Anmerkungen*, ohne Namen des Herausgebers oder Verlegers. Ich hoffe, dass der, welcher diesen Einfall gehabt hat, sich eines andern besinnen, und dem Verfasser selbst diese etwanige Besorgung, zusammt den hinzuzufügenden Anmerkungen, welche die seitdem mit seinen Begriffen von dergleichen Gegenständen vorgegangene Veränderung betreffen dürften, überlassen werde, doch unbeschadet der Anmerkungen, die der Herausgeber darüber gemacht haben mag, und die er auch ohne den Text, wie es ihm beliebt, bekannt machen kann; widrigenfalls die authentische Ausgabe in Collision mit der unrechtmässigen dieser allem Ansehen nach zum Nachtheil gereichen würde.

J. Kant.

Von dem jetzt in London herauskommenden Werke: *the general History of Europe or the entertaining travelor by Percival Barlow Esq.*, veranstaltet unterzeichnete Buchhandl. eine deutsche Uebersetzung unter dem Titel: *Barlow Geschichte von Europa, oder der unterhaltende Reisende*

FIGURE 4.9 Kant's 1790 public notice in the *Allgemeine Literatur-Zeitung*.

In its title appropriation of 'I. Kant' the pirated edition of Kant's texts masqueraded as a publication authorised by Kant himself. Given the non-disclosure of editor's and publisher's names, neither Kant nor the reading public at large would have been able to hold those print actors to account for the quality of its printing and the accompanying notes. It was left to Kant to reclaim his technologised autograph and assert his authority to comment on and update his writings. The presence of the author as a living being who evolved alongside and beyond the original publication, able to look back at different editions and assess their authenticity and limits, is critically staged in and by Kant's onymous note. In Kant's time, 'I. Kant' at once contributed to the problem of print proliferation as an exploitable brand name and acted as the material basis of the author's proffered solution, enabling the latter's assertion of authority to (dis)authenticate and (dis)avow textual publications.

Today, an Anglophone reader of Kant's essay on author's rights is likely to refer to Mary J. Gregor's English translation in *Practical Philosophy* of *The Cambridge Edition of the Works of Immanuel Kant.*[190] Between the publication of the contemporary translation and that of the late eighteenth-century German text is a supervening period of more than two hundred years with attendant transformations in, and transactions between, German, American, European and global Anglophone culture. With respect to legal culture, both Germany and the United States have established national traditions of copyright law with their pertinent statutes. Notwithstanding some evident differences between these regimes of author's rights and copyright, they partake in and reproduce a shared proprietary perspective on the literary work as the original creation of its author.[191] Under sections 2(1) and 2(2) of the *Urheberrechtsgesetz* ('Act on Copyright and Related Rights'), *Sprachwerke* ('literary works') and other *Werke* ('works') protected under the Act are defined as *persönliche geistige Schöpfungen* ('personal intellectual creations'), which coheres with the European standard of originality.[192] Section 7 clarifies that the *Urheber* ('author') is the *Schöpfer des Werkes* ('creator of the work'). The author has *das ausschließliche Recht, sein Werk in körperlicher Form zu verwerten* ('the exclusive right to exploit the work in its material form'), including *das Vervielfältigungsrecht* ('the right of reproduction'). Similar to UK copyright law, the German statute provides for a presumption of authorship based on the conventional appearance of the author's name on the published work.[193] As discussed in Chapter 1, section 102 (a)(1) of Title 17 of the United States Code provides that '[copyright] protection subsists … in original works of authorship fixed in any tangible medium of

[190] Gregor's translation was first published by Cambridge University Press, New York, in 1996. There is also the translation available on the digital archive 'Primary Sources on Copyright': see 'Kant: On the Unlawfulness of Reprinting, Berlin (1785)', Primary Sources on Copyright (1450-1900), eds L. Bently & M. Kretschmer, accessed 9 September 2024, www.copyrighthistory.org/cam/tools/request/showRecord.php?id=record_d_1785.

[191] For some comparative accounts of civil law and common law regimes of copyright, see Jane Ginsburg, 'A Tale of Two Copyrights: Literary Property in Revolutionary France and America', in *Of Authors and Origins: Essays on Copyright Law*, ed. Brad Sherman and Alain Strowel (Oxford: Clarendon Press, 1994); Alain Strowel, 'Droit d'auteur and Copyright: Between History and Nature', in *Of Authors and Origins: Essays on Copyright Law*, ed. Brad Sherman and Alain Strowel (Oxford: Clarendon Press, 1994); Bently et al., *Intellectual Property Law*, 36.

[192] Gesetz über Urheberrecht und verwandte Schutzrechte, sections 2(1) and 2(2).

[193] Ibid., section 10(1).

expression', including 'literary works'.[194] The US Supreme Court has clarified that authorship presupposes originality in the sense of 'independent creation plus a modicum of creativity'.[195] Similar to in Germany, the owner of literary copyright in the United States is able to exercise a number of proprietary rights, including the right to reproduce it.[196] In both jurisdictions, the literary work is apprehended to be its author's original creation. Though Kant dismissed uses of the property idiom to describe and regulate print publishing during the late eighteenth century, the myth of the proprietary author now prevails across copyright regimes.

The legal information included in the publisher's peritext in *Practical Philosophy* reflects, ratifies and reproduces the proprietary perspective on literature despite the death of the author Kant (who, in any case, contributed to the making of the original works at a time before copyright). On the same page bearing record of the publisher's identity ('Cambridge University Press'), year and place of first publication ('1996'; 'United States of America'; 'New York') and other related items we find the notice specifying that copyright in the volume, including the right of reproduction, has been vested in the publisher since it was first published: '© Cambridge University Press 1996 / This publication is in copyright. Subject to statutory exception and to the provisions of relevant collective licensing agreements, no reproduction of any part may take place without the written permission of Cambridge University Press.'[197] The form of the notice meets the requirements for giving 'reasonable notice of the claim of copyright'[198] to the public, namely the inclusion of the symbol ©, the year of first publication and the name of the owner of copyright, stated under section 401(b)(2) of the Title 17 of the United States Code. Having financed and directed the publication of *Practical Philosophy* in the United States, Cambridge University Press now holds a copyright in the 'compilation'[199] of Kant's works, which entails 'the collection and assembling of pre existing materials or of data that are selected, coordinated or arrange in such a way that the resulting work as a whole constitutes an original work of authorship'.[200] Like any 'literary work', the compilation is understood to be an 'original work of authorship' in which copyright protection subsists. For the purposes of copyright in compilation (not unlike in the instance of typographical copyright in the United Kingdom),[201] the publisher is understood to be the author-creator of the compiled work. *Practical Philosophy* is apprehended to consist in a literary compilation undertaken by and belonging to the university press.

[194] Title 17 of the United States Code, section 102.
[195] *Feist Publications Inc. v Rural Telephone Service Co. Inc.* 111 S.Ct. 1282 (1991), 1288. 499 U.S. 340 (1991), 1288.
[196] Title 17 of the United States Code, section 106.
[197] Kant, *Practical Philosophy*.
[198] See Title 17 of the United States Code, sections 401(b)(1)-(3) and 401(c).
[199] Ibid., section 103.
[200] Ibid., section 102.
[201] See Chapter 3.

Having switched hands, eyes and technology, Kant's essay on publisher's and author's rights, in its 1996 renewal, need not bear its original paratexts. The shift to digital typography printing has affirmed the obsolescence of the already dated mechanisms of catchwords and signature marks to guide the order of printing in the hand-press period.[202] Catered to an Anglophone readership accustomed to seeing and using serif typefaces, the 1996 essay is set in the ubiquitous Times New Roman font instead of the antiquated Breitkopf Fraktur, regardless of the author's preference for the latter. Similarly, the periodical's style of printing authorial names at the end of each contribution, as well as Kant's deliberate choice of his epistolary sign-off, are discarded in favour of the interests, considerations and circumstances of the university press and its appointed editors. No 'I. Kant' concludes Kant's essay in *Practical Philosophy*. Instead, appearing at the top of alternate pages of Kant's essay and his other works in the volume is the typographically centred running head 'IMMANUEL KANT'.[203] The other set of running heads bear the truncated work title: 'WRONGFULNESS OF UNAUTHORIZED PUBLICATION'.[204] Some relationship between author and work, between Immanuel Kant and the text, is reiterated across the pages and re-impressed on the reader as they flip from page to page. Whether this relationship is a *proprietary* relationship, one that reproduces the myth of proprietary authorship enshrined in copyright law, is left ambiguous, though not eliminated as a perceptual possibility. Since the cover page indicates at its top the full name of the series and edition, 'THE CAMBRIDGE EDITION OF THE WORKS OF IMMANUEL KANT', the first set of running heads may also act as a reminder of the author-centred series, at once affirming Kant's authority as author of the constitutive works and the university press's involvement in producing the edition. Again, in spite of the copyright notice (which extends from and reproduces the prevailing order of copyright qua intellectual property), it remains ambiguous whether or not the form and placement of the authorial name privileges any proprietary perspective on books and authorship. But the editorial decision against transposing 'I. Kant' to the present text arguably participates in an erasure of the function that Kant had assigned to the authorial name: a non-proprietary author-function of assuming and attributing responsibility for the text amidst print saturation.[205]

Despite this de-historicising omission, the new front matter of Kant's essay registers an awareness on the part of its contemporary literary producers of its medial-material conditions of possibility. The untitled prefatory note to *Practical Philosophy* locates the volume in an authoritative series of translations of Kant's

[202] See Chapter 3.

[203] Kant, 'On the Wrongfulness of Unauthorized Publication of Books (1785)'.

[204] Ibid.

[205] To the publisher's credit, 'I. Kant' does appear at the end of the open letters addressed to Friedrich Nicolai, which we discussed earlier: see Kant, 'On Turning out Books: Two Letters to Mr. Friedrich Nicolai from Immanuel Kant', 627.

oeuvre addressed to contemporary Anglophone scholars: 'The purpose of the Cambridge Edition is to offer translations of the best modern German edition of Kant's work in a uniform format suitable for Kant's scholars.'[206] Translating and compiling the dispersed works of Kant, previously published or unpublished, into a single series with a consistent format, including citation style and other scholarly aids, is the means by which the university press facilitates the study of Kant in the present, which is no less plagued by the problem of information overload than late eighteenth-century Germany was.[207] As a comprehensive volume containing 'all of Kant's writings on moral and political philosophy',[208] *Practical Philosophy* acts as one of the technologies with which to manage the surfeit of print and digital materials in the here and now. The very production of *Practical Philosophy* is credited to a socio-technological machinery composed of participants, both human and non-human, in addition to the original author and his manuscripts: 'The volume has been furnished with a substantial editorial apparatus including translators' introductions and explanatory notes to each text and a general introduction to Kant's moral and philosophy by Allen Wood.'[209] Supplemented with textual contributions by other authors and scholars, and also probably shaped by others in the list of 'General Editors'[210] and members of the 'Advisory board',[211] *Practical Philosophy* is not the 'personal intellectual creation' of an author. Rather, consistent with Kant's media-theoretical perspective on the book, the publication only emerges pursuant to the historical interactions between human bodies and technologies.

Given how entrenched the myth of proprietary authorship is, one might be tempted to read both the full authorial name, 'IMMANUEL KANT', and the author's portrait-style frontispiece as materials that reinscribe the author as creator and owner of the literary work. Rooted in biblical myth, the printed name 'Immanuel', meaning 'God is with us',[212] might suggest Kant to be a figure of sovereign authority who has created the work before us. The cover image consisting of Kant's illuminated head with a penetrating downward gaze, as if ably critiquing the grounds of his own existence, could be seen as some kind of visual supplement to the myth of the author as sovereign creator, or even personifying the Romantic ideal of poetic genius. But my claim is that this interpretation disregards the prefatory materials that reference and index the book's emergence from a literary apparatus. Rather than simply presenting a secularised portrait of 'God', the

[206] Kant, *Practical Philosophy*.

[207] See also Wellmon's study of information overload in the eighteenth century and the (re) conception of the modern research university as a technological solution: Wellmon, *Organizing Enlightenment*.

[208] Kant, *Practical Philosophy*.

[209] Ibid.

[210] Ibid.

[211] Ibid.

[212] See, for example, 'Immanuel', in Dictionary.com, accessed 9 September 2024, www.dictionary.com/browse/immanuel.

frontispiece is perhaps better understood to share an affinity with the copper frontispieces of the *Berlinische Monatsschrift*. In both instances, a 'special, deserving'[213] figure of enlightenment – that is, a key theorist and practitioner of enlightenment – is presented as being worthy of notice. Instead of someone whose image is 'not yet well known',[214] however, we have the already canonised author Kant, who, as early as 1785, had reckoned with the eighteenth-century print machinery on which the public use of reason depended. Though materially dependent on the book and the print machinery for individual and collective emancipation, the human being, '*who is now more than a machine*',[215] is asserted by Kant to be more important and able to steer the print machinery. Thus considered, the authorial name and portrait in the cover page is equally if not more suited to carrying forward the humanism in Kant's media theory.

In spite of much that resists the proprietary author-function, both at the rhetorical and material levels of Kant's essay and the accompanying paratexts of its various editions, Kant has at times been cast in the role of an intellectual forerunner, even proponent, of intellectual property in copyright scholarship.[216] The citationality (or, as Derrida puts it, 'iterability'[217]) of Kant's name and the texts bearing it, their material affordance to be transposed to an in-principle infinite number of signifying contexts, has allowed Kant to be (mis)read as an adherent of proprietary authorship and the contemporary juridical distinction between intangible property and its material embodiment. In a relatively recent instance, 'Kant' has acted as the third chapter title of Robert P. Merges' *Justifying Intellectual Property* (2011), a monograph in search of a conceptual foundation for intellectual property law.[218] Ignoring the tension between the concept of intellectual property and Kant's media-theoretically informed case for publisher's and author's rights, Merges opted to extend the coverage of Kant's property theory from the domain of physical objects to so-called intangibles such as literary or artistic works. Kant was characterised as a philosopher of liberal individualism, a worldview that began with 'a lone individual, on stage

[213] Friedrich Gedike and Johann Erich Biester, 'Vorrede', Münchener DigitalisierungsZentrum Digitale Bibliothek, 1783, accessed 9 September 2024, www.digitale-sammlungen.de/de/view/bsb10926840?q=%28Berlinische+Monatsschrift.+1.+1781%29&page=8,9. See Chapter 2.

[214] Gedike and Biester, 'Vorrede'.

[215] Kant, 'An Answer to the Question: What Is Enlightenment? (1784)', 22.

[216] Other than Robert P. Merges' work discussed later in the chapter, see Riccardo Pozzo, 'Immanuel Kant on Intellectual Property', *Trans/Form/Ação, São Paulo* 29, no. 2 (2006): 11–18; William Fisher, 'Theories of Intellectual Property', in *New Essays in the Legal and Political Theory of Property*, ed. Stephen R. Munzer (Cambridge: Cambridge University Press, 2001).

[217] Jacques Derrida, 'Signature Event Context', in *Limited Inc* (Evanston, IL: Northwestern University Press, 1988), 7.

[218] Robert P. Merges, 'Kant', in *Justifying Intellectual Property* (Cambridge, MA: Harvard University Press, 2011), 68–101. For Merges's comments on the book's aims and structure, see Ibid., 1–27.

with a single isolated object',[219] with which the individual's personality may be so bound up as to be injured by another's use without the former's consent. In Merges's reading of Kant's *Rechtslehre* ('Doctrine of Right') (1797), property was a right in the object with corresponding duties owed by others to respect the right-holder's claim over the object, the object being involved in the individual's exercise of one's own will.[220] While recognising Kant's focus on physical property in the doctrine of right, Merges sought to extend Kant's insights to 'intellectual creations' and 'intangible media': 'We are ... free to apply Kant's idea to the building blocks of intellectual creations, just as we do for other assets such as blocks of marble or land. Many people in the modern world may choose to express themselves in intangible media.'[221] Being dead for more than two centuries, Kant is now in no position to so deploy his epistolary signature as to reject the subordination of the text bearing his name to another's will.

Merges's treatment of Kant's 1785 essay presents an even more overt instance of the intellectual property scholar's cancellation and editing of Kant's text while staging it as authorised by the author Kant himself. As discussed in Chapter 3, Kant's essay dismissed from its outset the proprietary perspective on books and instead advanced a non-proprietary argument for the wrongfulness of reprinting. The former perspective arose within a parenthesis that doubted its credence: 'For the author's property in his thought (even if one grants that there is such a thing in terms of external rights) is left to him regardless of the unauthorized publication.'[222] The possibility of construing thought and personhood in terms of property is, as Barron puts it, but a 'throwaway remark Kant makes at the beginning of the Essay',[223] which Kant would show to be unnecessary to make out a case against unauthorised reprinting. Rather than dwelling on this scepticism, Merges elected to cross out the parenthetical remark so as to flatten out the contradiction between Kant's text and his interpretation of it: 'Though much has been made of the structure of this argument, with some scholars finding in it evidence of Kant's rejection of a property claim to authorial works, the introductory passage cited earlier seems clear enough to me. Eliminating the parenthetical, it says, plainly enough, "For the author's property in his thought or sentiments ... is left to him regardless of the unauthorized publication."'[224] Perhaps conscious of the violence done to the text, Merges went further to reinterpret the eliminated parenthetical remark as referencing the lack of copyright protection in Kant's time, at once substituting his own words for Kant's and presenting Kant as the author in whose name he was speaking: 'Kant was saying, in effect, "even if copyright is not in force in a given jurisdiction, counterfeiting is

[219] Merges, 'Kant', 72.
[220] Ibid. Merges refers to the translation in Kant, 'The Metaphysics of Morals (1797)'.
[221] Merges, 'Kant', 73–74.
[222] Kant, 'On the Wrongfulness of Unauthorized Publication of Books (1785)', 29.
[223] Barron, 'Kant, Copyright and Communicative Freedom', 41, fn. 137.
[224] Merges, 'Kant', 78.

still wrong." And it is wrong, he says, by virtue of the "author's property in his thought."'"[225] It was as if Merges had occupied the role of the medium, previously assigned by Kant to the publisher, and was acting on the author's behalf. All this was, of course, simply staged. There is too much in the texts bearing Kant's name to suggest the author was a supporter of intellectual property. That Merges still sought Kant's authorisation, or at least felt compelled to stage the latter's approval of his scholarship, attests to the present endurance and influence of the author-function.

Against such portrayals of Kant as justifying or anticipating the present dominance of intellectual property law and the enshrined myth of proprietary authorship, other Kantian copyright scholars have sought to recuperate Kant's 1785 essay as presenting a resolutely non-proprietary solution to the problem of reprinting in late eighteenth-century Germany. As discussed in Chapter 1, Drassinower, Borghi and Barron have mobilised Kant's concept of the book as speech act to rethink copyright law outside the utilitarian-proprietary paradigm.[226] Egalitarian authorship, truth and collective emancipation are some of the striking ideals that distinguish their respective projects, each of which builds in some way on Kant's recognition of publishing as involving the communication of a speech made to the public in the author's name. Separately but also in step with the three copyright scholars, Maria Chiara Pievatolo has thoroughly re-presented Kant's case against unauthorised reprinting as one that both eschews the idiom of intellectual property and remains deeply interested in enlightenment practice: Kant's 'justification of authors' right does not rely on intellectual property, but on the meaning and the function of both authors and publishers in the world of the public use of reason'.[227] It is the deeply social and ethical concern of Kant's perspective – that is, its interest in safeguarding the freedom of persons to make public use of their own reason so as to achieve personal and collective emancipation – that renders it a critical alternative to the utility-driven, liberal-individualist and proprietary account of copyright law. Read in the light of the 1784 enlightenment essay and other philosophical works bearing Kant's authorial name, Kant's 1785 essay affirms its non-proprietary commitment to public reason and human emancipation.

My claim is that much of the debate surrounding the relationship between Kant, his 1785 essay and the enterprise of intellectual property has proceeded without the participants' reflection on its material basis. The authorial name, no less than the assemblage of texts it adorns, has continually afforded the various (mis)interpretations of Kant. From a media theorist who simultaneously observed the unruliness of the eighteenth-century print machinery and affirmed the human being's power to steer it in favour of public enlightenment, Kant has inverted into a liberal-

225 Ibid.

226 See Chapter 1.

227 Maria Chiara Pievatolo, 'Freedom, Ownership and Copyright: Why Does Kant Reject the Concept of Intellectual Property?', *Società Italiana di Filosofia Politica*, 2010, 2.

individualist whose property theory lent support to the contemporary perspective on copyright as a species of intellectual property. This proprietary transformation of Kant has, in turn, provoked his rehabilitation and return to a humanist and enlightenment philosopher who envisioned a system of publishers' and authors' rights grounded instead in the author's personhood. But Kant exhibited in the texts bearing his name a far more profound understanding of the medial-material conditions in which authors operated than that evidenced in the recent copyright scholarship. The authorial name, be it 'I. Kant' or others appearing in other eighteenth-century publications, was understood and deployed by Kant to assume, ascribe, and exact responsibility for those publications. Alongside the *Berlinische Monatsschrift* and other pertinent eighteenth-century inventions (including the modern research university),[228] the authorial name acted as an enlightenment technology to manage the surfeit of print that threatened to overwhelm the human reader. Though a humanist who affirmed the author's right and authority to speak through the medium of print, Kant was also a media theorist and practitioner who was conscious of the human being's involvement in a medial environment and print machinery that determined humanity's projects. This is my Kantian addendum to the debate.

On 28 August 1799, there appeared in the *Intelligenzblatt* of the *Allgemeine Literatur-Zeitung* one of Kant's last public assertions of authorial responsibility for a text bearing his name (see Figure 4.10).[229] Earlier that year, another literary journal had published a book review that invited Kant, the author of *Kritik der reinen Vernunft* ('Critique of Pure Reason') (1781/1787), to comment on his pupil Fichte's *Grundlage der gesammten Wissenschaftslehre* ('Foundations of the Science of Knowledge') (1794), the latter of which purportedly advanced and fulfilled the former's transcendental philosophy.[230] Under the authority of his full name 'Immanuel Kant' (which similarly fronted the original and revised editions of the *Kritik*), Kant affirmed the *Kritik* to be a complete product of transcendental philosophy, and rejected Fichte's *Wissenschaftslehre* as a false practice of abstraction that denied the material basis of phenomena. For Kant, a 'pure theory of science [like Fichte's attempt] is nothing more or less than mere *logic*, and the principles of

[228] Other than Wellmon's monograph, see Multigraph Collective, *Interacting with Print: Elements of Reading in the Era of Print Saturation* (Chicago: University of Chicago Press, 2018).

[229] The original public declaration was untitled and published under the section II. *Erklärung*: see https://digipress.digitale-sammlungen.de/view/bsb10628812_00539_u001/1 (accessed 9 September 2024). For the English translation relied upon here, see Immanuel Kant, 'Public Declaration Concerning Fichte's *Wissenschaftslehre*, August 7, 1799', in *Correspondence*, ed. and trans. Arnulf Zweig (New York: Cambridge University Press, 1999), 559–61.

[230] See Immanuel Kant, *Critique of Pure Reason*, ed. and trans. Paul Guyer and Allen W. Wood (New York: Cambridge University Press, 1998); Johann Gottlieb Fichte, *The Science of Knowledge*, ed. and trans. Peter Heath and John Lachs (Cambridge: Cambridge University Press, 1982). For a discussion of the context in which Kant's public declaration arose, see Kant, 'Public Declaration Concerning Fichte's Wissenschaftslehre, August 7, 1799', 560–61, editorial fn. 1.

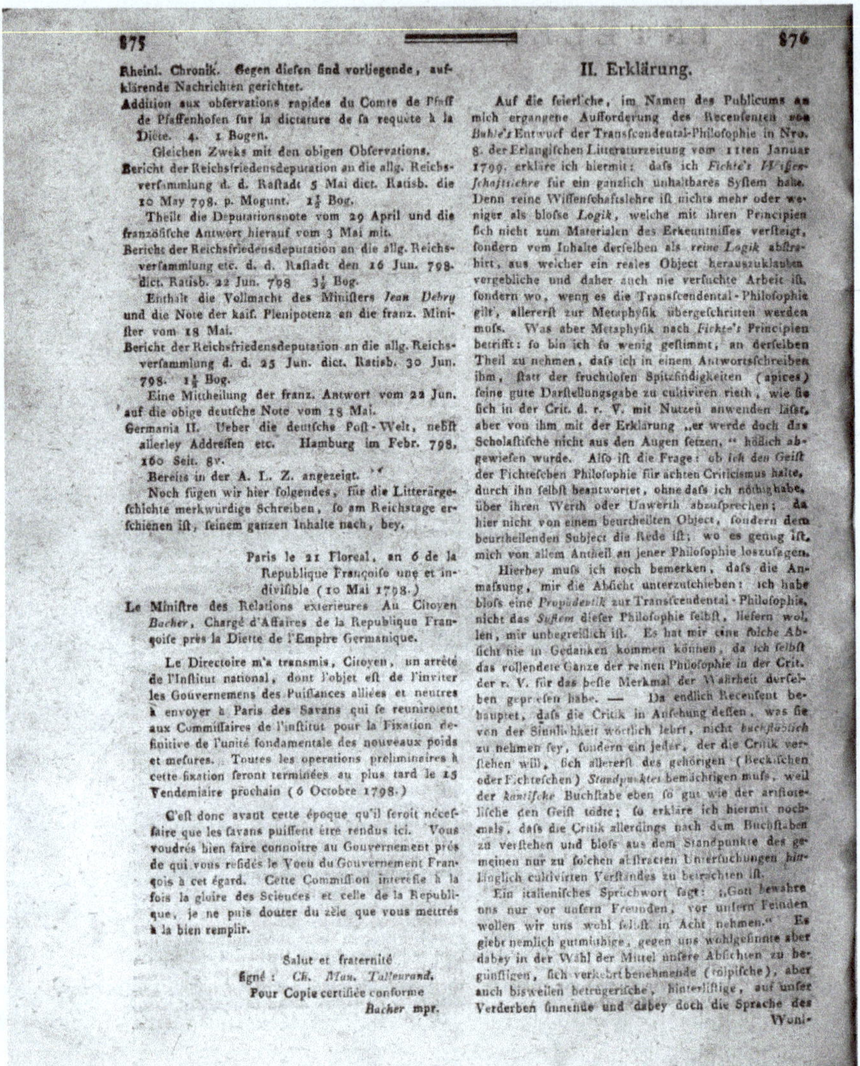

875

Rheinl. Chronik. Gegen diesen sind vorliegende, aufklärende Nachrichten gerichtet.

Addition aux observations rapides du Comte de Pfaff de Pfaffenhofen sur la dictature de sa requête à la Diète. 4. 1 Bogen.

Gleichen Zweks mit den obigen Observations.

Bericht der Reichsfriedensdeputation an die allg. Reichsversammlung d. d. Rastadt 5 Mai dict. Ratisb. die 10 May 798. p. Mogunt. 1½ Bog.

Theilt die Deputationsnote vom 29 April und die französische Antwort hierauf vom 3 Mai mit.

Bericht der Reichsfriedensdeputation an die allg. Reichsversammlung etc. d. d. Rastadt den 16 Jun. 798. dict. Ratisb. 22 Jun. 798 3½ Bog.

Enthält die Vollmacht des Ministers *Jean Debry* und die Note der kais. Plenipotenz an die franz. Minister vom 18 Mai.

Bericht der Reichsfriedensdeputation an die allg. Reichsversammlung d. d. 25 Jun. dict. Ratisb. 30 Jun. 798. 1½ Bog.

Eine Mittheilung der franz. Antwort vom 22 Jun. auf die obige deutsche Note vom 18 Mai.

Germania II. Ueber die deutsche Post-Welt, nebst allerley Addressen etc. Hamburg im Febr. 798. 160 Seit. 8v.

Bereits in der A. L. Z. angezeigt.

Noch fügen wir hier folgendes, für die Litterärgeschichte merkwürdige Schreiben, so am Reichstage erschienen ist, seinem ganzen Inhalte nach, bey.

Paris le 21 Floreal, an 6 de la Republique Françoise une et indivisible (10 Mai 1798.)

Le Ministre des Relations exterieures Au Citoyen *Bacher*, Chargé d'Affaires de la Republique Françoise près la Diette de l'Empire Germanique.

Le Directoire m'a transmis, Citoyen, un arrêté de l'Institut national, dont l'objet est de l'inviter les Gouvernemens des Puissances alliées et neutres à envoyer à Paris des Savans qui se reuniroient aux Commissaires de l'institut pour la Fixation definitive de l'unité fondamentale des nouveaux poids et mesures. Toutes les operations preliminaires à cette fixation seront terminées au plus tard le 15 Vendemiaire prochain (6 Octobre 1798.)

C'est donc avant cette époque qu'il seroit nécessaire que les savans puissent être rendus ici. Vous voudrés bien faire connoitre au Gouvernement prés de qui vous residés le Voeu du Gouvernement François à cet égard. Cette Commission interesse à la fois la gloire des Sciences et celle de la Republique, je ne puis douter du zèle que vous mettrés à la bien remplir.

Salut et fraternité
signé : *Ch. Mau. Talleyrand.*
Pour Copie certifiée conforme
Bacher mpr.

876

II. Erklärung.

Auf die feierliche, im Namen des Publicums an mich ergangene Aufforderung des Recensenten von *Buhle's* Entwurf der Transscendental-Philosophie in Nro. 8. der Erlangischen Litteraturzeitung vom 11ten Januar 1799. erkläre ich hiermit: dass ich *Fichte's Wissenschaftslehre* für ein gänzlich unhaltbares System halte. Denn reine Wissenschaftslehre ist nichts mehr oder weniger als blosse *Logik*, welche mit ihren Principien sich nicht zum Materialen des Erkenntnisses versteigt, sondern vom Inhalte derselben als *reine Logik* abstrahirt, aus welcher ein reales Object herauszuklauben vergebliche und daher auch nie versuchte Arbeit ist, sondern wo, wenn es die Transscendental-Philosophie gilt, allererst zur Metaphysik übergeschritten werden muss. Was aber Metaphysik nach *Fichte's* Principien betrifft: so bin ich so wenig gestimmt, an derselben Theil zu nehmen, dass ich in einem Antwortsschreiben ihm, statt der fruchtlosen Spitzfindigkeiten (apices) seine gute Darstellungsgabe zu cultiviren rieth, wie sie sich in der Crit. d. r. V. mit Nutzen anwenden lässt, aber von ihm mit der Erklärung „er werde doch das Scholastische nicht aus den Augen setzen," höflich abgewiesen wurde. Also ist die Frage: ob *ich den Geist* der Fichteschen Philosophie für ächten Criticismus halte, durch ihn selbst beantwortet, ohne dass ich nöthig habe, über ihren Werth oder Unwerth abzusprechen; da hier nicht von einem beurtheilten Object, sondern dem beurtheilenden Subject die Rede ist; wo es genug ist, mich von allem Antheil an jener Philosophie loszusagen.

Hierbey muss ich noch bemerken, dass die Anmassung, mir die Absicht unterzuschieben: ich habe bloss eine *Propädeutik* zur Transscendental-Philosophie, nicht das *System* dieser Philosophie selbst, liefern wollen, mir unbegreiflich ist. Es hat mir eine solche Absicht nie in Gedanken kommen können, da ich selbst das vollendete Ganze der reinen Philosophie in der Crit. der r. V. für das beste Merkmal der Wahrheit derselben gepriesen habe. — Da endlich Recensent behauptet, dass die Critik in Ansehung dessen, was sie von der Sinnlichkeit wörtlich lehrt, nicht *buchstäblich* zu nehmen sey, sondern ein jeder, der die Critik verstehen will, sich allererst des gehörigen (Beckischen oder Fichteschen) *Standpunktes* bemächtigen muss, weil der *kantische* Buchstabe eben so gut wie der aristotelische den Geist tödte; so erkläre ich hiermit nochmals, dass die Critik allerdings nach dem Buchstaben zu verstehen und bloss aus dem Standpunkte des gemeinen nur zu solchen abstracten Untersuchungen *hinlänglich* cultivirten Verstandes zu betrachten ist.

Ein italienisches Sprüchwort sagt: „Gott bewahre uns nur vor unsern Freunden, vor unsern Feinden wollen wir uns wohl selbst in Acht nehmen." Es giebt nemlich gutmüthige, gegen uns wohlgesinnte aber dabey in der Wahl der Mittel unsere Absichten zu begünstigen, sich verkehrt benehmende (tölpische), aber auch bisweilen betrügerische, hinterlistige, auf unser Verderben sinnende und dabey doch die Sprache des Wohl-

FIGURE 4.10 Kant's 1799 public notice in the *Allgemeine Literatur-Zeitung*.

logic cannot lead to material knowledge, since logic, that is to say, *pure logic*, abstracts from the content of knowledge; the attempt to cull a real object out of logic is a vain effort and therefore something that no one has ever achieved'.[231] Consistently, Kant disavowed the anonymous reviewer's suggestion that his *Kritik* was meant to be so read as to affirm its underlying 'standpoint' or 'spirit' rather than

[231] Kant, 'Public Declaration Concerning Fichte's *Wissenschaftslehre*, August 7, 1799', 559.

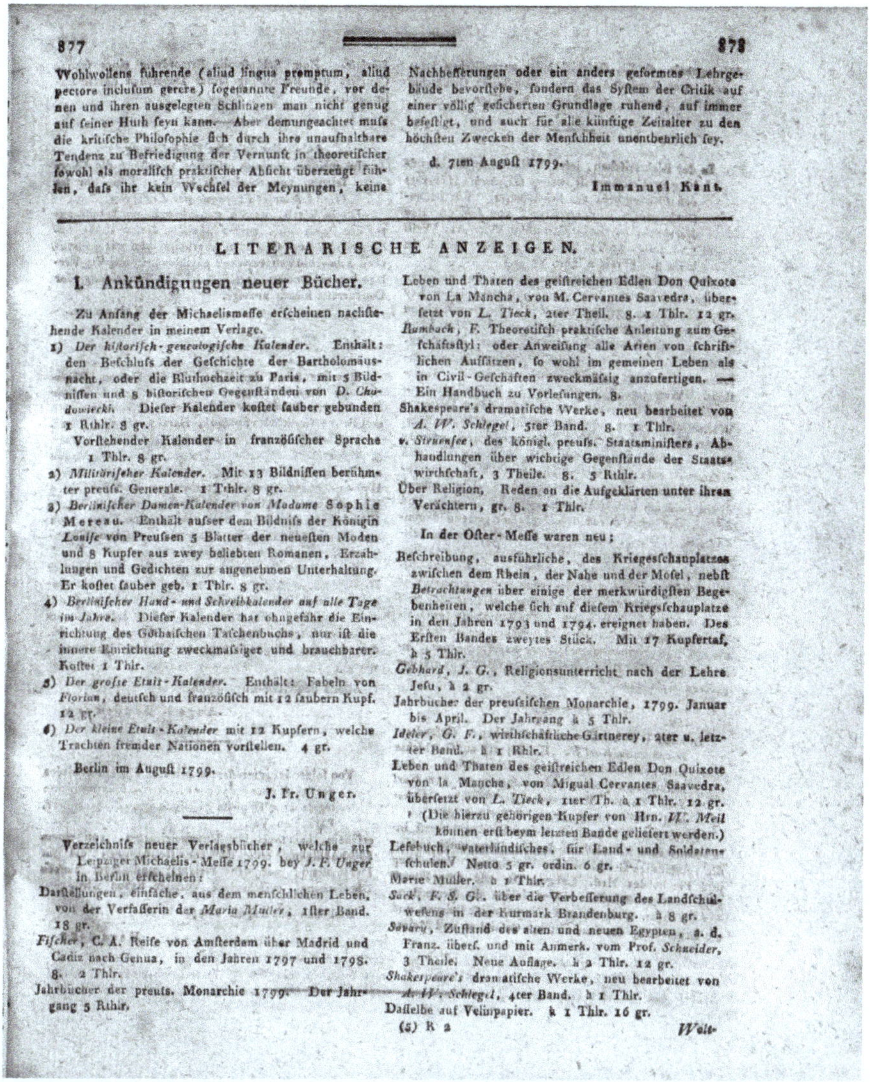

877 878

Wohlwollens führende (aliud linguâ promptum, aliud pectore inclusum gerere) sogenannte Freunde, vor denen und ihren ausgelegten Schlingen man nicht genug auf seiner Huth seyn kann. Aber demungeachtet muss die kritische Philosophie sich durch ihre unaufhaltbare Tendenz zu Befriedigung der Vernunft in theoretischer sowohl als moralisch praktischer Absicht überzeugt fühlen, dass ihr kein Wechsel der Meynungen, keine Nachbesserungen oder ein anders geformtes Lehrgebäude bevorstehe, sondern das System der Critik auf einer völlig gesicherten Grundlage ruhend, auf immer befestigt, und auch für alle künftige Zeitalter zu den höchsten Zwecken der Menschheit unentbehrlich sey.

d. 7ten August 1799.

Immanuel Kant.

LITERARISCHE ANZEIGEN.

I. Ankündigungen neuer Bücher.

Zu Anfang der Michaelismesse erscheinen nachstehende Kalender in meinem Verlage.

1) *Der historisch-genealogische Kalender.* Enthält: den Beschluss der Geschichte der Bartholomäusnacht, oder die Bluthochzeit zu Paris, mit 5 Bildnissen und 8 historischen Gegenständen von *D. Chodowiecki.* Dieser Kalender kostet sauber gebunden 1 Rthlr. 8 gr.

Vorstehender Kalender in französischer Sprache 1 Thlr. 8 gr.

2) *Militärischer Kalender.* Mit 13 Bildnissen berühmter preuss. Generale. 1 Thlr. 8 gr.

3) *Berlinischer Damen-Kalender von Madame* Sophie Mereau. Enthält ausser dem Bildniss der Königin *Louise* von Preussen 5 Blätter der neuesten Moden und 8 Kupfer aus zwey beliebten Romanen, Erzählungen und Gedichten zur angenehmen Unterhaltung. Er kostet sauber geb. 1 Thlr. 8 gr.

4) *Berlinischer Hand- und Schreibkalender auf alle Tage im Jahre.* Dieser Kalender hat ohngefähr die Einrichtung des Göthaischen Taschenbuchs, nur ist die innere Einrichtung zweckmässiger und brauchbarer. Kostet 1 Thlr.

5) *Der grosse Etuit-Kalender.* Enthält: Fabeln von *Florian*, deutsch und französisch mit 12 saubern Kupf. 12 gr.

6) *Der kleine Etuis-Kalender* mit 12 Kupfern, welche Trachten fremder Nationen vorstellen. 4 gr.

Berlin im August 1799.

J. Fr. Unger.

Verzeichniss neuer Verlagsbücher, welche zur Leipziger Michaelis-Messe 1799. bey *J. F. Unger* in Berlin erscheinen:

Darstellungen, einfache, aus dem menschlichen Leben, von der Verfasserin der *Maria Muller*, 1ster Band. 18 gr.

Fischer, C. A. Reise von Amsterdam über Madrid und Cadiz nach Genua, in den Jahren 1797 und 1798. 8. 2 Thlr.

Jahrbücher der preuss. Monarchie 1799. Der Jahrgang 5 Rthlr.

Leben und Thaten des geistreichen Edlen Don Quixote von La Mancha, von M. Cervantes Saavedra, übersetzt von *L. Tieck*, 2ter Theil. 8. 1 Thlr. 12 gr.

Rumbach, F. Theoretisch praktische Anleitung zum Geschäftsstyl: oder Anweisung alle Arten von schriftlichen Aufsätzen, so wohl im gemeinen Leben als in Civil-Geschäften zweckmässig anzufertigen. — Ein Handbuch zu Vorlesungen. 8.

Shakespeare's dramatische Werke, neu bearbeitet von *A. W. Schlegel*, 5ter Band. 8. 1 Thlr.

v. Struensee, des königl. preuss. Staatsministers, Abhandlungen über wichtige Gegenstände der Staatswirthschaft, 3 Theile. 8. 5 Rthlr.

Über Religion, Reden an die Aufgeklärten unter ihren Verächtern, gr. 8. 1 Thlr.

In der Oster-Messe waren neu;

Beschreibung, ausführliche, des Kriegesschauplatzes zwischen dem Rhein, der Nahe und der Mosel, nebst *Betrachtungen* über einige der merkwürdigsten Begebenheiten, welche sich auf diesem Kriegsschauplatze in den Jahren 1793 und 1794. ereignet haben. Des Ersten Bandes zweytes Stück. Mit 17 Kupfertaf. à 5 Thlr.

Gebhard, J. G., Religionsunterricht nach der Lehre Jesu, à 2 gr.

Jahrbücher der preussischen Monarchie, 1799. Januar bis April. Der Jahrgang à 5 Thlr.

Ideler, G. F., wirthschaftliche Gärtnerey, 2ter u. letzter Band. à 1 Rthlr.

Leben und Thaten des geistreichen Edlen Don Quixote von la Mancha, von Migual Cervantes Saavedra, übersetzt von *L. Tieck*, 1ter Th. à 1 Thlr. 12 gr. (Die hierzu gehörigen Kupfer von Hrn. *W. Meil* können erst beym letzten Bande geliefert werden.)

Lesebuch, vaterländisches, für Land- und Soldatenschulen. Netto 5 gr. ordin. 6 gr.

Marie Muller. à 1 Thlr.

Sack, F. S. G., über die Verbesserung des Landschulwesens in der Kurmark Brandenburg. à 8 gr.

Savary, Zustand des alten und neuen Egypten, a. d. Franz. übers. und mit Anmerk. vom Prof. *Schneider*, 3 Theile. Neue Auflage. à 2 Thlr. 12 gr.

Shakespeare's dramatische Werke, neu bearbeitet von *A. W. Schlegel*, 4ter Band. à 1 Thlr.

Dasselbe auf Velinpapier. à 1 Thlr. 16 gr.

(5) R 2 *Welt-*

FIGURE 4.10 (*cont.*)

its letter, asserting instead that it was to be understood 'literally', 'exactly' and without additional supplement nor revision:

> Since the reviewer finally maintains that the *Critique* is not to be taken *literally* in what it says about sensibility and that anyone who wants to understand the *Critique* must first master the requisite *standpoint* (of Beck or of Fichte), because *Kant*'s precise words, like Aristotle's will destroy the spirit, I therefore declare again that the *Critique* is to be understood by considering exactly what it says and that it requires

> only the common standpoint that any mind sufficiently cultivated in such abstract investigations will bring to it.[232]

Faced with another's (mis)use of his authorial name to align his work with Fichte's idealist project, Kant's response was to so redeploy his full authorial name – including his unabbreviated forename, as if leaving no room for ambiguity – as to publicly declare his project's commitment to materiality.

In the light of Kant's comments on and uses of the authorial name across his texts, it is probable that Kant intended for his 1785 account of books in terms of publishers' and authors' names to be taken quite literally and materially. It was through the printing of names on textual publications that the system of publishers' and authors' rights could endure and advance public enlightenment. In Kant's media theory and practice we find an acute appreciation of the authorial name's role in enforcing authorial responsibility that anticipated Foucault's and Chartier's later recognition of the materialities of the author-function. Before the authorial name came to be equated with the proprietary author, it implemented an ethically and socially concerned author-function in late eighteenth-century Germany that Kant recognised to be essential to the public use of reason. This historical status of the authorial name discloses not only the failure of copyright to reckon fully with the materiality of literature but also the contingency of the myth of proprietary authorship that the law continues to preserve.

[232] Ibid., 560.

Conclusion

The Ethics of Digital Authorship

AFTER ENLIGHTENMENT

A technological gap has opened in the interval of more than two centuries since the original publication of Kant's text. Literary production has undergone radical changes that contest print's predominance during the German Enlightenment. The socio-technological assemblage of print actors and technologies seems to have long given way to an apparatus, or apparatuses, of new literary actors, objects, and techniques that properly define the digital present.[1] Consider the fact that today's authored manuscripts tend not to be handwritten, but instead are often typed on the computer with its installed word processor. The dominant writing technologies of professional authors are no longer pen and paper, but rather the keyboard and screen, and the latter's virtual space is a computer graphic with its own medial-material conditions of possibility that differ from those of the paper page.[2]. Alongside the making of manuscripts, the mass (re)production of books has technically departed from the procedures extending from Gutenberg's system of movable type. Whereas the turning out of books used to rely on hand, steam and electric letter-presses, it now occurs mainly through offset lithographic and digital printing. In the case of electronic books, or e-books, no equivalent method for producing physical

1 This has also been called the 'late age of print': see Jay David Bolter, *Writing Space: Computers, Hypertext, and the Remediation of Print*, 2nd ed. (Mahwah, NJ: Lawrence Erlbaum Associates, Publishers, 2001); Ted Striphas, *The Late Age of Print: Everyday Book Culture from Consumerism to Control* (New York: Columbia University Press, 2009).

2 For an account of the electronic remediation of print, see Bolter, *Writing Space*. Before the predominance of computers, mechanical typewriters already were becoming the preferred tools of writers, initiating or aggravating the de-personalisation of writing with the appearance of homogenous typed characters and erasure of individual handwriting. On the relationship between the typewriter and the human being, see Martin Heidegger, *Parmenides*, trans. André Schuwer and Richard Rojcewicz (Bloomington: Indiana University Press, 1992), 80–81; Friedrich Kittler, *Gramophone, Film, Typewriter*, trans. Geoffrey Winthrop-Young and Michael Wutz (Stanford, CA: Stanford University Press, 1999), 183–263.

paper copies in bulk is required. Any digital device with a screen and the requisite software may access the e-book.[3] Where printed books are made searchable and viewable on the Internet via mass digitisation projects, the techniques of photographic scanning and data processing via optical character recognition software are relied upon for the remediation of print. In terms of skills and instruments, or *technē* and technology, the making of identical book commodities has long departed from the 'first assembly-line'[4] of Gutenberg's letterpress.

Though at present we may still be surrounded by print publications, such printed matter are often not products of the eighteenth-century print machinery that generated the *Berlinische Monatsschrift*, nor even the predominant literary medium in our media ecology. The ambiguity surrounding print's place in the digital environment, its seeming endurance and extinction, was observed by Jay David Bolter at the turn of the new millennium: 'Although print remains indispensable, it no longer *seems* indispensable: that is its curious condition in the late age of print. Electronic technology provides a range of new possibilities, whereas the possibilities of print seem to have played out.'[5] In line with Kittler, I would stress that the rise of digital media is so indebted to print technology and its crucial role in the history of engineering that it would be misleading to represent digital pathways as distinct from the possibilities of print.[6] Nonetheless, the uncertain status of the print medium in contemporary culture is haunted by the possibility that the medial-material conditions for literary (re) production worldwide have already mutated, and are probably continuing to diverge, from those of late eighteenth-century Germany.

Further work should be done to diagrammatise the digital machinery or network that presently defines literary and cultural production. The print machinery mapped out in this book is but a stimulus for future projects on the continuously evolving medial infrastructure in which information is generated, disseminated and experienced by humans with their technologies. It is perhaps only by taking the material dimension of literature and other cultural forms seriously, as opposed to neglecting or suppressing it, that authorship and copyright studies may redress the proprietary bias in the law's present treatment of authors and works. To conclude this study of and alongside Kant, I perform a medial analysis of a digital text, namely the exemplary work of Wikipedia, likewise focusing on its paratextual materialities and implications on copyright's proprietary account of authorship. This may serve as a starting point for research into the present – and future – of authorship and copyright.

3 For a history of the e-book, see Striphas, *The Late Age of Print*, 19–46.

4 Marshall McLuhan, *The Gutenberg Galaxy* (Toronto: University of Toronto Press, 2017), 124.

5 Bolter, *Writing Space*, 2.

6 Friedrich Kittler, 'The Perspective of Print', trans. Geoffrey Winthrop-Young and Michael Wutz, *Configurations* 10, no. 1 (2002): 37.

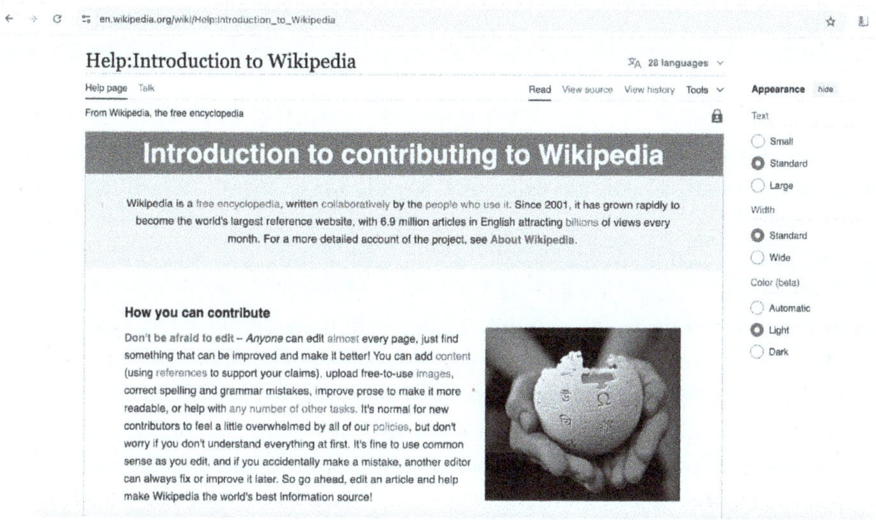

FIGURE C.1 Main page of Wikipedia.

MULTITUDINOUS AUTHORSHIP OF WIKIPEDIA

Visibly more so than a printed text bearing an author's name, the digital encyclopaedia Wikipedia stands at odds with the Romantic conception of the author as creator of the unique literary work. The home page of the English website reads, 'Welcome to Wikipedia, the free encyclopedia that anyone can edit.'[7] With 'edit' substituting for 'write', the putative origins of the literary work in the writer and their act of writing gives way to an always-already secondary, derivative act of revision without end. Clicking on the hyperlink attached to 'anyone can edit', we are led to one of its many 'help pages' introducing and encouraging the socially inclusive activity of 'contributing to Wikipedia' (see Figure C.1).[8] Viewers are assured '[not to] be 'afraid to edit – *Anyone* can edit almost every page; just find something that can be improved and make it better!'[9] The exclusivity of the Romantic author qua genius, whether in the Wordsworthian construct of the exceptional artist or in the Fichtean guise of the giver of singular form, is displaced by an ethic of inclusion that defines the digital *demos* of Wikipedians. On the right of the passage is a photograph of an anonymous pair of hands carefully holding an unfinished jigsaw-sculpture of a globe comprised of written scripts from multiple languages, as if emblematising the ongoing work of the Wikimedia Foundation to build a world representative of its

7 'Main Page', Wikipedia, last accessed 9 September 2024, https://en.wikipedia.org/wiki/Main_Page.

8 'Help: Introduction to Wikipedia', Wikipedia, last accessed 9 September 2024, https://en.wikipedia.org/wiki/Help:Introduction_to_Wikipedia.

9 Ibid.

culturally diverse participants. Both the text and the image are effectively deployed to convey and reinforce the collaborative and collective authorship of the world's largest encyclopaedia.

Wikipedia registers in its name the technological basis of its public or multitudinous authorship. A wiki is a piece of software, first launched in 1995, whereby digital users may create and edit any page of a website using a browser.[10] The editorial speed and efficiency that the content management system grants to collaborative projects, too, is nominally registered: the Hawaiian phrase 'wiki wiki' means 'superfast'.[11] Wikipedia adopts a wiki-based program, MediaWiki, for its articles, discussions and other collectively constituted pages.[12] Initially developed to expedite the creation of content for another online encyclopaedia authored by academic experts, Wikipedia quickly outgrew, outlived and displaced its host Nupedia.[13] As of August 2024, the English Wikipedia alone has 6,879,979 articles, averaging 533 new articles per day.[14] There are 47,927,179 registered users, with a minority of 115,260 having made edits within the last 30 days.[15] The Wikipedia community, whose members are known to one another as 'Wikipedians', is comprised of volunteers who, variously, edit and maintain the articles and contribute to community discussions.[16] In lieu of expertise, the world's largest online encyclopaedia is continually made and remade by a multitude of persons operating with and alongside their digital devices and programs.[17]

Wikipedia's distinctively collective model of authorship has not escaped the attention of copyright and intellectual property scholars.[18] From a legal perspective, the Wikipedia project is of interest for its ambivalent relationship with the copyright

[10] Ward Cunningham, Jimmy Wales, and Larry Sanger, "Wiki Pedia," C2, January 2001, http://wiki.c2.com/?WikiPedia. For a recent edited collection of essays on Wikipedia's two-decade history, see Joseph Reagle and Jackie Koerner, eds., *Wikipedia @ 20: Stories of an Incomplete Revolution* (Cambridge, MA: The MIT Press, 2020).

[11] Joseph Reagle, 'Wikipedia: The Happy Accident', *Interactions* 16, no. 3 (2009): 44.

[12] 'MediaWiki', Wikipedia, last accessed 9 September 2024, www.mediawiki.org/wiki/MediaWiki.

[13] Nupedia was shut down in September 2003: see Dariusz Jemielniak, *Common Knowledge? An Ethnography of Wikipedia* (Stanford, CA: Stanford University Press, 2014), 11.

[14] 'Wikipedia: Statistics', Wikipedia, last accessed 9 September 2024, https://en.wikipedia.org/wiki/Wikipedia:Statistics.

[15] 'Wikipedia: Wikipedians', Wikipedia, last accessed 9 September 2024, https://en.wikipedia.org/wiki/Wikipedia:Wikipedians#:~:text=This%20page%20in%20a%20nutshell,edit%20during%20the%20last%20month. Unregistered users, too, can make edits.

[16] For a six-year ethnographic study of the Wikipedia community, see Jemielniak, *Common Knowledge?*.

[17] As I discuss later, Wikipedia has nonetheless been criticised for its geographical, racial and gender bias. On Wikipedia's gender imbalance, see Heather Ford, *Writing the Revolution: Wikipedia and the Survival of Facts in the Digital Age* (Cambridge, MA: The MIT Press, 2022).

[18] See, for instance, Matthew Rimmer, 'Wikipedia, Collective Authorship and the Politics of Knowledge', in *Intellectual Property Reform: Fostering Innovation and Development*, ed. Christopher Arup and William van Caenegem (Cheltenham: Edward Elgar Publishing Limited, 2009), 172–98; Susan Corbett, 'Creative Common Licences, the Copyright Regime and the Online Community: Is There a Fatal Disconnect?', *The Modern Law Review* 74, no. 4

system, at once resisting the law's proprietary frame of understanding and reinforcing it through the very mechanisms adopted to overcome its limits. In spite of the perpetual revisability of its pages, Wikipedia presently affirms, as part of its legal policy, the extension of copyright protection to its articles by virtue of the international copyright regime. 'The text of Wikipedia is copyrighted (automatically under the Berne Convention) by Wikipedia editors and contributors and is formally licensed under one or several liberal licences.'[19] For permissions to be granted for the public's reuse of the articles, including their copying, distribution and modification, of the articles, the text itself is legally viewed as consisting of original literary works in which their editors, as author-creators, hold copyright. A dual-licencing regime, composed of the Creative Commons Attribution-ShareAlike 4.0 International License (CC BY-SA) and the GNU Free Documentation License (GFDL), and enforced through the terms and conditions on which Wikipedians agree to have their pages published, ensures the public's unmonetised access to these works. Creative Commons licences have evolved as a critical response to the recent encumbering of cultural forms, particularly online works, with increasingly restrictive private property rights that limit or obstruct the public's access to those works.[20] And yet, the licenced works belonging to the 'Creative Commons', those freely circulating in the public domain, are subjected to certain conditions in the licences. In the instance of Wikipedia's CC BY-SA, such conditions include the need to attribute the original authored work, and to similarly bind future uses of the 'derivative' work. Further, the Creative Commons regime not only presumes and legitimates copyright law but further bases its issuance of permissions upon the latter's proprietary system of rights.[21] In so sustaining the derivative regime, Wikipedia and other users of such licences could be said to inhibit alternative imaginings of literary and cultural regulation that do not take the possessive-individualist author-owner as their fundament.

Notwithstanding Wikipedia's embedment in the copyright regime, my claim is that the processes by which its pages are made and unmade fundamentally challenge the proprietary model of authorship, inviting, even necessitating, its rethinking. The principle and fact of collective participation in the digital-encyclopaedic production, which relies on a multitude of contributors interacting with the virtual platform, brings into focus the insufficiency of copyright's fiction of the work's origination in an independent, personal author. Rather than yielding piecemeal

(2011): 503–31; Daniela Simone, 'Wikipedia', in *Copyright and Collective Authorship: Locating the Authors of Collaborative Work* (Cambridge: Cambridge University Press, 2019), 72–99.

[19] 'Wikipedia: Copyrights', Wikipedia, last accessed on 9 September 2024, https://en.wikipedia.org/wiki/Wikipedia:Copyrights.

[20] See Corbett, 'Creative Common Licences, the Copyright Regime and the Online Community'.

[21] Ibid.

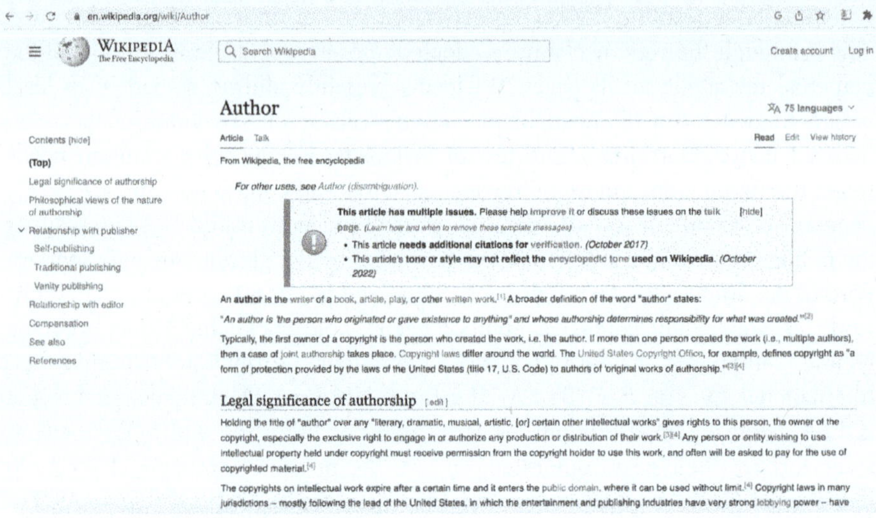
en.wikipedia.org/wiki/Author

WIKIPEDIA
The Free Encyclopedia

Search Wikipedia

Create account Log in

Author

75 languages

Contents [hide]
(Top)
Legal significance of authorship
Philosophical views of the nature of authorship
Relationship with publisher
Self-publishing
Traditional publishing
Vanity publishing
Relationship with editor
Compensation
See also
References

Article Talk Read Edit View history

From Wikipedia, the free encyclopedia

For other uses, see Author (disambiguation).

This article has multiple issues. Please help improve it or discuss these issues on the talk page. *(Learn how and when to remove these template messages)* [hide]

- This article **needs additional citations for** verification. *(October 2017)*
- This article's **tone or style may not reflect the** encyclopedic tone **used on Wikipedia**. *(October 2022)*

An **author** is the writer of a book, article, play, or other written work.[1] A broader definition of the word "author" states:

"An author is 'the person who originated or gave existence to anything' and whose authorship determines responsibility for what was created."[2]

Typically, the first owner of a copyright is the person who created the work, i.e. the author. If more than one person created the work (i.e., multiple authors), then a case of joint authorship takes place. Copyright laws differ around the world. The United States Copyright Office, for example, defines copyright as "a form of protection provided by the laws of the United States (title 17, U.S. Code) to authors of 'original works of authorship.'"[3][4]

Legal significance of authorship [edit]

Holding the title of "author" over any "literary, dramatic, musical, artistic, [or] certain other intellectual works" gives rights to this person, the owner of the copyright, especially the exclusive right to engage in or authorize any production or distribution of their work.[3][4] Any person or entity wishing to use intellectual property held under copyright must receive permission from the copyright holder to use this work, and often will be asked to pay for the use of copyrighted material.[4]

The copyrights on intellectual work expire after a certain time and it enters the public domain, where it can be used without limit.[4] Copyright laws in many jurisdictions – mostly following the lead of the United States, in which the entertainment and publishing industries have very strong lobbying power – have

FIGURE C.2 Author page of Wikipedia.

revisions to copyright law's doctrines, tests, and threshold requirements,[22] the inherent sociality and multiplicity of literary production suggests the need to move beyond the proprietary matrix in which the literary work is presently imagined, that is, as a mere literary commodity governed by an economic logic of rewards and incentives. Despite the anonymity of their production, the digital works of Wikipedia bear the potential to be rethought as a contemporary information technology that, not unlike Kant's printed mater, responds to the profoundly social problem of information overload.

A DIGITAL MACHINERY BEHIND 'AUTHOR'

Let us return to the interface of Wikipedia and its constitutive text and paratexts. If we type 'author' or 'authorship' in the search bar at the top of any Wikipedia page, we shall find an article on the matter that discloses some of the socio-technological bases on which the authorship of Wikipedia proceeds (see Figure C.2).[23] Before one even begins to read the propositions on authorship therein gathered, a caveat in the form of a text box announces its presence with a white exclamation mark in an orange circle to the left of the text. Apparently, the article has 'multiple issues',

[22] See, for instance, Simone, 'Wikipedia'.

[23] 'Author: Old revision', Wikipedia, last modified 20 January 2023, https://en.wikipedia.org/w/index.php?title=Author&oldid=1134784210. This analysis is based on the page last edited by Axinomancy9 on 20 January 2023, which remains accessible via the 'View history' tab. For the latest version of the article, see 'Author', Wikipedia, last accessed 9 September 2024, https://en.wikipedia.org/wiki/Author.

including its lack of citations for 'verification' (that is, for users to check that the information therein presented derives from a 'reliable source'[24]) and its failure to adopt the mandated 'encyclopedic' or 'formal tone'.[25] Instead of simply retrieving the information on the page, the reader is asked to 'improve it' or to discuss the issues on the 'talk page', both options facilitated with hyperlinks to the editing and discussion tabs of the article. Rather than present its content on authorship as stable, reliable knowledge, the article points to its state of incompletion and the means of resuming its production.

The article discloses various facets of authorship that already exceed copyright law's focus on authors as creators and first owners of intangible works. Though barely more than a hundred words, its opening paragraph offers four understandings of authorship whose corresponding citations doubly point to the multiple textual sources from which it is pieced, and to the bibliographic system that binds together Wikipedia and other publications, print or digital. Foregrounded, first, is a commonplace understanding of the author as a literary author, one authorised by the Cambridge Dictionary, a reference book that meets Wikipedia's requirement of verification. 'An author is the writer of a book, article, play, or other written work [Footnote 1: a hyperlink to the dictionary website].'[26] As if cognisant of the medial limits of this entry, the article provides a second definition that identifies the author as the personal point of origin of any work. It further ascribes to this creator responsibility for the work, thereby recognising an ethical understanding of authorship. 'A broader definition of the word "author" states: "An author is 'the person who originated or gave existence to anything' and whose authorship determines responsibility for what was created" [Footnote 2: a reference to Frank N. Magill's *Cyclopedia of World Authors* (1974)].'[27] Finally, the paragraph concludes by restating various aspects of the legal account of authorship, including the law's recognition of authors as first owners of copyright in the work, the doctrine of joint authorship, the possibility of doctrinal variations across copyright regimes and the US account of copyright as protecting authors of 'original works of authorship [Footnotes 3 and 4: two references to a digitised version of a print circular from the United States Copyright Office, and to Title 17 of the United States Code]'.[28] The footnotes attached to these four accounts of authorship – text-based, originalist, ethical and legal – evince the chain of relations between texts from which the paragraph

[24] 'Wikipedia: Verifiability', Wikipedia, last accessed 9 September 2024, https://en.wikipedia.org/wiki/Wikipedia:Verifiability.

[25] 'Wikipedia: Writing better articles', Wikipedia, last accessed 9 September 2024, https://en.wikipedia.org/wiki/Wikipedia:Writing_better_articles.

[26] 'Author: Old revision', Wikipedia, last modified 20 January 2023, https://en.wikipedia.org/w/index.php?title=Author&oldid=1134784210.

[27] 'Author: Old revision', Wikipedia, last modified 20 January 2023, https://en.wikipedia.org/w/index.php?title=Author&oldid=1134784210.

[28] 'Author: Old revision', Wikipedia, last modified 20 January 2023, https://en.wikipedia.org/w/index.php?title=Author&oldid=1134784210.

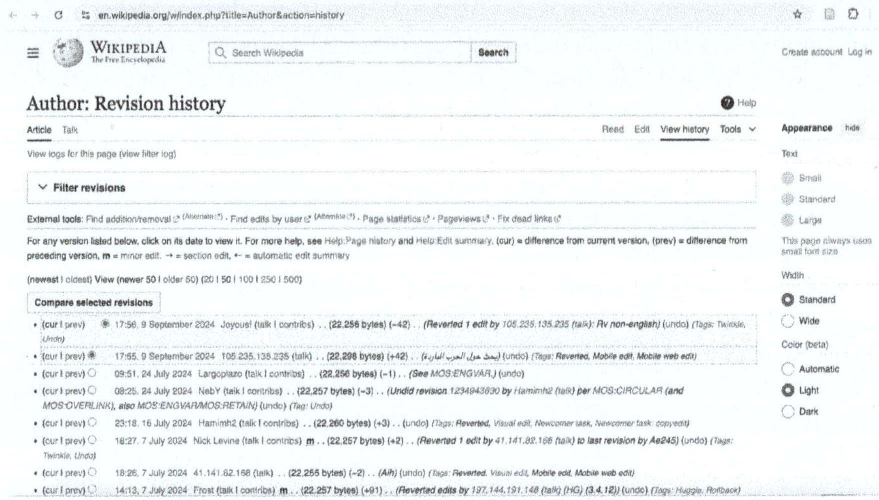

FIGURE C.3 Revision history of the author page of Wikipedia.

emerges. Rather than reinforce the myth of proprietary authorship, these references give credence to Barthes' view of the text as 'a tissue of quotations drawn from the innumerable centres of culture'.[29]

A digital machinery precedes, and is registered in, the Wikipedia article on authorship. Clicking on the 'View history' tab of the article allows us to glean that it has been edited more than 1,500 times since 30 August 2001 (see Figure C.3).[30] Known to Wikipedians as an authoritative record of all the page edits made and unmade, each timestamped and attributed to its user-contributor, this 'Revision history' sheds light on the history and process of its production. A quick scan of the page would reveal the absence of need for the contributors – including 'HeyElliott', Daask', and 'Largoplazo' – to base their usernames on their legal or formal names. Wikipedia does not verify the legal identities of its users.[31] This policy (or lack thereof) has allowed Wikipedians not only to retain their anonymity as virtual users but also to use false credentials to buttress their contributions to articles and discussion pages.[32] Indeed, the contributors may not even be human. On 11 November 2022, 'ClueBot NG', an approved program that makes 'repetitive

29 Roland Barthes, 'The Death of the Author', in *Image Music Text*, trans. Stephen Heath (London: Fontana, 1977), 146.

30 'Author: Revision history', Wikipedia, last accessed 9 September 2024, https://en.wikipedia.org/w/index.php?title = Author&action = history

31 The account is now blocked indefinitely for being a 'suspected sockpuppet' of another user, that is, one of multiple Wikipedia accounts created to circumvent its sanctions or policies: see 'Wikipedia: Sockpuppetry', Wikipedia, last accessed 9 September 2024, https://en.wikipedia.org/wiki/Wikipedia:Sockpuppetry.

32 See, for instance, 'Essjay controversy', Wikipedia, last accessed 9 September 2024, https://en.wikipedia.org/wiki/Essjay_controversy. For an extended reading of the event and its disclosure

automated or semi-automated edits that would be extremely tedious to do manually',[33] undid an act of vandalism by one 'Brian.Reinwald', who had, gratuitously, added a version of his own name to the page. Wikipedia allows bots to assist and automate edits of its pages, provided that the bots' users have sought the requisite approval to do so.[34] Instead of performing independent acts of creation, Wikipedia editors operate with and alongside machines to advance the project.

Scrolling down the page and clicking on each of the revised entries appearing in reverse chronology, we shall find that the four definitions of authorship were proposed by different users at different points in time. These definitions did not even appear in the same sequence or in the same form but had been inserted in a non-linear way and altered by multiple hands. When the page was first created on 30 August 2001 by 'Rmhermen', there was but a bare description of the author as 'a person who writes some text' and the generic examples of 'poetry or prose, technical [text] or literature'.[35] The more substantial, and corroborated, definition based on the Cambridge dictionary entry only appeared recently: on 20 October 2022, input by one 'Naomikrate'.[36] Even then, it was worded differently. Instead of concluding with the phrase 'or other written work', the sentence ended with 'mostly written work'. Whereas the present phrase strictly restricts authorship to that of textual production, the initial phrase recognised that non-cultural productions could well fall within its semantic ambit. It was only on 28 December 2022, with a grammatical edit by 'Quin Mas', that the definition of authorship shifted from one that was merely textually centred to another that is, now, exclusively textual.[37]

Before Naomikrate had made their edit, the 'second' and 'third' definitions affixed with the encyclopaedia reference were already present on the page. They appeared as early as more than a decade ago. On 16 June 2012, one 'Wahrmund' (German for 'true mouth') added the reference to Magill's 1974 *Cyclopedia of World Authors*.[38] Because the same definition sans encyclopaedia reference had already been present on the page, it remains unclear how far the definition was, indeed, supported by Magill's work. To clarify this it would be necessary to consult Magill's work. But no other Wikipedian has questioned Wahrmund's edit. As regards the fourth legal

of the Wikipedia community's attitudes towards rules of conduct and interpersonal trust, see Jemielniak, *Common Knowledge?*.

33 'User: ClueBot NG', Wikipedia, last accessed 9 September 2024, https://en.wikipedia.org/wiki/User:ClueBot_NG.

34 'Wikipedia: Bot policy', Wikipedia, last accessed 9 September 2024, https://en.wikipedia.org/wiki/Wikipedia:Bot_policy.

35 'Author: Old revision', Wikipedia, last modified 30 August 2001, https://en.wikipedia.org/w/index.php?title=Author&oldid=234349.

36 'Author: Difference between revisions', Wikipedia, last modified 20 October 2022, https://en.wikipedia.org/w/index.php?title=Author&diff=prev&oldid=1117156607.

37 'Author: Difference between revisions', last modified 28 December 2022, https://en.wikipedia.org/w/index.php?title=Author&diff=prev&oldid=1130104248.

38 'Author: Difference between revisions', Wikipedia, last modified 16 June 2012, https://en.wikipedia.org/w/index.php?title=Author&diff=prev&oldid=497913123.

definition of authorship, a version of it had appeared less than two weeks before Naomikrate's intervention. On 8 October 2022, 'Tropicalkitty' had furnished the definition as the opening paragraph of the first section entitled 'Legal significance of authorship'. But this definition would be moved to the untitled introductory paragraph above by Naomikrate on the same day (20 October 2022) and at the same time (06:39 UTC) as when the latter had inserted the Cambridge dictionary definition.[39]

As systematically registered on the history page, the article on authorship has undergone multiple revisions, involving both human users and non-human digital technologies, over two decades. The opening paragraph, alone, has entailed the contributions of no fewer than five Wikipedians, who had relied upon the pre-existing reference books, in digital and print forms, along with the citation system, to produce the definitions. Our retrieval of such a history is premised on our own embedment in the digital machinery that made the article. There could have been no 'authoring' of the page on 'author' without the digital machinery of Wikipedia. And it is this very same socio-technological apparatus that renders the work endlessly revisable. In contrast to copyright law's fiction of a stable literary work with a determinable point of origins, the work of any Wikipedia article is, in principle, unfinished. Each article opens unto the future, inviting further contributions from any connected to its generative machinery.

TOWARDS A MEDIA HISTORY OF THE DIGITAL ENCYCLOPAEDIA

The ethics of authorship arises as an important yet unresolved question in the Wikipedia article and the paratextual indices of its making. In the third definition of authorship stemming from Magill's *Cyclopedia*, responsibility for the work is tied to its origination in the author. Not simply a basis on which to grant proprietary rights, authorship is suggested to bear an ethical dimension that remains undetermined. As discussed in Chapter 4, Kant had attempted to (re)assert his presence 'in' the text through his printed authorial name as a technique for managing information overload during the German Enlightenment. For Kant, responsibility extended to accounting for the interventions made and published under one's authorial name. Wikipedia departs from the printed work as understood by Kant in its absence of requirement to specify an editor's legal name or to verify their credentials. Composed and endless subject to revision by a multitude of authors, human and non-human, the digital text does not lend itself to be ethically assessed from the standpoint of the personal author. On what other grounds, then, might the responsibility for Wikipedia's making and its effects in the world be understood?

39 'Author: Old revision', Wikipedia, last modified 20 October 2022, https://en.wikipedia.org/w/index.php?title=Author&oldid=1117158108.

In step with the preceding analysis of Kant's essay, I claim that the ethics of Wikipedia authorship should be understood in reference to its material form and historical conditions of possibility. Specifically, a media history of Wikipedia, as a digital text that extends from a literary-scientific tradition of the encyclopaedia, could clarify its ethical role in the digital public sphere. The genre of the encyclopaedia dates back to as early as the first century AD.[40] Often regarded as the first surviving encyclopaedia of Western civilisation (though this perception has also been contested for its anachronism),[41] Pliny the Elder's *Historia Naturalis* is an illuminating precedent. Composed of thirty-seven books (ten published in Pliny's time and the remainder by his namesake nephew), the ancient Roman inventory of details and facets of the natural world, ranging from cosmology to geography, humanity, zoology, botany, medicine, minerals, art and more, has been read in two principal ways that may inform our understanding of the present digital text.[42]

First, from an informational perspective, the *Historia Naturalis* functions as technology that exhaustively compiles in a single site the innumerable records of natural knowledge, sorting them into lists of structured items in its numbered volumes. In so doing, the ancient encyclopaedia anticipates by two millennia Wikipedia's project of summarising knowledge, general and specialised alike, and presenting them in variously categorised articles. By virtue of differences in medial form, the paratexts facilitating information retrieval from the *Historia Naturalis* and Wikipedia differ. Originally appearing in the form of Roman scrolls and subsequently reproduced in codex forms leading up to modern print editions,[43] the Pliny text utilises a *summarium*, a list in the first volume outlining the contents of the remaining thirty-six volumes, to guide the reader.[44] For instance, a reader interested in learning about the making and use of papyrus and parchment in antiquity could be directed by the list to the thirteen volume, particularly to those passages pertaining to 'Papyrus; employment of paper; when begun; how manufactured; 9 kinds;

[40] See Aude Doody, *Pliny's Encyclopedia: The Reception of Natural History* (Cambridge: Cambridge University Press, 2010).

[41] On the difficulty, and risks, of assimilating Pliny's text, a text from Roman antiquity, to the genre of the encyclopedia as a modern category, see Doody, *Pliny's Encyclopedia*, 11–39. Other scholarship directs us instead to the sixteenth century as the time when the first encyclopedia, namely Paul Scaliger's *Encyclopaedia, seu orbis terrarium* (1559), emerges: see Robert Collison, *Encyclopedias: Their History Throughout the Ages* (London: Hafner, 1966).

[42] See 'Links to translation of Pliny the Elder, "Natural History"', Attalus, last accessed 9 September 2024, www.attalus.org/info/pliny_hn.html.

[43] Cornelia Vismann, *Files: Law and Media Technology*, trans. Geoffrey Winthrop-Young (Stanford, CA: Stanford University Press, 2008), 41–47. On Pliny's note-taking methods (as recounted by his nephew), including his oral dictation of passages of interest from source texts to a secretary or slave, who then transcribed them onto wax tablets and, later, papyrus rolls, see Ann M. Blair, *Too Much to Know: Managing Scholarly Information before the Modern Age* (New Haven, CT: Yale University Press, 2010), 80–81.

[44] Pliny, *Natural History in Ten Volumes*, trans. H. Rackham, vol. I (Cambridge, MA: Harvard University Press, 1938), 24–167.

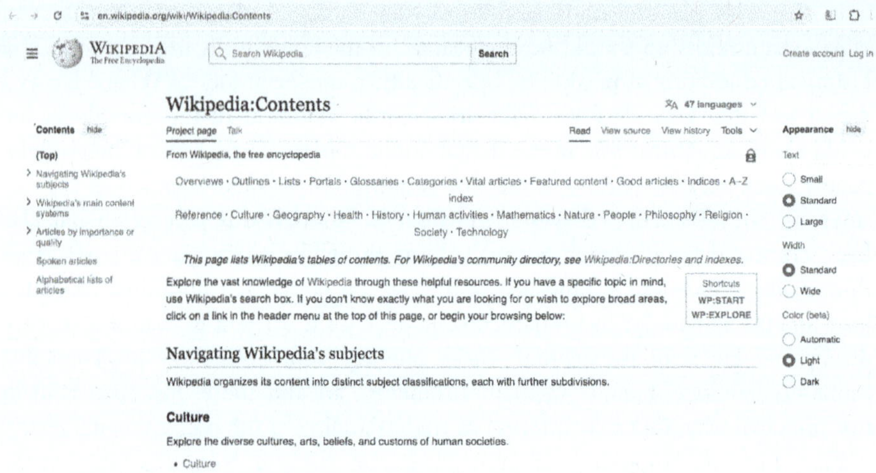

FIGURE C.4 Contents of Wikipedia.

mode of testing papers; defects of papers; paper-glue'.[45] Unlike the *Historia Naturalis* and modern print encyclopaedias, Wikipedia does not have a static list or table of contents as part of its front matter. Instead, its online articles are presently grouped and divided, at the first level, into twenty-four categories that are not unified under an overarching principle of classification, as if recalling Borges's monstrous animal taxonomy of the Chinese encyclopaedia (see Figure C.4).[46] Listed horizontally, and across two lines, the categories begin with some foregrounding content that are valued for meeting high editorial standards ('Vital articles', 'Featured Content', 'Good articles'), which are abruptly followed by other indexical categories ('Overviews', 'Outlines', 'Lists', 'Portals', 'Glossaries', 'Categories', 'Indices', 'A-Z index', 'Reference'), as if recognising the insufficiency of the present index. Only thereafter do we see some common subject categories ('Culture', 'Geography', 'Health', 'History', 'Human activities', 'Mathematics', 'Nature', 'People', 'Philosophy', 'Religion', 'Society', 'Technology'). Clicking on any of these hyperlinked categories will lead us to other pertinent pages composed of more hyperlinked words and phrases that, in some way, relate to the initial term. From 'Culture', we could move to 'literature' as a subcategory including both 'fiction' and 'non-fiction'; before turning, for instance, to the latter page that provides

[45] Ibid,, 69. For criticisms of inaccuracies in Pliny's account and his failure to credit sources, see Adam Bülow-Jacobsen, 'Writing Materials in the Ancient World', in *The Oxford Handbook of Papyrology*, ed. Roger S Bagnall (Oxford: Oxford University Press, 2009), 5–8.

[46] 'Wikipedia: Contents', Wikipedia, last accessed 9 September 2024, https://en.wikipedia.org/wiki/Wikipedia:Contents. See Foucault's famous reading of Borges's discussion of the Chinese encyclopaedia in Michel Foucault, *The Order of Things: An Archaeology of the Human Sciences* (London: Routledge, 2002), xvi–xxvi.

another monstrous list of genres, forms and formats, including the 'encyclopedia'; the clicking of which could direct us back to 'Wikipedia' as one of the 'digital and open-source versions in the 21st century ... [that have] vastly expanded the accessibility, authorship, readership, and variety of encyclopedia entries'.[47]

Perhaps more so than the horizontal list of twenty-four categories, accessibility to Wikipedia's articles is secured by the search bar at the top of every Wikipedia page. As demonstrated in our search for the article on 'author' and 'authorship', the search function allows the reader to find the pertinent page or pages relating to any given term. Indeed, external search engines such as Google Search act as one of the chief gateways to Wikipedia. Presently, a Google web search query on 'author' produces about 5,850,000,000 results. Out of these, the first result to appear immediately after the definition in Oxford Languages is a link to, and excerpt from, the Wikipedia page on authorship. Search engines and digital indices composed of, and building upon, hyperlinks – that is, cross-references that afford immediate access to relevant items of information – are now some of the key devices by which Wikipedia and other sites present themselves to their reader-users.

Before further clarifying the place of Wikipedia in the medial history of information, we should note, too, that Pliny's text has been incisively critiqued to be a product, and an agent, of ancient Roman imperialism.[48] Approached not simply as a compulsive aggregation of facts but rather as a cultural artefact arising from within a place at a certain time, a reference book such as Pliny's catalogue of natural knowledge could index the cultural tendencies and geopolitics in which it participated. As a classicist Trevor Murphy has demonstrated, the information recorded in *Historia Naturalis* reflect the values of its author and the Roman culture to which he belonged. Far from being dead, or rather in spite of his absence from the text à la Barthes, the author leaves behind in it a ghostly presence, in the form of material residues of the epitextual background in which he and his privileged contemporaries operated. Consider, for instance, Pliny's account of the accomplishments of human race in the seventeenth book, in which the Roman statesman Cicero, amongst others of his glorious countrymen, received superlative praise:

> But what excuse could I have for omitting mention of you, Marcus Tullius? or by what distinctive mark can I advertise your superlative excellence? by what in preference to the most honourable testimony of that whole nation's decree, selecting out of your entire life only the achievements of your consulship? Your oratory induced the tribes to discard the agrarian law, that is, their own livelihood; your advice led them to forgive Roscius the proposer of the law as to the theatre, and to tolerate with equanimity the mark put upon them by a distinction of seating; your

47 'Encyclopedia', Wikipedia, last accessed 9 September 2024, https://en.wikipedia.org/wiki/Encyclopedia.

48 Other than Trevor Murphy's work discussed below, see also Sorcha Carey, *Pliny's Catalogue of Culture: Art and Empire in the Natural History* (Oxford: Oxford University Press, 2003); Doody, *Pliny's Encyclopedia*, 58–75.

> entreaty made the children of the men sentenced to proscription ashamed to stand for office; your genius drove Catiline to flight; you proscribed Mark Antony. Hail, first recipient of the title of Father of the Country, first winner of a civilian triumph and of a wreath of honour for oratory, and parent of eloquence and of Latin literature; and (as your former foe, the dictator Caesar, wrote of you) winner of a greater laurel wreath than that of any triumph, inasmuch as it is a greater thing to have advanced so far the frontiers of the Roman genius than the frontiers of Rome's empire.[49]

Pliny's catalogue of the natural world, whilst beginning from the heavens and ending with a marvel at its minerals, had Rome as its evaluative centre. The achievements of the Roman empire, and those of its celebrated public figures, are selectively monumentalised in the reference book. As Murphy has sharply noted, Pliny's text institutionalised the common knowledge of his fellow citizen-readers of ancient Rome, presupposing and perpetuating a community of readers with shared values and endorsements of their civilisational achievements.[50] A critical archaeology of the reference book could disclose the Roman imperialist bias that informs, and is supported by, its production and transmission of knowledge.[51]

This second *political* perspective on the Pliny text is no less valuable to our present assessment of the digital encyclopaedia. Wikipedia purports to be a radically democratic project to which any user can contribute as editor. But do the actual composition of editors, and the contents of their articles, indeed reflect and align with the declared ethos? Despite our characterisation of the Wikipedia authorship as based in a collaborative multitude, for some time now critical literature on the encyclopaedia has disclosed its geographical, racial and gender bias.[52] According to recent surveys, less than a quarter of Wikipedians are women, and the article contents tend to be gendered, provoking the holding feminist 'edit-a-thons' to correct the bias in coverage.[53] In 2015, a *New Statesman* journalist compared the edit counts of two Wikipedia pages on pornographic actresses and female poets, which emblematises the encyclopaedia's poor representation of topics of feminine interest: 'The list of poets has been edited 600 times, by near 300 editors. The list of female porn stars is a newer page but over 1,000 editors have edited it more than

[49] 'Book 7, sections 117–18', Attalus, last accessed 9 September 2024, www.attalus.org/translate/pliny_hn7b.html.

[50] Trevor Murphy, *Pliny the Elder's Natural History: The Empire in the Encyclopedia* (Oxford: Oxford University Press, 2004), 16.

[51] See Michel Foucault, *The Archaeology of Knowledge* (London: Routledge, 2002).

[52] See, for instance, Mark Graham et al., 'Uneven Geographies of User-Generated Information: Patterns of Increasing Informational Poverty', *Annals of the Association of American Geographers* 104, no. 4 (2014): 746–64; Mackenzie Emily Lemieux, Rebecca Zhang, and Francesca Tripodi, '"Too Soon" to Count? How Gender and Race Cloud Notability Considerations on Wikipedia', *Big Data & Society* 10, no. 1 (2023): 1–14; Pablo Beytía and Claudia Wagner, 'Visibility Layers: A Framework for Systematising the Gender Gap in Wikipedia Content', *Internet Review Policy* 11, no. 1 (2022): 1–22.

[53] See Ford, *Writing the Revolution*.

2,500 times.'[54] Let us add that the 'author' page of Wikipedia neither refers to any related work by a woman author nor recognises the struggles of women writers in literary production and regulation. Wikipedia's problematic gendering has recently been traced to its infrastructure: its policies, logics and codes.[55] For instance, Wikipedia's overlapping policies of 'neutral point of view', 'no original research' and 'verifiability' have tended to restrict the production of content to a mirroring of pre-existing sources and publications that, in themselves, reflect and contribute to male bias. Dependent on a gendered body of knowledge that remains to be fixed, Wikipedia is conditioned to perpetuate its bias and, particularly in the light of its popularity, to reinforce the marginalisation of women in knowledge production. In an unequal world, these policies act as the means by which the Wikipedia justifies its irresponsible contributions to gender inequality and other social problems. A fuller account of the ethical dimension of the encyclopaedia would have to address its necessary embroilment in emancipatory struggles of the present.

To conclude this analysis, Wikipedia may be further compared with some of its key eighteenth-century print predecessors to deepen our understanding of its informational function. As helpfully outlined by Wellmon, the European Enlightenment saw the purposeful making and conceptualisation of encyclopaedias to manage the surfeit in print, some key examples of which could be understood as evidencing three distinct generic models.[56] The first model is a *cartographic* understanding of the encyclopedia as a text that helped readers to navigate the surfeit of print. Denis Diderot's and Jean d'Alembert's co-edited *Encyclopédie* (1751–1772) was an organised abbreviation and collation of 'all knowledge that now lies scattered over the face of the earth'.[57] The project aimed to produce not so much an exhaustive record of knowledge as a practical survey of it for learners. As understood by its co-editor d'Alembert, the *Encyclopédie* acted as 'a kind of world map'[58] that oriented its readers to the terrain of the various existing knowledge systems and their potential points of intersection. Its other co-editor Diderot understood the value of their cartographic work in a future of ever-accruing print publications that would inhibit humanity's learning:

54 Jenny Kleeman, 'The Wikipedia Wars: Does It Matter If Our Biggest Source of Knowledge Is Written by Men?', *The New Statesman*, 26 May 2015.

55 See Heather Ford and Judy Wajcman, '"Anyone Can Edit", Not Everyone Does: Wikipedia's Infrastructure and the Gender Gap', *Social Studies of Science* 47, no. 4 (2017): 511–27.

56 Chad Wellmon, *Organizing Enlightenment: Information Overload and the Invention of the Modern Research University* (Baltimore, Maryland: John Hopkins University Press, 2015), 77–107.

57 Denis Diderot, 'Encyclopedia', in *Rameau's Nephews and Other Works*, ed. and trans. Jacques Barzun (New York: Doubleday, 1956), 291; cited in Wellmon, *Organizing Enlightenment*, 83.

58 Jean le Rond d'Alembert, *Preliminary Discourse to the Encyclopedia of Diderot*, trans. Richard N. Schwab (Indianapolis, IN: Bobbs-Merrill Educational Publishing, 1983), 47–48; cited in Wellmon, *Organizing Enlightenment*, 83.

> As long as the centuries continue to unfold, the number of books will grow continually, and no one can predict that a time will come when it will be almost as difficult to learn anything from books as from the direct study of the universe. It will be almost as convenient to search for some bit of truth concealed in nature as it will be to find it hidden away in an immense multitude of volumes. When that comes, a project, until then neglected because the need for it was not felt, will have to be undertaken.[59]

Diderot's insistence on the difficult project of securing writers to contribute to the *Encyclopédie* over the two decades from 1751 evidenced his belief that the text was a solution to the escalating problem of print proliferation in his time.

The second model of the encyclopaedia is a *systemic* or *formal* understanding of the text as presenting the underlying logical structure that unified true claims to knowledge. Advanced in opposition to exhaustive projects of encyclopaedias (many of which collapsed by the early nineteenth century),[60] the systemic standpoint sought not to be comprehensive in its content and cross-references but to clarify the systemic unity of knowledge. Building upon Kant's concept of the system as 'the unity of the manifold cognitions under one idea',[61] Wilhelm Traugott Krug advanced an encyclopaedic account of the sciences based on what he regarded as their basic structure.[62] 'Krug organized sciences according to common elements that were preestablished as the basic characteristics of a science: their basic concepts, content, boundaries, relationships to other sciences, current states, and the methods and literary aids for engaging them.'[63] The encyclopaedic impulse was to uncover, or perhaps to project, a rational order of articulable categories to which knowledge belonged.

Whereas the first and second models of the encyclopaedia still revolved around the print medium as the principal means of knowledge dissemination, the third *ethical* model of the encyclopaedia was evidenced in teaching practices increasingly adopted in German universities during the 1780s and 1790s. From this perspective, the encyclopaedic drive towards uncovering the systemic unity of knowledge and sciences was understood as an ideal scientific disposition to be imparted to and embodied by persons. Recalling the emphasis in Pliny's text on providing a 'general

[59] Diderot, 'Encyclopedia', 314; cited in Wellmon, *Organizing Enlightenment*, 85.

[60] See, for instance, Friedrich Martini, *Allgemeine Geschichte der Natur in alphabetischer Ordnung* (Berlin: Joachim Pauli, 1774) ('Universal History of Nature in Alphabetical Order'); Heinrich Köster, Martin Gottfried and Johann Friedrich Ross, eds, *Deutsche Enzyklopädie, oder Allgemeines Real-Wörterbuch aller Künste und Wissenschaften* (Frankfurt am Main: Varrentrap Sohn & Wenner, 1778–1807) ('German Encyclopedia, or Universal Dictionary of All Arts and Sciences'); cited in Wellmon, *Organizing Enlightenment*, 88–90.

[61] Immanuel Kant, *Critique of Pure Reason*, ed. and trans. Paul Guyer and Allen W. Wood (Cambridge: Cambridge University Press, 1998), 691.

[62] See Wilhelm Traugott Krug, *Versuch einer systematischen Enzyklopädie der Wissenschaften* (Leipzig: Winckelmann & Barth, 1796) ('Attempt at a Systematic Encyclopaedia of the Sciences'); discussed in Wellmon, *Organizing Enlightenment*, 94–96.

[63] Wellmon, *Organizing Enlightenment*, 94.

education' (*enkyklios paideia*) to its readers, 'encyclopedic lecture courses'[64] introducing the ethos that purportedly motivated all the sciences were offered by the University of Jena and other German universities towards in the last two decades of the eighteenth century. These lectures stressed, and enacted, the university's function of cultivating students as scholars interested in, and competent to, generate scientific knowledge.[65] 'The study of the science of sciences excites, enlivens, and maintains the drive to infinite expansion, as well as perfected unity and the organic mutual determination of all knowledge. It gives all students a purposeful direction.'[66] August Wilhelm Schlegel stressed the importance of this scientific spirit within the wider medial and social context in which such encyclopaedic lectures were given.[67] Understood not simply as a curated repository of knowledge but rather as a subject's propensity for the assimilation and production of knowledge, the encyclopaedia was similarly advanced as a solution to the problem of the expanding book trade and the superficial modes of reading and it encouraged. As Schlegel observed,

> Twice a year the great book fair flood (not even counting the smaller, monthly floods with which the journals are washed up) casts on land the newly birthed books in great balls from out of the great ocean of writerly shallowness and banality. These are then ravenously devoured by the great mob of the reading world, but without affording any nourishment. And they are just as quickly forgotten and fade away into the filth of the reading libraries and with the next trade fair the whole cycle begins again.[68]

To respond effectively to the surfeit of print, Schlegel argued that individuals had to possess and enact the encyclopaedic disposition, or what he understood to be the 'method and spirit of the sciences',[69] which would allow them to grasp the organic unity of the sciences while contributing to their development in time.

From the distance of the twenty-first century, the three models of the eighteenth-century encyclopaedia, particularly the second formal version, may seem quite removed from their present digital counterpart. No search for systemic unity is apparent in the multitudinous making of more than six million Wikipedia articles, each often the product of innumerable revisions that, instead, work on the less ambitious long-term collective task of improving its readability, coherence and cross-checkability. Wikipedia's editing policy page presents a typical image of an article's history:

64 Wellmon, *Organizing Enlightenment*, 96.

65 The scholars giving these lectures in Jena included Christian Gottfried Schütz, Johann Heinrich Gottlieb Heusinger and Carl Christian Schmid: see Wellmon, *Organizing Enlightenment*, 97–101.

66 Carl Christian Erhard Schmid, *Allgemeine Encyklopädie und Methodologie der Wissenschaften* (Jena: Akademische Buchhandlung: 1810) ('Universal Encyclopaedia and Methodology of the Sciences'), 7, iii; cited in Wellmon, *Organizing Enlightenment*, 100.

67 On Schlegel's lectures on the literature and the encyclopaedia, see Wellmon, *Organizing Enlightenment*, 101–07.

68 Wellmon, *Organizing Enlightenment*, 102.

69 Ibid., 104.

> [One] person may start an article with an overview of a subject or a few random facts. Another may help standardize the article's formatting or have additional facts and figures or a graphic to add. Yet another may bring better balance to the views represented in the article and perform fact-checking and sourcing to existing content. At any point during the process, the article may become disorganized or contain substandard writing.[70]

The human contributors are often not systems-oriented philosophers, but instead 'amateur volunteers'[71] who edit pages in their spare time.

Likewise, in respect of the cartographic and ethical models, Wikipedia only subscribes to each in limited ways. The article on 'author', which includes references to Barthes' and Foucault's key works, may well act as a starting guide to the field on authorship and copyright. However, its utility as a map is presently restricted by its scope. As foregrounded in another orange-coloured 'dispute tag'[72] dating back to August 2021, the section on '[p]hilosophical views on authorship' restricts itself to what the editor has called 'postmodern'[73] theories of authorship, and thus 'needs expansion'.[74] Its omission of female and feminist perspectives on authorship and literary production, on the other hand, is not at all mentioned. Further, Wikipedia's disconnection from the university, which tends to prefer instead its system of peer review, diminishes its role in the training of students to embody what Schlegel and the contemporaries celebrated to be the encyclopaedic spirit. Often dismissed by academic experts as lacking rigor in its production, Wikipedia may not seem to exemplify the sort of scientific ethos, the 'method and spirit of the sciences',[75] advanced by the late eighteenth-century German philosophers.

And yet, across the divide of more than two centuries, Wikipedia joins hands with the eighteenth-century encyclopaedic publications and teaching practices to address a familiar problem of information overload. In the present 'information age'[76], it is not simply a glut of print that confronts the learner but also a supersaturation of information relayed through digital-communicative channels.[77] The staggering sum of six million Wikipedia articles may seem, of itself, to contribute to the problem of excess. But in perceptual terms, the on-screen appearance of the pertaining

70 'Wikipedia: Editing policy', Wikipedia, last accessed 9 September 2024, https://en.wikipedia.org/wiki/Wikipedia:Editing_policy.

71 Jemielniak, *Common Knowledge?*, 22.

72 'Wikipedia: Template index/Disputes, Wikipedia, last accessed 9 September 2024, https://en.wikipedia.org/wiki/Wikipedia:Template_index/Disputes.

73 'Author: Old revision', Wikipedia, last modified 20 January 2023, https://en.wikipedia.org/w/index.php?title=Author&oldid=1134784210.

74 'Author: Old revision', Wikipedia, last modified 20 January 2023, https://en.wikipedia.org/w/index.php?title=Author&oldid=1134784210.

75 Wellmon, *Organizing Enlightenment*, 104.

76 On the information age, see Blair, *Too Much to Know*; Wellmon, *Organizing Enlightenment*.

77 For a recent account of the bodily exhaustion induced by information overload, see Tung-Hui Hu, *Digital Lethargy: Dispatches from an Age of Disconnection* (Cambridge, MA: The MIT Press, 2022).

Wikipedia page with at least a basic understanding of the subject matter whose key word the user had input in Google Search (or Wikipedia's search bar) does mitigate the issue of information superabundance. A working map, possibly even directing the reader-user to some of the peer-reviewed publications preferred by universities and scholarly experts, is available at the fingertips of the digital user.[78] In so connecting to, and selectively foregrounding, the bibliographic network of textual publications, the Wikipedia article helps to orient readers to the field of authorship. Such references, if followed through, could act as the means by which to disclose and displace the ideological and socio-political limits of the Wikipedia text.

If Wikipedia eschews the traditional markers of expertise such as credential controls and peer review, it is because the encyclopaedia prioritises the democratisation of knowledge production. In lieu of the truth-seeking ethos of eighteenth-century encyclopaedic practices, the Wikipedia community embodies, and advances, a mass-participatory ethos of authorship where anyone may contribute to the formation and development of its pages. Kantian critical debate is not absent from the project but rather informs both the continual revision of its articles and the disputes recorded in the discussion tabs. The evolution of the authorship page from one comprised of only two lines to a multi-sectioned piece with supporting references was accompanied by more than 1,500 edits made in response to the limits of prior versions. If we click on the 'talk' tab of the article, we shall find various suggestions, offered by other Wikipedians, on ways in which the article could be expanded. To cite three of these: 'Another term, someone could elaborate on is "collective authorship". Thanks.' 'It would be useful to further comment on authorship with regards to the use of pseudonyms. An important question in that field would be, how the adoption of a (non-narrator) persona by a writer affects the author of his/her text: Is a person writing once under his/her real name and once under an adopted name still the same author; or is it two different authors that are writing and just happen to spring from that same person?' 'The lead image was changed from a portrait of Mark Twain to an image of Toni Morrison, then reverted. I believe the original edit was constructive for a few reasons . . . I suggest that the change to Morrison be restored.' All three suggestions identify certain limits of the article – namely, its focus on sole authorship, onymous authorship and male authorship – and call for their displacement. It is through such discursive contributions, and the accompanying editorial acts, that Wikipedia's digital machinery is immanently steered to enhance the quality of its articles and exercise its function of organising knowledge amidst information overload. A democratic model of critical public debate, taking place within and documented by the digitally mediated pages of Wikipedia, reflects the mass-participatory ethos

[78] Included in the Wikipedia page on authorship, for instance, is a reference to Alexander Nehamas, 'What an Author Is', *The Journal of Philosophy* 83, no. 11 (1986): 685–91.

of the twenty-first-century encyclopaedia: 'the free encyclopedia that anyone can edit'.[79]

Following the guide of the recent feminist-technological literature, further assessments of Wikipedia's function as a contemporary information technology that democratically inflects Kant's project of enlightenment should look closely at its constitutive infrastructure. How far do the policies of allowing Wikipedians to make their contributions without verifying their legal identities or credentials, and of requiring instead that these contributions be traceable to existing publications, advance its function of assisting user-readers with the problem of information overload? Do the presentation of distinct usernames and, in the instance of users without accounts, the publishing of their IP addresses, fulfil the same function of ensuring authorial accountability as the printed authorial name in Kant's account? Should the mass-participatory ethos of Wikipedia be allowed to override the concern for individual authorial responsibility? Or ought more controls be put in place to cultivate such responsibility? How far should Wikipedia's existing policies, logics and codes be preserved in the light of feminist, racial and decolonial critiques? Could the digital encyclopaedia further evolve to accommodate alternative modalities of authorship? A media history of Wikipedia, one adequate to address these deeply ethical questions, remains to be written.

Contemporary euphoria and anxieties surrounding the evolution of the internet, its promise of disseminating knowledge to the masses and its threat of dispossessing readers of their rational faculties, are preceded by similar concerns with print technology expressed in the late eighteenth century. Kant and other contributors to the *Berlinische Monatsschrift* understood that the print machinery had to be strategically steered to advance practices of critical public debate essential to individual and collective emancipation. Their interventions in the name of enlightenment, a project that depended on the interaction between humans and print media, called for a renewed attention to those medial-material bases for recording and transmitting knowledge. The historical case of authorship in the German Enlightenment suggests that we should neither romanticise nor demonise technology, but rather critically cultivate our contact with it.[80] Such cultivation would require that we develop a medial-theoretical and -historical competence to situate contemporary knowledge forms such as Wikipedia, alongside and against their predecessors, so as to clarify their continuities and differences. More so than the proprietary idiom of copyright, it is this medial-material literacy that enables us to respond to the ethical stakes and demands of authorship in the digital present.

79 'Main Page', Wikipedia, last accessed 9 September 2024, https://en.wikipedia.org/wiki/Main_Page.

80 Chad Wellmon, 'Why Google Isn't Making Us Stupid. . .or Smart', *The Hedgehog Review* 14, no. 1 (2012): 66–80.

Index

authorship
  author-function, 2, 11–13, 16, 119–22, 124, 126, 128, 130–31, 138, 151, 158, 160, 162, 166
  history, 4, 7, 9–10, 13
  proprietary, 1–2, 4, 6–8, 23–24, 55, 76, 83, 114–16, 118, 121, 126, 130, 139, 142, 149, 157–60, 162, 166, 174
  responsibility, 134, 163, 166, 176, 186
  Romantic genius, 2, 6, 15

book history, 2, 11, 23, 46, 60, 74, 127

copyright
  history, 1, 7, 9–10, 126
  Kantian copyright scholarship, 9–10, 17, 75, 134, 162
  law, 1–2, 4, 29–31, 33, 36, 38, 41, 44, 50, 52–53, 55, 76–77, 82–83, 85, 88, 91–92, 98–99, 118, 120–21, 130–31, 135, 141, 156, 158, 162, 172–73, 176
  utilitarian, 2–3, 6, 28–29, 31, 33–34, 37, 40, 53, 84, 162

digital
  encyclopaedia, 169, 180, 186
  machinery, 168, 174, 176, 185
  mass digitisation, 21–22, 24–26, 31, 50, 168
  present, 167, 186

German Enlightenment, 2, 55, 65, 74, 76, 86, 98, 145, 149, 167, 176, 186

Johann Gottlieb Fichte, 5–6, 8, 15, 85–88, 91–94, 96–98, 102, 106–7, 110, 112, 114–15, 132, 135, 139, 141, 163, 165

literary studies, 2, 11, 17, 46, 119, 121

materiality
  of literature, 1, 11, 14, 166
  medial-materiality, 1–2, 7, 9–10, 18, 55, 67, 73–74, 76, 95, 98, 145, 158, 163, 167–68, 186
  visual, 9, 82, 84–85, 95, 97, 102, 107, 109, 115, 145
media theory, 2, 10–11, 14, 46, 51, 121, 145, 160, 162, 166

paratexts, 2, 13, 18, 55, 68, 70, 73–75, 98, 122, 158, 160, 172, 177
  authorial name, 2, 10, 17, 116–18, 120–22, 124–25, 129–30, 135, 138–39, 142, 146, 148–49, 158–59, 162–63, 166, 176, 186
  catchwords, 2, 55, 68–70, 73, 98, 128, 158
  footnotes, 9, 42, 48, 56, 60, 67, 95, 97, 139, 173
  front matter, 2–3, 10, 13, 17, 55, 67, 70, 72, 98, 107, 116, 119, 122, 127–28, 130, 142, 151, 158, 178
  hyperlinks, 173, 179
  signature marks, 2, 55, 69–70, 73, 98, 128, 158
  typeface, 10, 18, 47, 78, 82, 84–85, 96–100, 102–3, 105–7, 109, 112, 115, 128, 139
  typesetting, 2, 10, 17–18, 78, 96–97, 99
print
  actors, 10, 14–15, 124, 130, 155, 167
  agency, 10, 16
  book, 1, 3, 7–10, 15, 23, 42, 46–47, 53, 72, 86, 95, 97, 105, 107, 115, 138, 142, 151
  machinery, 2–3, 11, 55, 74, 76, 86, 112, 121, 130–31, 135, 138, 145–46, 154, 160, 162, 168, 186
  matter, 6, 16, 21, 56, 59, 65–66, 70, 73–74, 97, 145, 168
  medium, 10, 16, 23, 114, 168, 182
  system, 13, 48, 131, 151

CAMBRIDGE INTELLECTUAL PROPERTY AND INFORMATION LAW

Titles in the Series (formerly known as Cambridge Studies in Intellectual Property Rights)

Graeme W. Austin, Andrew F. Christie, Andrew T. Kenyon and Megan Richardson
Across Intellectual Property: Essays in Honour of Sam Ricketson

Brad Sherman and Lionel Bently
The Making of Modern Intellectual Property Law

Irini A. Stamatoudi
Copyright and Multimedia Products: A Comparative Analysis

Pascal Kamina
Film Copyright in the European Union

Huw Beverley-Smith
The Commercial Appropriation of Personality

Mark J. Davison
The Legal Protection of Databases

Robert Burrell and Allison Coleman
Copyright Exceptions: The Digital Impact

Huw Beverley-Smith, Ansgar Ohly and Agnès Lucas-Schloetter
Privacy, Property and Personality: Civil Law Perspectives on Commercial Appropriation

Catherine Seville
The Internationalisation of Copyright Law: Books, Buccaneers and the Black Flag in the Nineteenth Century

Philip Leith
Software and Patents in Europe

Geertrui van Overwalle
Gene Patents and Clearing Models: Patent Pools, Clearinghouses, Open Source Models and Liability Regimes

Lionel Bently, Jennifer Davis and Jane C. Ginsburg
Trade Marks and Brands: An Interdisciplinary Critique

Jonathan Curci
The Protection of Biodiversity and Traditional Knowledge in International Law of Intellectual Property

Lionel Bently, Jennifer Davis and Jane C. Ginsburg
Copyright and Piracy: An Interdisciplinary Critique

Megan Richardson and Julian Thomas
Fashioning Intellectual Property: Exhibition, Advertising and the Press, 1789–1918

Dev Gangjee
Relocating the Law of Geographical Indications

Andrew Kenyon, Megan Richardson and Ng-Loy Wee-Loon
The Law of Reputation and Brands in the Asia Pacific

Edson Beas Rodrigues, Jr
The General Exception Clauses of the TRIPS Agreement: Promoting Sustainable Development

Annabelle Lever
New Frontiers in the Philosophy of Intellectual Property

Sigrid Sterckx and Julian Cockbain
Exclusions from Patentability: How Far Has the European Patent Office Eroded Boundaries?

Sebastian Haunss
Conflicts in the Knowledge Society: The Contentious Politics of Intellectual Property

Helena R. Howe and Jonathan Griffiths
Concepts of Property in Intellectual Property Law

Rochelle Cooper Dreyfuss and Jane C. Ginsburg
Intellectual Property at the Edge: The Contested Contours of IP

Normann Witzleb, David Lindsay, Moira Paterson and Sharon Rodrick
Emerging Challenges in Privacy Law: Comparative Perspectives

Paul Bernal
Internet Privacy Rights: Rights to Protect Autonomy

Peter Drahos
Intellectual Property, Indigenous People and their Knowledge

Susy Frankel and Daniel Gervais
The Evolution and Equilibrium of Copyright in the Digital Age

Edited by Kathy Bowrey and Michael Handler
Law and Creativity in the Age of the Entertainment Franchise

Sean Bottomley
The British Patent System during the Industrial Revolution 1700–1852: From Privilege to Property

Susy Frankel
Test Tubes for Global Intellectual Property Issues: Small Market Economies

Jan Oster
Media Freedom As a Fundamental Right

Sara Bannerman
International Copyright and Access to Knowledge

Edited by Andrew T. Kenyon
Comparative Defamation and Privacy Law

Pascal Kamina
Film Copyright in the European Union (second edition)

Tim W. Dornis
Trademark and Unfair Competition Conflicts: Historical-Comparative, Doctrinal, and Economic Perspectives

Ge Chen
Copyright and International Negotiations: An Engine of Free Expression in China?

David Tan
The Commercial Appropriation of Fame: A Cultural Analysis of the Right of Publicity and Passing Off

Jay Sanderson
Plants, People and Practices: The Nature and History of the UPOV Convention

Daniel Benoliel
Patent Intensity and Economic Growth

Jeffrey A. Maine and Xuan-Thao Nguyen
The Intellectual Property Holding Company: Tax Use and Abuse from Victoria's Secret to Apple

Megan Richardson
The Right to Privacy: Origins and Influence of a Nineteenth-Century Idea

Martin Husovec
Injunctions against Intermediaries in the European Union: Accountable but Not Liable?

Estelle Derclaye
The Copyright/Design Interface: Past, Present and Future

Magdalena Kolasa
Trade Secrets and Employee Mobility: In Search of an Equilibrium

Péter Mezei
Copyright Exhaustion: Law and Policy in the United States and the European Union

Graham Greenleaf and David Lindsay
Public Rights: Copyright's Public Domains

Ole-Andreas Rognstad
Property Aspects of Intellectual Property

Elena Cooper
Art and Modern Copyright: The Contested Image

Paul Bernal
The Internet, Warts and All: Free Speech, Privacy and Truth

Sebastian Felix Schwemer
Licensing and Access to Content in the European Union: Regulation between Copyright and Competition Law

Daniela Simone
Copyright and Collective Authorship: Locating the Authors of Collaborative Work

Emily Hudson
Drafting Copyright Exceptions: From the Law in Books to the Law in Action

Graeme Gooday and Steven Wilf
Patent Cultures: Diversity and Harmonization in Historical Perspective

Mark Burdon
Digital Data Collection and Information Privacy Law

Tanya Aplin and Lionel Bently
Global Mandatory Fair Use: The Nature and Scope of the Right to Quote Copyright Works

Edited by Niklas Bruun, Graeme B. Dinwoodie, Marianne Levin and Ansgar Ohly
Transition and Coherence in Intellectual Property Law: Essays in Honour of Annette Kur

Alexander Peukert
A Critique of the Ontology of Intellectual Property Law

Brent Salter
Negotiating Copyright in the American Theatre: 1856–1951

Patrick R. Goold
IP Accidents: Negligence Liability in Intellectual Property

Péter Mezei
Copyright Exhaustion: Law and Policy in the United States and the European Union (second edition)

Jose Bellido and Kathy Bowrey
Adventures in Childhood

Henning Grosse Ruse-Khan and Axel Metzger
Intellectual Property Ordering Beyond Borders

Brad Sherman
Intangible Intangibles: Patent Law's Engagement with Dematerialised Subject Matter

Joshua Yuvaraj and Rebecca Giblin
Copyright Reversion: Reclaiming Lost Culture and Getting Authors Paid

Benjamin Goh
The Materiality of Literature: Rereading Authorship and Copyright with Kant

Printed by Integrated Books International,
United States of America